T0128468

Merchant of Time

The Round Table

J.N. Carroll

authorHOUSE®

AuthorHouse™
1663 Liberty Drive
Bloomington, IN 47403
www.authorhouse.com
Phone: 833-262-8899

Published by AuthorHouse 04/19/2024

ISBN: 979-8-8230-0562-3 (sc)
ISBN: 979-8-8230-0561-6 (hc)
ISBN: 979-8-8230-0560-9 (e)

Library of Congress Control Number: 2023906491

Print information available on the last page.

To my daughters,
Sunrise and Sunset,

If you wake up
with fleas, look around;
there's probably a dog,

or a cat,
or a rat,
or a bat.

How 'bout that?

John showed me exceptional kindness and hospitality while I was playing in the Cape Cod Baseball League. His simple adages and unique perspective helped give me a foundation to be successful in life. As simple as it is, I will always remember him telling me over and over again ".... just do the right thing". Those words speak true to his character.

Parker Rigler
Ex-Professional Baseball Player in the Chicago White Sox Organization

I met John in Fort Lauderdale in 1988. He taught me the art of sales. More importantly, he always stressed, "pursue your dreams!" My life's passion had always been horses! With his encouragement I competed as an equestrian rider and trainer for years. Today I can be found professionally judging top ranked horse events around the country. John and I have managed to keep in touch the past thirty years. I fully appreciate his impact on my life.

Lisa Forman
U.S.E.F & U.S.H.J.A. "R" judge
Owner of SignatureSpurs.com
Prestige Italia Saddle Fitter & Sales

CONTENTS

Section III |

| Provincetown

Section IV |

| Las Vegas

Section V |

| Back to the Castle

SECTION I |

| PROLOGUE

Eyes Wandering

In the pale yellow glimmer reflecting off the wet road, a cluster of oak leaves swirled around the red sports car and then stuck to the windshield until the wipers swept them away. The tired Alfa Romeo sputtered and almost stalled, as if it knew what was coming. There wasn't much room between the dashboard and my six-foot frame, but there was no turning back. It had to be that night. I pressed the clutch and slammed the car into gear. The back tires fought for traction on the narrow winding road. Giant oak trees, near-stripped of their fall foliage, leaned from side to side like spectators watching a back-of-the-pack runner finishing a long race. My heart pounded as the car rounded a corner and the fork in the road appeared.

The Alfa was going too fast, and the rock seemed much larger than it did when I first found this spot, just last week.

I closed my eyes, took my foot off the gas pedal, and slammed into the gigantic boulder. It was a deafening crash, as expected, but the rest was a surprise.

Instead of screaming to a dead stop, my red missile crashed nose first through a split-rail fence, smashing into a soggy field thirty feet ahead of the rock.

When my heart slowed, I knew I was okay. I pushed at the wedged door, jammed from the impact, and got out to inspect the damage. The front end was beyond recognition, and the tires were flat, but the damn engine was purring.

I took a lug wrench from the trunk, knelt at the front of the car, and smashed the oil pan until black liquid streamed out. Before long, the engine smoked, shuddered, and died.

The nighttime mist turned into a cold rain, but I was happy, my mission accomplished. As I turned from the wreck to head toward the nearest town, I locked eyes with a golden Labrador sitting across the road. My plan hadn't called for a witness, not even a canine. Unbothered by the weather, the dog simply observed me.

The tilt of his head asked, "What was that?"

I took both hands out of my pockets and broke into a sprint.

I didn't know where I was going, but I was running toward the future.

A Month Earlier | September 1979

The alarm blared at seven, as usual. I then sat up, rubbed the sleep from my eyes, and groaned. The only shower in the house would be tied up for a half hour as my younger brother and sisters got ready for school.

At least it was Friday. The Bay State League's football season would kick off this weekend, and everyone in Natick, Massachusetts, took pride in the student athletes. My dad coached the high school's baseball, football, and basketball teams, so I was always excited about a new season. It was in my blood.

Dad's voice filled the kitchen as he strategized for tomorrow's game. And even though he was a regular phone-pacer, Mom still put on quite the show as she prepared breakfast for the kids, ducking and dodging the cord.

"Morning, Coach," I said as I walked in. I then grabbed the milk, smelled it before pouring a glass, and put a few pieces of bread into the toaster. Upstairs, the younger kids threatened each other over the bathroom. And while my mom was busy packing lunches for them, she gave me one of those smiles that said, "I know what you're thinking, and I wish I could help."

Dad then put the phone down. "Walpole is a powerhouse this year," he said. "Those kids are a lot bigger than ours. Tomorrow's going to be tough."

"Don't worry," I told him. "Natick's coach is all over it."

He smiled, yelled, "Bye, kids!" to the gang clambering down the stairs, and then headed for the door.

As he was leaving, ten-year-old Blaine reached for a piece of toast, knocked over my milk, and yelled, "Fumble." We all laughed, even Mom, who grabbed a towel to mop it up.

Joanne was a high school junior and said, "Good luck today, Jake," as the three of them scrambled for coats and books.

"Yeah, knock 'em in the head," seven-year-old Sessy said.

"It's 'knock 'em dead,'" Mom corrected.

Sessy smiled. "Whatever. Bye, Mom. Bye, Jake."

When the door slammed, the house fell quiet. At the kitchen table, Mom flashed that smile again. "Honey, is everything all right?"

I looked down at the tiled floor and then back up at her. "It will be, Mom. I just need a chance, that's all—a chance to make a sale. Don't worry, I'll make it happen."

She reached across the table and squeezed my hand, leaving a five-dollar bill behind. She then stood and took the breakfast dishes to the sink.

"Thanks, Mom. I'll pay you back."

2

Wearing blue bell-bottoms, a white dress shirt, and Coach's blue tie, I headed out to the 1969 Alfa Romeo in the driveway, my pride and joy. I had earned it selling Electrolux vacuum cleaners. I was one of the top twenty-five reps in New England last year. The job taught me to work hard but, more importantly, to work smart. And it wasn't smart to keep slogging door-to-door through New England winters.

So I went to real estate school and snagged one of the last one-shot brokers' licenses. It was just before the commonwealth started requiring a salesman's license and a year's apprenticeship as prerequisites. I landed a position in a fine Framingham real estate office, Price & Ross. I was twenty-one years old, as green as green could be, and in a firm of forty, all middle-aged women. It was a start in a direction. And any direction was fine for me prior to this gig, but the excitement of a new job had quickly dissipated. I had run out of patience and money. And I hadn't seen a paycheck in a long time.

As I thought all this over, the Alfa took a while to start. But the engine finally caught, coughing up a cloud of black smoke. I then headed toward the center of Natick, the gas gauge on empty. While I drove the single "Midnight Confessions" by the Grass Roots crackled from the radio, lifting my mood. It was time for my apprenticeship to end, time to make some money, and time to have a heart-to-heart with the owner of the brokerage, Marilyn Price.

And while my mood was lifting, I noticed that the line of cars waiting at Maybardi's Service Station was nuts. No one could explain where all the gas had gone, not even President Jimmy Carter. At eighty-five cents a gallon, it was still hard to find sometimes. My friends thought that the US was stockpiling reserves for a war in the Middle East. A new dictator, Saddam Hussein, had seized control of Iraq, Ayatollah Khomeini was holding sixty-three Americans hostage in Iran, the Russians had just invaded Afghanistan, and I was going to be late for work because I couldn't gas up.

When I finally reached the pump, Mike Maybardi told me five gallons was the limit. And that was okay by me. It left just enough from Mom's handout for one hot dog at Casey's.

"What does Coach think about our chances tomorrow?" Mike asked.

I shrugged. "You know my dad, no predictions. He says winning is a result of effort and pride, a byproduct of doing things right."

"Well, see you at the game. Go Natick!" Mike yelled. His voice was hardly audible as I pulled out of the station.

I waved, and the lineup at the pump, in my rearview mirror, made me think about the "haves" and "have-nots" of the world. I knew which group I wanted to join, and I had already planned my showdown with Marilyn Price.

3

In the Price & Ross parking lot, the Alfa trembled, backfired, and spat out a plume of black smoke. It was a fitting announcement. Here was a guy who meant business. There would be no more, "Jake, honey, dash out and get us some coffee," "Jake, I have a showing; run my Lincoln to the carwash," or "Jake, be a dear and watch my kids while I go to a closing."

With that in mind, I knocked on the open door of Marilyn Price's private office, where she was reviewing paperwork. "Come in, Jake," she said, flashing a smile that complemented her success. "What can I do for you?"

Marilyn was fortysomething and looked fine. She had shoulder-length blond hair, blue eyes, and a petite figure, which was flattered by a designer outfit. Looking at her, I forgot my mission for a split second but recovered.

"Marilyn, for months, I've done whatever anyone asked. I helped whenever I could, and I never complained. Yet, any time a new client calls or an opportunity shows up, I'm passed over. I'm here to say that it's my turn to prove myself. I know I can sell. Now I need to know if you're going to give me a shot."

As I spoke, her engaging smile faded. She then stood to face the window, looking out over the highway. "You know, Jake, I wasn't much older than you are, with a degree from Boston College, when I started working here. It was Ross Realty then, and Bill Ross ran a no-nonsense, roll-up-your-sleeves office. I was the first female ever hired. And if I told you no one took me seriously, I'd be putting it mildly. Christ, it was unusual for a woman to drive a car in those days, let alone compete in a man's workplace."

Her tone was calm and thoughtful as she gazed at the traffic crawling by, no letup in sight. "I know it's tough to break in. But you've got to stay

5

positive and, above all else, do your homework. If you do, you'll be ready when your chance comes."

She then gestured for me to join her at the window. "Look at that. Thousands of people drive by every day on their way to work so they can support their families. Every one of them needs a place to go at the end of the day. It's the American dream, Jake, to own a home, to own a bigger home, and to own a better home. That's what we're here for. To help all those people fulfill their dreams."

She swept her hand across the scene. "The successful agent makes his or her fortune out there, not in any office. So go make it happen. The sales are waiting for you. Tell all those people that Jake Arril is on this earth to help them fulfill their God-given right to pursue the American dream."

I knew she was good, but I didn't know she was that good. "Marilyn?"

"Yes?"

"How did you end up owning the company?"

She turned to me; her smile slowly reappeared. "By taking no prisoners, kicking ass, and letting no one stand in my way."

"I get it." I headed for the door. "The money's out there, not in here. So just wait and see; I'm going to be the best damn agent you've ever known, Marilyn. I'll work morning to night. No job is too big or small."

"Jake," she called, "will you do something for me now?"

"Name it."

"Be a dear, run over to Dunkin' Donuts, and get the girls and me the usual."

4

I practically ran the hundred yards to the donut shop. Fresh-brewed coffee and sugar had never smelled so good. The money was waiting outside the walls of the office, not inside.

I saw it now.

When I arrived, Dunkin' Donuts was almost empty. I noted a pair of women who appeared to be in their fifties chatting away at a small table. And I fired off a memorized list of beverages and snacks for the firm. I was certain at least one of them needed a bigger, better house. And since it would be a few minutes for the order, I thought I'd put Marilyn's wisdom into action.

"Good morning, ladies. Beautiful day, don't you think?"

With a half-glance in my direction, one replied, "Mhm. I'll have a regular coffee, with a blueberry muffin."

The other followed her friend's assumption, "Make mine a bran."

I returned to the counter to pick up my order. "Table over there wants two regulars, a blue, and a bran," I said before leaving.

Once in the parking lot, I paused to let a new Ford Ranchero—half pickup, half car—pull into a parking space. Gloria Gaynor's "I Will Survive" blared from its stereo. When the driver trotted off to the donut shop, I peered in the passenger side to admire the interior. I then caught my reflection in the window. It was time for an image check. I wore a pullover sweater and an outdated tie, and I had long hair reaching down my back. It was no wonder those two women thought I worked there. *Time for a new suit, shirt, shoes ... maybe start with a haircut.* It was time to make money, but I was still holding the damn coffees.

Friday afternoons were usually quiet around the office, most of the staff off getting their hair done for a night out at some fancy restaurant or

7

a show. I handed a coffee to Sally, Marilyn's personal assistant, who was on the phone. She smiled and blew me a kiss.

Marilyn's desk was surrounded by her three top guns, a trio responsible for most of the firm's sales. I'd been told that in most sales organizations, 10 percent of the staff produces 50 percent of the business, and top producers tend to be a high-maintenance group. Massaging egos and catering to pet peeves, Marilyn was a champ at keeping these three happy—at least most of the time.

I put the coffees on the desk, nodded to the cream of the crop, and mouthed to Marilyn, "Thanks. See you Monday."

I stepped outside again and sucked in the cool air. I looked around at a new world, or perhaps it was my vision that altered. Either way, I was hungry for the opportunities that awaited me.

5

◆

Friday afternoon was a good time to drop in on Mario and Antonio Panniello, who owned the garage at the Citgo gas station. I'd bought the Alfa from Mario about a year before, and the brothers usually found time to give it a once-over at the end of the week. If it had serious problems, I didn't want to find out about them in the middle of a New England blizzard. Like a sick kid threatened with a doctor's visit, the Alfa started right away.

Traffic was heavy on the highway; the prospect of a nice weekend had people leaving work early, heading to the beaches of Cape Cod or the mountains up north. I took a detour on the way to Mario's, turning right on Concord Street toward my old neighborhood in Framingham. Stopping in front of 24 Belvedere Road, I felt a bit sentimental. It had been years since I'd seen the old place, and old it was: faded white with black trim, pigeons' nests crammed under the eaves, bird crap staining the corners of the roof. I could still picture Coach on a ladder, pushing the nests out with a broom, muttering, "filthy rats."

One morning, as I supported the bottom of the old two-piece ladder, the wood snapped and the ladder broke. Twenty-five feet in the air, Coach held on for dear life. I ran onto the neighbor's lawn as the ladder pulled away from the house and froze in an upright position. Coach sliding halfway down jumped, narrowly missing the cracked asphalt driveway. He landed on the grass, where he executed a perfect somersault. Jumping to his feet, he pointed his finger at me and said, "Ya gotta know how to fall, Jake." The pigeons were hysterical.

As I drove back to Concord Street, the old neighborhood looked beaten up, yet so many great childhood memories were born there:

9

black-and-white TV, Red Sox games on the radio, hot summer nights on the porch with a Wallace's ice-cream cone. Things were a lot simpler then.

Feeling nostalgic, I pulled onto Thelma road, recalling fond memories of my best friends George, Karl, Pat, and Mike: the gang. This neighborhood hadn't fared any better. Where their houses once stood were now empty lots. I headed for downtown Natick, the Alfa on its best behavior. I drove passed Dug Pond, where I'd spent many hot summer days swinging from ropes tied to massive oak trees and dropping into the cool water. Trout fishing opened here in April. With frost on the ground and mist rising from the water, the line would tug as trout nibbled the bait. Driving past People's Cemetery, I tried to ignore the fresh flowers on new graves. I was still young enough to excuse myself from the "debt to be paid by all men."

Like most Boston suburbs, Natick's center featured a firehouse, a red-brick library, a bank, and a couple of restaurants. At the edge of town, I put on my right blinker, passed a few body shops, and pulled up to Casey's, the world's best diner. Originally horse-drawn around town by Joe Casey's grandfather and then his father, the eatery had come to rest in this gravel lot. Its sliding door opened to twelve round stools and an ancient hand-rubbed wooden bar. The smells inside meant home.

The flat steel griddle, scraped clean since lunch, was polished and lined with containers of chopped onions, mushrooms, sliced tomatoes, fresh burgers and cheese, tuna salad, egg salad, mayo, and relish—a hungry man's paradise. Behind the bar stood Joe Casey, a big man with thinning hair wearing an apron and a smile. He put a paper plate, napkin, and fork on the bar and punched my shoulder.

"What'll it be today, my boy?"

"One all-around with onions, please, Joe."

"Anything to drink?"

I shook my head. "No thanks."

Grinning, he lifted the lid from a hot copper box and reached in for two steamed buns, then snagged a couple of dogs with a fork. He topped them off with catsup, mustard, and chopped onion, then plopped them on the paper plate. As I inhaled half of a dog, he snapped open a can of Coke, winked, and said, "On the house, kid."

I loved everything about Casey's. At the takeout window, people patiently waited for their orders, as Joe's friendly demeanor made conversation easy. Most were townies—carpenters, doctors, teachers, and janitors—born and raised in Natick and proud of it. Once home to Champion Sporting Goods, the town was dubbed the "Home of Champions" years ago. Though the factory had long since moved away, the name stuck, and the town lived up to it, turning out some of New England's finest athletes.

Photographs of Natick's notables hung on the cracked leather walls. The screening process was tough, the qualifications known only to the Casey family, but I knew two things for sure: they'd all contributed to Natick athletics, and they were all dead.

I finished the Coke, retasted the onions when I burped, and waved to Joe, who was occupied at the takeout window. He gently paused his customer midorder. "Tell Coach I wish him good luck this season."

I nodded and ducked out the door. I could've eaten a hundred of those dogs.

6

Main Street traffic was backed up, but no one seemed to mind. Drivers chatted across lanes, waving when one finally moved. Slowly passing the fire department, I spotted a former teammate washing down a truck. "Hey, Slats," I hollered, "good thing we're not in the starting lineup against Walpole tomorrow!"

"Natick wouldn't stand a chance!" Slats called back. Slats had wanted to be a fireman since we were kids. I was glad to see him happy.

Past the congestion, I headed to Mario's, though it felt like I was going to the dentist. When I turned into the old Citgo at the intersection of Routes 9 and 30, familiar chimes rang as the Alfa ran over the cable next to the pumps.

In an open service bay, under a car hoisted six feet in the air, the younger of the two brothers yanked on something with a wrench.

"Need help, Tony?" I asked. He put the wrench down and grinned. "Take the rest of the day off," I joked. "You know what? Go back to Italy. I'll finish up whatever you and Mario have going. How tough can this stuff be?"

When Antonio first arrived in America, just a few years earlier, I introduced him to English, including a few choice phrases. I had known his older brother a lot longer.

"Where's Mario anyhow?"

Tony led me through the garage, ducking under a bright yellow Fiat that was suspended on a lift.

"Fiat: Fix It All the Time. Right, Tony?"

"Pieces of shit. Can't be made in Italy." He pulled two icy beers from a cooler, snapped off the caps with a bottle opener, and handed me one. "Salut."

We found Mario at the back of the garage, inspecting a blue Ferrari, a 1969 246 Dino, named for Enzo Ferrari's son. With its V6 engine and steel bodywork, it was a resurgence car for Ferrari, the first all-around street supercar the company had offered to compete with Porsche in years. It was a collector's car; only thirty-nine hundred had ever been produced.

Next to the Ferrari sat a silver Porsche 911 Turbo, the newest design in what many considered the world's finest sports car. Built in 1975 but not available in the United States until the following year, it boasted a top speed of 160 mph and went from 0 to 60 in 4.9 seconds. It was a rocket with a five-speed manual shift for the serious driver.

Both cars looked as if they'd just come from the showroom, posed for the cover shot on a high-end automotive magazine. In his blue jumpsuit with his name printed on the pocket, Mario looked like he belonged in the picture too.

"Jake, what's up?" he asked, his expression serious.

"The car is dying, man. She's hard to start, smells like oil, and shakes like she's gonna fall apart whenever I take a corner or hit a bump."

Mario shrugged, and we headed toward the front, but the Alfa wasn't where I'd parked it. I was excited for a few seconds, thinking it had been stolen, but then the familiar cable chimed as Tony drove toward us from the pumps. He winked, and I knew he'd filled the tank.

We stood around staring at the Alfa until Tony pushed down on the left front end and let it go. The car made a sick metal-on-metal sound. When he pushed again, the Alfa bounced like an overgrown Slinky. He shook his head, looked at Mario, and walked away.

"Frame's broken," Mario said. "Not good."

"How not good is it? What's it gonna cost?"

He muttered in Italian and drove the car into the service bay, where Tony had just lowered the yellow Fiat from the lift. Once the Alfa was in the air, Mario grabbed a light with a long extension cord and hooked it to the underbelly, and both brothers inspected the damage.

"Jake"—Mario cranked his neck so I could see the effect of his eyebrows rising—"what you been doing to this car? The frame's split. You been four-wheeling?"

"No, I haven't been four-wheeling. How bad is it? It can be fixed, right?" This time Mario walked away.

13

"Insurance," Tony said. I didn't get it.

"This car is done. Cost more to fix than it's worth. Insurance."

I still didn't get it. And I didn't like the idea of being broke without transportation.

"Insurance," Tony said again. "No big deal. We do it all the time." He took my arm and led me back to the blue Ferrari and the silver Porsche. "Remember the cars out front when you bought the Alfa last year?" I nodded, no closer to getting the point. "Jake." He motioned to the cars before us. Still nothing.

"I didn't see a blue Ferrari or a silver Porsche."

Tony used a screwdriver to scrape paint from the underside of the Ferrari's passenger door. Ferrari red. He pointed. "Remember the black Porsche?"

I got it. "These are the cars that were here last year? With different paint?"

Tony shook his head. "Not just different paint. Better. Insurance makes them better."

I stared at him.

"The Ferrari has been totaled three times this year. Mario collects from insurance, buys it back at auction, fixes it, wrecks it, collects again, buys it back again ... Get it?"

I definitely got it, though it was more than I wanted to hear.

Tony pressed a finger to his lips. "This car's worth thirty grand. Mario's collected eighty so far."

"Do something quick," Tony advised. "Your Alfa's not safe."

7

I parked in front of the house—no need to spill more oil on the driveway—and went in through the garage. At 7:00 p.m., the dogs from Casey's were a distant memory. I was famished.

Blaine and Sessy were watching a new TV show, *The Dukes of Hazzard*, and Mom was at the sink, rinsing up the remnants of supper. I gave her a hug and a peck on the cheek, "Anything left?"

"Dinner's in the oven, honey. How was your day? Any luck?"

"No, Mom." I took my plate of chicken with boiled potatoes and carrots to the table. "Today won't make my top-ten list."

When her smile faded, I added, "Don't worry. Something will break soon."

I had barely finished my food when a car horn sounded from our driveway. I went to the door and held up one finger to my best friend, Frankie D., then dashed upstairs for a quick change into blue jeans, a sweatshirt, and a pair of Converse sneakers. "Thanks for supper, Mom."

Frankie was in his usual pleasant mood. "What's up, Captain Real Estate? Any property left to sell in Boston?"

The blue cooler in the backseat was no doubt packed with iced-down Budweisers.

"What d'ya wanna do?" he asked.

The million-dollar question. We'd asked it every Friday night for the past five years. But we both knew we were heading for the parking lot by the football field, where students would be gathering as usual.

Frankie parked in the far corner of the gravel lot, away from most of the students, and pulled out a couple of beers. "Man, remember when we played the opener?"

We snapped the beers open and drank, the eight-track and cassette decks from cars around us sending out a blend of Rod Stewart, Michael Jackson, and the Doobie Brothers. Frankie punched me on the shoulder, hard. "What's up, pal?"

"I don't know. Sometimes I think I'm going to end up here forever, and it drives me crazy. It was a great place to grow up, but I don't feel like I'm going anywhere."

"What about the real estate gig?"

"I don't want to hang onto the past, Frankie. I just want a future. Let's just get out of here".

"Quick trip to McDonald's?"

I shook my head, and we drove back to the house in silence. We sat in the driveway long enough to feel how far away my mind was from where we were.

Frankie's voice brought me back down to earth. "You know, I'm a townie. I'll stay here forever. But you've always been different. I love you, man, but you gotta do what's right for you. Stop sweating it; you'll figure it out."

I got out of the car and walked to the house. At the front door, I turned and watched as the taillights disappeared down the driveway.

8

In sweats and sneakers, I went downstairs just before the sun rose. Coach was sipping his coffee, studying game plans methodically laid out on a clipboard.

"Ready for today?" I asked as I filled a glass from the faucet.

"It's all in the preparation, Jake. Games are won and lost before the players take the field."

He looked up as I downed the water. "Where are you going?"

"Thought I'd take a bike ride before the game. Good luck today, Coach."

I loved everything about my ten-speed Motobecane: sewn-up racing tires, custom seat, toe clips. Some days I'd ride from early morning until night, feeling a freedom only the bike could deliver.

Pedaling out into the beautiful September day and turning onto Cottage Street toward the Charles River, I settled into a comfortable rhythm. The towering oaks had just started to sport their fall foliage, and though the sun effortlessly pierced through the blue sky, a chill filled the morning air.

The trees blurred as the miles passed. My breathing, my heartbeat, and the click of the gears brought my mind to a blissful state. This must be what the priests call peace. The stress of the week was, at least temporarily, on hold.

Hours later, the morning chill disappeared. While dismounting back in the garage, I used my sleeve to wipe the sweat off my face; I was drenched. At the end of the driveway sat the Alfa, like a dog who'd been scolded. *Bad car.*

From the kitchen table, Blaine asked, "Is it raining, Jake?"

"Naw," Sessy answered for me. "He's just slimy from his bike ride."

As I headed to the sink for more water, the telephone rang and both kids bolted for it. After a struggle, Blaine grudgingly let his younger sister answer. "Arril residence," she said sweetly, still glaring at her brother, "how may I help you?" She smiled as she handed me the phone. "Jake, it's for you."

As I put the phone to my ear, a voice grew in volume and familiarity. "Are you there?"

My boss had never called me at home. "I'm here, Marilyn. What's up?"

As I listened, Mom came into the kitchen, Sessy barely visible behind her. "Blaine, did you hit your sister?" Her tone was halfhearted as her eyes settled on me.

"Don't worry, Marilyn," I said. I'll handle it. I won't let you down." I'd barely hung up before I let out a war cry.

"Natick scores!" Blaine whooped. "Right, Jake?"

"That was my boss," I told Mom. "I have a listing appointment with a serious seller in Marlborough. She wants me to handle it alone. In two hours."

Mom hugged me. "I knew you'd get your chance, honey. You deserve it."

Sessy looked baffled. "Jake, are we still going to the game?"

The game. I'd been going to the season opener my whole life. "I have an important meeting, Ses. You guys go, and I'll get there as soon as I can." Turning back to Mom, I said, "Gotta get ready. Gotta stop by the office to get the paperwork before the appointment."

My words sounded like someone else's. How many times had this exact scene played out in my mind? Finally, it was real.

I was in the car in a flash. Without thinking, I took the longer route through Natick Center, down Speen Street to Route 30, past honking cars, men pumping fists, an entire town decked out in red and blue for the start of the new season. But my mind was focused: my shot had arrived at last.

With money in my pocket, I'd be able to deal with the Alfa's problems, even get myself a proper sport coat. I figured I'd go to the Chestnut Hill Mall, walk into Brooks Brothers, and get two—no, three—of everything. Passing the shop, I thought about the Panniello brothers. Maybe I'd put the Porsche—no, the Ferrari—on hold. Out front of the shop, a few cruisers, an ambulance, and a crowd had gathered. Mario was talking earnestly with a couple of cops. My jaw dropped as I slowed. A yellow Fiat apparently had lost control while driving into the station. It had plowed into a silver Porsche 911 Turbo and, yep, a dark blue Ferrari.

They'd done it again.

9

The Alfa started to act up on Route 9. It stuttered on acceleration, and the burning oil smell got stronger. "Don't quit on me now," I begged. I then breathed a sigh of relief as I pulled into the office parking lot. At least I'd made it that far.

Marilyn's personal assistant was alone in the office. She smiled when I walked in, offering me a manila envelope.

"This is it, Sally."

Her smile faded. "Are you nervous, Jake?"

"No, I'll be okay." After a half-laugh, I added, "Just hope my car makes it."

"I'll be here until five. Call if you need anything and, hey, good luck."

I left the office and habitually glanced across the lot at the coffee shop. *Today I'm after a different kind of dough.*

The car started with a bang and a puff of black smoke. I drove past Timothy's, the first nightclub I'd gone to after turning eighteen, and Sheraton Tara, the grandest hotel in the area. I never bothered to learn the names of all the ponds and lakes on the route. Too many to count. Thirty minutes later, the smell of burning oil made my eyes sting. I reached Marlborough, host to an unsightly string of manufacturing plants, many making shoes, dating back to the Civil War. Just off Main Street, I pulled over in front of the Frye Boot Building, a three-level brick-front collection of stores, to check the directions Sally gave me earlier.

Good thing I was close; the car was filling with smoke. *I'll show up with my car on fire. That oughta tell them I'm serious.*

Five minutes and a couple of wrong turns later, I parked in front of 19 Drydon Road: a brown, two-story structure, its porch screens torn. The lawn was a combination of dirt and overgrown weeds; three tin trashcans overflowed at the curb. Frankly, it was a shithole.

A sorry-looking tree, the single highlight of the property, had grown over the roof, and flourishing vines spilled from the gutters. Ropes dangling from the tree must have held a swing at some point; now they looked primed for a dual hanging. Three rusted bicycles with flat tires leaned against the house. Pigeon shit decorated the second story, a lovely brown-on-white pattern.

If I'd weighed a few more pounds, the rotten wooden steps would have collapsed. The doorbell didn't work, so I knocked; this was answered by a series of low barks and growls. *I guess they don't need the doorbell anyway.* Moments later, I laid eyes on my first potential client. He was in his forties, with thinning hair and a grayish-black mustache. Barefoot, wearing gray sweatpants and a red checkered shirt, he stood about five feet ten inches tall, weighing in at a good 250 pounds.

"Mr. Alvarez, I'm Jake Arril from Price & Ross."

Alvarez was doing his best to restrain a black German shepherd who wanted nothing more than to rip my throat out. I took a healthy step back.

"For Christ's sake, Maria, come get Satan. The real estate guy's here." I took a few more steps back down to the driveway.

"Don't pay him no mind," Alvarez said, "he wouldn't hurt a squirrel." Slipping a collar around the dog's neck, he added, "Doesn't like salesmen, though." His smile showcased a gold front tooth. "You go on inside. I'll hold on to Satan."

The dog went nuts and lunged again as I scrambled into the house. The smell of cat piss and spicy rotten garbage made me gag as my eyes adjusted to the dimness.

Compared to this scene, the outside of the place was a palace.

Mrs. Alvarez sashayed down the stairs in a fluffy pink bathrobe and slippers, a burning cigarette in one hand, a can of Coke in the other. In her midthirties, she'd apparently had three and a half rough decades. With a cough and a half-smile, she pointed me toward the living room.

Her husband followed. "Juan Alvarez," he said with a heavy Spanish accent, "and my wife, Maria."

After a drag from her cigarette, Maria motioned toward a chair draped with a bedspread. "Have a seat."

I sucked it up and sat, fearing what might live in the folds.

"Mr. Jake, how long you been selling real estate?" His gold tooth was all I could see, or even think about. "You look young."

Maria put down her soda can, set the burning cigarette in an ashtray, and leaned against the wall, her arms folded.

I leaned forward. "Mr. Alvarez, believe me, Price & Ross wouldn't give me the time of day if the principals didn't have confidence in my abilities. Everyone wins when a property sells, and *only* when it sells. We pay all advertising costs. My job is to bring you potential buyers until you have a check in your hand." The stench was giving me a headache. "My age is actually an advantage to you and Mrs. Alvarez. I'm single and motivated. I get results for my clients." Juan's face told me the spiel had hit its mark.

"Mr. Jake, I leave my country years ago because there was no work. I end up here, work in the factory, make shoes. Now all the factories are closed. No work here anymore. We need to sell this big house."

"Well, let's see what we have and talk price." I stood slowly, resisting the impulse to check the seat of my pants. "If you'll show me around, I'll give you my opinion."

I noticed burned-out lightbulbs in lamps with no shades, though you'd need to completely dampen the light in here to disguise the layer of solidified dust, which covered almost every surface I could see. A week's worth of dirty dishes in the kitchen sink was the least of that room's problems; the litter box looked like it serviced a dozen cats and hadn't been emptied in years. The smell of cat piss was staggering.

Upstairs, the three bedrooms were littered with dirty laundry piled on unmade beds. While inspecting what was ostensibly the master bedroom, I heard the toilet flush.

Juan had taken a detour.

Maria smiled, nodded toward the bed, and winked.

I was horrified. Worse, I knew it showed. She shrugged and left the room. Juan met us in the hallway, wiping his hands on his shirt. "Want to see the bathroom, Mr. Jake?"

"Nah. Seen one, seen them all."

I followed Maria downstairs, with Juan safely in tow. Back in the living room after the grand tour, I pulled the listing contract from my folder and did what I'd been taught: Assume the sale. Never ask for the business; *assume* the business.

The three of us sat on the sofa, me in the middle, and I laid the contract on the coffee table. "Okay, Mr. and Mrs. Alvarez, what do you have in mind for an asking price?"

Juan stood and began pacing, running his hands through his sparse hair. "One hundred and sixty-five thousand dollars." He stopped abruptly. His eyes were shifting from Maria to me, uncertain of whom to look at.

I knew in that instant the listing was mine. Other reps had told me that sellers always shoot for the moon. My job was to bring them back to earth—get them to set a realistic price so the property would actually sell.

"With all due respect, Mr. Alvarez," I said, leaning back into the sofa, "the house needs work. Potential buyers will see that, and they'll know what the work will cost."

Juan frowned and turned toward Maria, who was busy lighting a new cigarette from the still-burning end of the last one. At least the smoke masked some of the cat piss odor. "Well, Mr. Jake," he said, "what do you think our house is worth?"

Distracted by a wet feeling on my back, I completely forgot what I was doing, then collected myself. "How quickly do you want the home to sell?"

I'd been taught to ask the question, and I knew the answer. Like most in their position, Juan and Maria needed the house sold fast.

We sat in silence for a few minutes. I was still wondering why the hell my back was wet. "I'd feel confident listing your house at one hundred forty-five thousand dollars," I said eventually. "That's a fair price. And remember, every day that goes by with the house unsold costs you money."

Juan said something in Spanish to his wife, then, "Okay, Mr. Jake. Sell our house, please." With that, he stuck out his hand.

Ten minutes later, excited to have the listing, I forgot about the creature from hell on the porch. I slammed the door just in time as the beast lunged for my nuts.

Juan apologized as he grabbed Satan by the neck, swearing at him in Spanish.

I made a run for it. "Good-bye, Mr. Jake. See you soon."

I started the Alfa, ecstatic, my first deal in the can. Pulling into the office parking lot, I ignored the smoke in the car. I ran for the door, knowing I'd succeeded. I'd brought the prize home.

Sally was on the phone until she saw my smile. Hanging up, she said, "Do we have another Top Gun around here?"

"Signed, sealed, and delivered." I pulled out the paperwork. "Should we call Marilyn and give her the good news?"

"She's on the Cape, sailing Nantucket Sound, but I'll be talking with her tonight." Sally walked around the desk and gave me a bear hug.

I lifted her and swung her around. When I finally put her down, she sniffed her right hand.

"Jake, honey, what is that? It smells like cat piss."

"Christ, I knew I felt something. It's from the sofa at my listing." She frowned and went to the washroom.

I pulled off the sweater, inspected the wet stain on the back, then checked my reflection in a wall mirror. Cat hair covered my ass and the backs of my legs. "Sorry about that, Sally," I said on my way out the door.

I threw the wadded sweater into the back of the Alfa. As I drove, the car began to fill with smoke again, so I rolled down the windows. A rusted frame, cat piss, and burning oil—all good. Nothing could get me down. I'd just pulled off my first real estate deal.

10

Mario was engrossed in conversation with a gray-haired guy in a suit, and Tony was in the garage, grinning. He waved me inside, gripping two cans of beer. I took one and asked, "Who's that with Mario?"

"Insurance."

"I can't believe you guys did it again. What's that, the third time those cars have been wrecked?"

"Fourth. Now Mario buys them back, changes insurance, has another accident." Tony's grin expanded. "Great country you have here."

I did the math. The profits on this move would net Mario thirty grand on each car, and he'd done it four times. "Why don't the insurance companies catch on?" I asked.

"Try to prove it wasn't bad luck. Busy road, busy station, different drivers. Bad luck." Tony raised his beer "Mario's building a villa back home in Italy, all because of those two cars."

He sniffed his beer, then looked around the station. "You smell something bad?" I moved a few steps away and shrugged.

Mario shook the insurance guy's hand and watched him back out of the station. Heading into the service bay with his arms outstretched, he asked, "What am I to do? Nothing but bad luck."

He slapped both our backs before grabbing a beer.

"Hey Mario, there's so much smoke inside the Alfa I can barely see out the windshield."

He took a hard swallow and frowned. "Jake, the car is done. Like I told you, insurance." He gulped the last of his beer and threw the can in the trash before walking away.

The discussion was over. If the brothers could help, they would, but they couldn't.

"Ciao, Antonio, a domani," I said in my best Italian accent.

"Insurance, Jake. Only thing to do."

It was almost 5:00 p.m. when I pulled onto Speen Street and suddenly wondered who'd won the game. If Natick won, the townies would be hanging out in the parking lot at Casey's, telling football stories from years gone by.

The diner's lot was almost empty. I thought about grabbing a couple of dogs and getting a rundown on the game and the score, but then realized I was broke. Besides, I needed a shower.

The new For Sale sign on Cottage Street didn't trouble me. Once word got out, I'd get plenty of listings. I already had one in the bag.

Coach was pushing the lawnmower, blowing off steam. Some guys drink, some smoke, my father opted for physical labor. I parked in front to spare the driveway from my beater's leaking oil.

"Hey, Dad, missed the game. Guess it didn't go so well."

I'd learned years ago that if we win, it's Coach. Lose, it's Dad.

"Mental mistakes!" He put the mower in neutral, shaking his head. "The Sisters of the Poor could have beaten us today."

Another fact I learned years ago: no team on earth has less talent than the Sisters of the Poor.

"Get 'em next week, Dad." At the front door, I added, "I'll get changed and help."

He signaled "no" with a wave. Coach always told his players, "Leave it all on the field. Give a hundred percent and then forget about it." But he wasn't all that keen at taking his own advice. He wanted to be alone to relive each play that went wrong.

Inside, Mom was heading upstairs with a basket of fresh laundry. "Well?" she asked. "How did it go?"

I gave her my best poker face, but she waited me out. When I broke into a smile, she screamed. "You did it? Tell me you did it, Jake. No BS."

"Yep. No BS." Her hug almost broke my neck. Sessy and Blaine came running toward the racket. "Your big brother made a real estate deal today." Mom's pitch raised half an octave. "Aren't you proud?"

Little Sess wrinkled her nose as she covered her ears. "We lost today, Jake. The nuns from the church could've beat us up."

Blaine high-fived me. "Good job, Jake. How much did you make?" At ten, he already knew how to cut to the chase.

"Let me put the laundry away dear, and then I want to hear all about it."

Sessy looked up at me, her face even more contorted, "No offense, but you stink."

Blaine pinched his nose as they ran from the room, yelling, "Cat pee! Cat pee! Cat pee!"

The commotion stopped Mom halfway up the stairs. "How in the world did you get cat piss all over you? Put those clothes in the basement."

On the kitchen table, one Natick Pizza box was empty; the other held two green pepper slices. Pepperoni was always the first to go. I was pretty sure Coach bought green peppers only so there'd be leftovers.

I threw my balled-up sweater and shirt into the basement, smelled my hands, and thought better about grabbing the slices. By the time I got back from my shower, only one was left. Blaine was in the TV room watching a ball game, happily eating the other one.

I polished off the last slice with three bites as Dad came through the garage door.

"Two bucks a slice," he said. "Half-price today."

I didn't even have enough to cover that. "What happened today, Dad?"

"We weren't ready mentally."

Coach attributed all losses, in all sports, to mental mistakes. The body would do whatever the mind commanded. If the mind wasn't right, the body wouldn't perform.

"How did it go for you today, Jake? Any luck?"

Mom answered for me. "He made his first deal today. Isn't that great?"

Blaine walked into the kitchen and shook the empty pizza box, frowned at me, and went back to the game.

"That is great! So when do you get paid?"

"Not until the house sells. The six percent commission gets divided between the listing firm and the selling firm. Each agent splits that share with the office."

"So how much will you make?" Dad pressed.

"For God's sake, don't be so nosy." Mom winked. "The important thing is he got his first deal."

"It's complicated." I told Dad.

The fact was, I didn't have a clue. I'd never had to worry about a commission up until this point.

"Well, keep up the good work, Jake. Your mother and I are always happy to see you succeed." Dad sauntered into the TV room to watch the game with Blaine.

"Tell me all about it, honey," Mom said as she joined me at the table. "I'm so proud of you."

"Thanks, Mom."

I condensed the day into a ten-minute story. I walked back to my room with a notepad and pencil, determined to figure out my commission. Joanne was on the phone in our parents' bedroom, but she'd obviously heard the conversations downstairs; she gave me a thumbs-up as I passed.

I mouthed "thanks," went into my room, and closed the door. Sitting on the edge of my bed, I jotted down the numbers. If the house sold for $145,000, the 6 percent commission would come to $8,700. If Price & Ross made the sale, the full amount would stay in-house. But if another office sold the property, Price & Ross would take only 3 percent. And if I split that 3percent with the firm, I'd earn 1.5 percent: $2,125—but only if the firm split was 50/50, and only if the house sold at the list price.

I stared at the numbers. There sure were a lot of ifs on the page.

The black 1973 Cadillac Coupe de Ville in the driveway meant that J. B. was driving. Frankie was riding shotgun, and through the tinted windows, I could see someone else in the backseat. Frankie opened his door and leaned forward so I could climb in. It never made sense to me that such a big car had only two doors.

The backseat passenger was Robby Dunlop, or Dunny—the team's star running back when we were in school a hundred years ago. He cracked me on the shoulder, and it hurt like hell, but some code prevented a guy from saying so.

I settled into the sofa-like seat and thumped Frankie on the back of the head.

"Good evening, girls."

"Long time, no see," J. B. said from behind the steering wheel.

We'd all been like brothers in high school, swearing we'd never break the bond. But time had other plans. We'd drifted apart over the last few years.

As J. B. backed out and started down Cottage Street, Dunny handed me a beer.

"Didn't see you at the game," he said. "What a mess."

"How bad was it?" I asked after a gulp. Frankie half-turned. "Thirty-two to six."

"I can't remember losing by that much, ever," Dunny added.

That was a big loss for Natick. Coach would probably want to clean out the garage tomorrow.

"Where were you?" Frankie asked.

"I had a listing appointment in Marlborough."

"No shit." Frankie looked genuinely excited. "Did you get it?"

"Yep. First one."

J. B. adjusted the rearview mirror so he could see into the backseat. "How much?"

"A hundred and forty-five thousand."

Frankie's smile revealed his cracked front tooth, a souvenir from last year's skiing accident in Vermont. "Must be a nice house. My old man just got our place appraised at a hundred."

"Your house is a lot better than this piece of shit," I said, "and it's in Marlborough."

"A hundred, a hundred-forty," Dunny said. "What difference does it make? I'll never have enough bread to buy my own place." Dunny was a mechanic at a service station. After a swallow of beer, he added, "Looks like I'll be a lifer at my parents' house."

"For that kind of money, you can get a three-bedroom in Wayland," J. B. said into the rearview mirror. "And Marlborough ain't no Wayland."

I got a little pissed off. "Are you saying I listed it too high? What do you guys know about real estate?"

Nobody answered.

J. B. fumbled in his pockets, leaning left and then right, and the car swerved into the other lane.

"Watch what you're doing!" Frankie yelled. "We've got open beers here."

At six foot five and 250 pounds, J. B. could've crushed Frankie, but he was a gentle giant. He never played sports in school but spent his time with the kids in the drama department, taking an occasional odd role that required someone his size. He always hung out with beautiful girls from the neighboring town of Wayland, where long blond hair and blue eyes seemed to be requirements for residency, but he never had a girlfriend.

J. B. finally ended his search, triumphantly handing a bag of pot to Frankie.

We pulled into the parking lot next to the football field. Old habits die hard. Frankie rolled a joint and passed it around, and the Caddy filled with the pungent smell of weed. "Remember when we stole all the school bells?" Dunny asked. "They had to use the intercom to tell us when classes were over."

"Coach was pissed," I said. "Good thing we never got caught."

J. B. laughed. "What about the time we went skinny-dipping in the country club pool and the cops came?"

I nearly choked. "I was so freaked. I jumped that eight-foot fence without my clothes."

"That's nothing," Frankie added, "I got stuck halfway over. Jake was yelling, 'Hurry up!' and the cops were yelling, 'Freeze!'"

Dunny just about busted a gut. "Then the fence broke and you fell onto the golf course. I remember the cop yelling, 'I hope you broke your fucking ass!'"

When the four of us finally stopped roaring, Dunny asked, "How the hell did you two get home that night? It's a long walk. And you were naked."

We all roared again when I described stealing laundry from the clothesline behind one of the houses on the golf course. "Never did get our clothes back."

When the laughter died down, we sat sipping our beers, lost in memories. A rap on the driver's window snapped us back. J. B. lowered it for a couple of cuties.

"Any of that pot for sale, J. B.?"

J. B. shook his head as smoke billowed out through the open window.

"Oh, c'mon J. B. One joint. Pleeease."

J. B. reached into the bag and handed her a big bud. "Tell your sister I'll call her soon."

The girls headed off, giggling.

"Let's get out of here," Frankie said, "before every kid in town shows up. All I need is to get popped for selling pot."

J. B. always developed a slight lisp when he got high. "Not selling," he said, "giving."

"Great," Frankie said, sounding a little pissed, "that ought to get us a reduced sentence."

"Where should we go now?" Dunny asked as J. B. pulled out of the lot.

For me, the moment had already passed. We weren't kids anymore.

"Just take me home," I said. "Let's call it a day."

12

The house was quiet, Coach and Blaine on the sofa watching the Red Sox play Baltimore. I sank into the recliner next to them.

"The Orioles are tough," Coach said. "Even with our powerhouse lineup—Lynn, Rice, and Yastrzemski—we don't have the legs to catch them this year." Blaine struggled to stay awake.

I sank deeper into the chair. "Yaz got his three thousandth hit against the Yankees the other night. It was great."

Any blow dealt to the Yankees was great. The fact that Yaz was born in New York only made it sweeter. Boston die-hard fans would never forgive the Yankees for stealing the Great Bambino—Babe Ruth—years ago. This year, Freddy Lynn and Jimmy Rice were battling it out for the league's top batting average, home runs, and RBIs. Even so, Coach was right. The Sox couldn't finish strong this season. Damn Yankees. Damn curse.

I stood and gently shook my kid brother, "Come on, big guy, time for bed."

During a fitful sleep, my mind replayed the day's events: Mario, Tony, and the Alfa; Maria Alvarez's not-so-subtle gaze upon the unmade bed; and finally—*finally*—my first deal. It seemed I had barely slept at all when the phone jolted me awake on Sunday morning, but the clock on the bedside table swore it was ten thirty.

"Arril residence," Sessy recited, "may I help you?" Then there came the sound of the phone hitting the floor. "Jake, it's your office!" Sessy shouted.

I threw on clothes and ran downstairs. "Hello," I said, trying to untangle the cord.

"Jake, this is Marilyn. I want to know one thing. Is there an oilfield or a goldmine in the backyard of the Alvarez property?"

She didn't wait for a response.

"If not, I'd like to know how the hell you came up with that price." I couldn't find any words, and she still didn't seem interested.

"You have got to be shitting me, Jake. The place isn't worth half that amount. What were you thinking?"

Again, she wasn't actually expecting an answer.

"I've got to kill that listing or we'll be the laughingstock of the real estate world."

Kill the listing?

"I don't know how I'm going to get out of that contract, but my name—my firm—won't have anything to do with this mess. Maybe I'll tell them you're on drugs—or just plain crazy."

I waited, not even trying to come up with a word anymore.

"Good-bye and good luck, Jake. You're fired."

13

"Are they excited about your listing, Jake?" Mom was at the kitchen table, having coffee and toast, when I finally hung up the phone.

"Yep, they're excited all right." I headed for the stairs. "I think they want to make me a partner or something."

"That's great news, honey. Let's tell your father."

"Not just yet, Mom. Not till I get the details."

I went upstairs to shower. And to figure out what the hell had just happened.

I was no closer to understanding anything when I went back downstairs and poured a bowl of cereal. Mom did her best to look busy, but after folding a kitchen towel three times, she asked, "What happened, honey?"

I almost choked on my cereal. "Well, my deal is no longer a deal. I overpriced the place. The firm won't honor the contract. And the boss fired me."

She joined me at the table. "What are you going to do now?"

"No clue, Mom. Maybe I'll sell my blood. They pay ten bucks a pint. How many pints you figure I've got in me?"

She frowned, "Nothing worthwhile comes easily, Jake. You've worked hard, and this isn't fair, but don't quit on yourself. You're never beaten unless you quit." She gave my hand a gentle squeeze, then stood and left the room.

Reading the sports section in the living room, Coach paid no attention when I dug out the classifieds. Jobs were available for construction workers, nurses, and executives willing to relocate. Plenty of positions were posted under "Sales": insurance agents, pharmaceutical reps, car salesmen, travel agents. The list went on and on, but nothing looked even remotely promising for me. I was about to put the newspaper down when a blocked advertisement caught my eye:

IMMEDIATE OPENINGS FOR AMBITOUS PRECONSTRUCTION SALES REPS FOR BERKSHIRE MOUNTAIN RESORT. WE PROVIDE TRAINING, ACCOMODATIONS, AND CLIENTS. MASS. REAL ESTATE LICENSE REQUIRED. JOIN THE EXCITING WORLD OF TIME SHARE.

In smaller print was the contact, Herbie Starr, with a telephone number. I tore out the ad and stuffed it into my pocket.

SECTION II |

| On the Road

Jiminy Peak

14

Two weeks later, insurance check cashed and $2,000 in my pocket, I stood on the Mass Pike with my thumb out. Wearing a brown turtleneck, blue jeans, cowboy boots, a three-quarter-length calfskin coat and a Red Sox cap, I hoped Sox Nation would help me hitch to Hancock, Massachusetts. The team had faded at the end of the season, but this neck of the woods would always be Sox territory, and I needed a 250-mile ride.

It took a couple of weeks to deal with the insurance company after the Alfa's unfortunate mishap, but once I waived all claims for medical assistance, the check came through. Saying good-bye to my family was tough, but I held it together, realizing I might be back in a week. The whole deal sounded too good to be true.

Herbie Starr told me I'd live in the resort rent-free, have prospects delivered daily, and earn a commission on each sale. He'd been vague about what might constitute a sale, saying only that a condo that usually changed hands by way of a single deed could now be sold fifty-two times, one for each week of the year. If an owner didn't want to use his own condo during his week, he could swap time with like-minded folks.

It was all pretty confusing, but after the telephone interview, Herbie assured me a spot in the village, provided I arrived by October 1.

Natick had rebounded from its season opener with wins against Wellesley and Dedham, and Coach juggled his Tuesday schedule to drive me as far as the Mass Pike.

When we approached the toll booth, he fumbled in his pockets, finally asking, "Do you have thirty-five cents?"

"Dad, when I come back, I'm going to take you and Mom to the best stores and buy whatever you want."

He grinned. "But do you have the toll?"

He pulled over just past the Route 9 access. "I love you, son. Be careful and call if you need us."

At nine thirty, the morning air was chilly. After about fifteen minutes, a middle-aged guy in a van pulled over, "Where you headed?"

"West," I said, "to a new job."

I thanked him as I opened the passenger-side door. The van reeked of cigarettes. I took a deep breath in and climbed into the van.

"How far you going?"

"Next exit," he spoke through his cigarette, "got a short circuit in my breaker system. Nothin' to worry about, kid; we'll make it all right."

After small talk about the Sox and the future of the Pats, he dropped me and all my worth, neatly stuffed into my red backpack, on the side of the road again. If all the rides turned out to be local traffic, the trip would take a while.

The day had begun to warm up, and the sky was blue, but clouds building to the west looked ominous. An hour passed before I caught another lift, and I spent six hours after that alternately waiting on the roadside or riding with folks who were kind, lonely, or both. A pickup that pulled over near Pittsfield dropped me at Jiminy Peak at about five o'clock.

"They want to make a resort out of this place," the driver said. "Don't think it'll work."

The sun was setting over the beautiful Berkshires, but the mountain in front of me was black. With my backpack secured, I headed for the lodge. It seemed like forever since I'd left home.

As I walked the side road toward the mountain, I passed a small white building with two glowing neon signs reading, "Pat's Place" and "Budweiser." I considered stopping for a cold one but decided to push ahead. It was too early to ski, yet one section of the mountain was lit. As I rounded the last corner, the clubhouse greeted me with a Welcome sign. The few cars parked in front were noticeably new; one was painted a color I hadn't seen on a car.

The reception area was unmanned, but the guys at the back of the bar/restaurant were having a great time, their laughter erupting every few seconds, almost drowning out Bob Marley. As I approached, the music shifted to Donna Summer and somebody upped the volume. The place had a great sound system.

One of the partiers stood, lip synching "Hot Stuff" into a beer bottle, gyrating from one appreciative onlooker to the next. When he reached the biggest one in the bunch, he ran his fingers through the guy's hair, sat on his lap, and blew a kiss to his admirers. The whole gang was howling.

The big guy lurched to his feet, launching Donna Summer airborne, and the crowd went berserk.

"Don't play hard-to-get, Charlie," called a smaller, middle-aged guy. "We can't be picky up here."

After another chorus of laughter, someone else said, "That's it for today, guys. See you tomorrow. Eight sharp."

"You're too hard on them," Charlie said. "After all, they know everything. They don't need more training. Why don't we let them sleep in, Herbie?"

The head honchos, Charlie Furano and his right-hand man, Herbie Starr.

"Eight o'clock, girls!" Herbie hollered.

Charlie sat at the bar, lit a pipe, and blew a cloud of smoke toward the ceiling.

"Herbie, is it my imagination or is a new pup standing in my salesroom?"

Herbie Starr didn't look at all like I'd pictured during the phone interview. Just under five and a half feet tall and slim, with piercing green eyes and a pencil-thin mustache, he was bald but for a rim of black hair.

Charlie was five-ten and wide, with a large head and wiry brown hair. His big nose had obviously been broken more than once.

Herbie's smile featured a gap between his two front teeth. "Jake Arril, right?" I put out my hand, but he didn't take it.

"We only shake hands over money. You going to give me money?" I didn't know what to say.

He turned toward the bar. "Come meet your new boss."

Charlie seemed more interested in the bowl of his pipe than his new recruit.

"This is Jake Arril," Herbie said. "Real estate and a door-to-door sales gig. Thinks he has what it takes." Charlie didn't react.

"Thanks for the opportunity," I said. "I'm a fast learner, a hard worker, and I want to make a lot of money. I won't let you down."

Charlie seemed pleased with the job he'd done on his pipe. He repacked the bowl with fresh tobacco and lit up. "First of all," he said, not looking at me, "I didn't give you the opportunity. He did." He nodded toward Herbie. "Second, I'm not looking for hard workers. You want to work hard, go do construction or lay bricks. I need smart workers, fuckers who can sell." I thought maybe I should respond, but Charlie wasn't through. "Lastly, the fact that you want to make a lot of money means nothing. I want people who *need* to make a lot of money. I only make money when you do. And I *will* make a lot of money, puppy."

He meant every word.

"Time to bed you down," Herbie said, then turned to Charlie. "Sweets has his girlfriend in town. The only open spot is with Niles …"

Charlie almost smiled, "Go ahead. Put him in 101. Let him spend a night with Niles."

Herbie handed me a key. "Don't fuck around with this guy. See you in the morning."

I started for the door but then stopped. "Where am I going?"

"Young pup," Charlie muttered in a disgusted tone while shaking his head.

Herbie led me into the darkness outside. "You're going to have to figure things out. Your mother isn't here to babysit. Now, there's only one road—one way in, the other way out. See those cottages?"

He pointed toward a few dimly lit windows a couple hundred yards down the dirt road. "That key opens one of them. Find it, you have a bed. Don't sleep in the woods. Welcome to the club, kid. See you at eight."

Jiminy Peak sat in a bowl called the Jericho Valley, and on that cloudy, moonless night, it was dark. Really dark. When a sizeable something rustled in the bushes, I picked up the pace, and in no time I saw the hand-carved sign for Unit 101. The Moody Blues blasted from inside.

I dug in my pocket for the key but remembered the warning about my new roommate. I decided to knock. How bad could this Niles guy be?

Tired and hungry, I didn't wait long to knock again. This time the door flew open. There stood Niles, in army fatigues, an olive-green T-shirt and combat boots.

"Who the fuck are you, maggot?"

15

"Just kidding," Niles said, laughing. "Herbie called to say you were here. Throw your stuff in the spare room and come have a beer. I'll rustle up some grub."

I started to take off my shoes, but he told me not to. "The place gets cleaned every other day. We have a service. For ten bucks, they'll do the laundry too, but I don't bother. We have a washer and dryer."

The spare room had a freshly made king-size bed and an attached bathroom. I dumped my backpack and went to the kitchen. "Grab a cold one," Niles said. "Be with you in a second. Don't want the fine cuisine to burn."

He was frying hamburger in a large skillet, an unopened can of Franco-American spaghetti on the counter. "Hungry?"

As he pulled a second can of spaghetti from the cabinet, I realized who he was.

"Caught your act at the clubhouse, Donna Summer. You must sell out every night."

Niles opened both cans and added the spaghetti to the browned meat. The pasta sizzled. "You're off to a good start," he said. "Dinner and a show."

The meal smelled pretty damn delicious. He filled two plates, set them on the table, and offered his hand. "John Niles. Pleased to meet you."

We shook, and he added, "Make yourself at home. For thirty days anyhow. Or until Charlie gets pissed off at you."

The food tasted great. "What do you mean, thirty days?" I asked between mouthfuls.

"Figures they didn't give you the scoop. Charlie either gets this thing running in thirty days or he's out."

"Out?"

"He promised the owner of this joint that sales would be running thirty days from now. If not, we'll all be back in Boston, selling cars."

Niles took a gulp of beer. "If we could get some UPs"—he drew a *U* and a *P* in the air—"we could pull it off. The program makes a lot of sense."

My plate was empty. "What's an UP?"

Niles hadn't touched his food. He grabbed another beer from the fridge. "An UP is a prospect, someone who can buy something so we can make some fucking money."

I thought about asking for his plate of food but then noticed he'd squished his cigarette out in the pasta.

"I've already been here thirty days," he said. "Show up every morning at eight sharp. And I've had five UPs the whole time."

"How many did you sell?"

"Two. Made a grand. Don't get me wrong; the commission is great. But we need more UPs."

I cleared the plates and looked at the fridge.

"Help yourself," he said.

With a fresh beer in hand and a full belly, the worries of the last few weeks began to fade.

"And I don't know how much longer any of us can stand Charlie," Niles said as he went into the living room, "he's driving everybody crazy."

He clicked on the TV and found game six of the World Series. The Orioles had jumped to a 3–1 lead, seeming to have the series in the bag, but then Pittsburgh rallied, winning game five. This game was in the ninth inning, and it looked like they were headed for game seven in Baltimore. Sister Sledge's *We Are Family* was on the lips of every Pirates fan.

Lighting a new cigarette, Niles asked, "Do you wanna see the place? Or do you just wanna crash?"

Fortified by the beer and the notion of a new beginning, I said, "Let's have a look around, see what you've got here."

"Let's stop next door; maybe Sweets and his girlfriend will join us."

Niles knocked once. When no one answered, he went in. I couldn't believe my eyes. In the living room stood a beautiful blond twentysomething, six feet tall, wearing black lingerie. Next to her was a little guy, maybe five feet three inches, midforties, with shoulder-length blond hair. He might have weighed 125 pounds soaking wet. He stood naked but for a white cowboy hat he held over his crotch and two gold chains draped around his neck.

"For Christ's sake, Niles," he said, "why the hell don't you knock?"

I turned to leave, but Niles said, "Sweets. Hi, Becky. Welcome back."

"Hey Niles," she answered calmly. "Did you miss me?"

By the time I faced them again, they'd put on robes. Hers was shiny, pink, and short. His was black and covered his feet. He turned to grab a cigarette, revealing pink letters across the back: *SWEETS.* He looked like an aging porn star.

Niles dropped into a chair and pointed me to the sofa. "Guys, meet Jake, a new addition to the list of the banished and forgotten."

"And tortured." Sweets extended his hand, exhaling a cloud of white smoke. He was definitely no spring chicken.

Becky took my hand next, holding on a bit too long. "Finally, new stock worth looking at. Maybe I'll stick around." She winked before heading to the kitchen.

"Knock it off, honey, or the new stock might think you're a tramp." Sweets joined me on the sofa. "I'm Bobby Ditaccio," he said, "Sweet Bobby D. Just Sweets to my friends. Where the hell did Charlie and Herbie find you?"

I started to answer, but he interrupted. "Never mind that for now. Let's head to Pat's. We'll get chummy over a few cold ones."

Becky returned with a glass of orange juice. "Yippee," she said flatly. "Another big night on the town. Let me grab my dancing shoes."

She dropped the robe as she sauntered into the bedroom, giving us a back-door view. Nice ass, blond hair hanging to the middle of her back. A beauty. I peeled my eyes away in time to see Sweets eyeing me. He smiled and went into the bedroom.

"A racehorse," Niles said as he stood. "Pure thoroughbred. Let's go. They can catch up."

16

As we walked toward the main lodge, I wished I had a warmer coat, and the cowboy boots were starting to hurt. I asked about the work crew on the lighted part of the mountain.

"The alpine slide," Niles said. "When there's no snow, people come here just for the slide—little sleds on two racing tracks that run from the top of the mountain, hand brakes for control. Pretty cool."

Behind us, headlights bounced on the rutted dirt road. Sweets and Becky pulled up in a lime green 1976 Cadillac Eldorado, its top down in spite of the night chill.

"Need a lift to town, cowboys?" Becky opened the passenger door and tilted her seat forward.

Inside the enormous car, Willie Nelson and Waylon Jennings crooned "Mammas Don't Let Your Babies Grow Up to Be Cowboys." We all belted out the chorus, but Niles changed "cowboys" to "time-share salesmen." We were roaring by the time we got to Pat's and piled out of the Eldorado. Becky slipped her arm around my waist and rested her head on my shoulder. Her perfume was nice—really nice.

"Aw, Jake," she said, "you always bring me to the best places."

Pat's was what I expected. Wooden tables and chairs, a handful of guys at the bar under a red neon Budweiser sign, an old man was tossing darts on the far side of the room, a few others shooting pool. At a corner table sat Charlie, smoking his pipe over a cup of coffee, while Herbie chowed down on a basket of wings.

Niles's voice broke through the bar noise. "Fearless leaders."

Becky pulled her chair close to mine. "I'm cold, Jakey. Will you keep me warm?" Sweets didn't seem to mind. Maybe it was just her way.

"Any UPs coming tomorrow?" Niles asked.

Herbie looked at Charlie, who shrugged. "All it takes is one, if you make it count."

"Yeah, but we need bodies," Niles fired back. "Maybe we should change the premium. Or the marketing."

Herbie's eyes shot daggers at Niles, but it was too late. Charlie laid his pipe in the ashtray. "If things aren't going your way, Niles, why don't you pack up? Go home and sell Buicks. A hundred guys are waiting to take your place."

Niles didn't back down. "I gotta tell you, sitting up here in the woods seeing one or two UPs a week is driving me nuts. How many times do we need to hear Herbie's five steps? I'm starting to fucking dream about them. And that's not good, Chaz. You know what I'm saying?"

Becky's mouth was touching my ear. "What do you dream about, Jake?"

Charlie went back to his pipe. "We'll get the tours. I'm meeting with Brian tomorrow. Maybe you're right. Maybe the premium isn't strong enough."

He stood to leave, and Herbie looked sadly at his half-eaten basket of wings.

A tall, lanky guy with a full head of slicked-back black hair walked up to the table. "Pat, my good man," Niles said, "set up my posse with a pitcher of your finest lager." Eyeing Herbie's wings, he added, "and we will finish the remainder of that fine Jewish man's dinner."

Becky frowned. "That's gross, Niles. Herbie probably breathed all over it."

"Sis, you didn't see what I ate in 'Nam. Trust me, this is dinner at the Ritz."

I'd never met anyone who'd actually gone to war. "You were in 'Nam?" I was fifteen when the draft was abolished.

Sweets moaned. "Don't get him started."

Niles snapped to attention and saluted. "Sergeant John Niles, US Marines. Hoorah!"

Pat showed up with the pitcher. "You start that shit again in my restaurant, Niles, and I swear I'll toss you for good. My customers come here to chill out. They don't need to listen to your crap."

Niles poured the beer—Becky's first, his own last—then stood and raised his mug.

"Semper fi, motherfuckers!"

One pool player set down his stick. "Semper fi, brother!"

Niles downed the beer, then sat and filled up again. "Why the hell weren't you there?" he asked Sweets.

"I told you. I'm a diabetic. C'mon, John, let's not scare the recruit away on his first day."

Niles tamped out a cigarette. "Everything you have or ever will have was defended by me and my brothers," he said to me. "Don't ever take that for granted."

Sweets was hell-bent on changing the subject. "Jake, what do you know?"

"Yes, Jake, let's hear about you." Becky had moved her chair even closer to mine. She was practically on my lap.

"Not much to tell," I said, surprised by the attention. I was content to sit on the sidelines, watching. "Grew up just outside of Boston, went to college for a few years, it didn't work out, and I've been kicking around since, trying to make a buck." I finished my beer, and Niles poured a refill.

Under the table, Becky's hand rested on the inside of my right leg. My beer almost spilled. Needing to change the subject fast, I asked about Herbie's five steps, but Niles had wandered over to the pool players, exchanging a few words and a brotherly hug with his "Semper fi" buddy.

Becky rubbed the inside of my leg. If Sweets noticed, he didn't let on.

"The five steps!" Niles yelled. "The path to success. One: meet and greet. Blow the first impression and you'll fail. Two: make a friend. Forget the salesman/client shit. Every fact you find out about your new friend is ammunition. Three—"

Sweets took over. "Break the pact. UPs usually come in pairs, and the pairs always have a pact: They will *not* buy anything. Let them know you expect them to join today. Not tomorrow, next week, or next year. *Today.*"

Niles circled his hand in the air, pointed at the empty pitcher, and Pat delivered a full one. He also brought a pepperoni pizza, setting it down in front of Becky. "On the house, honey," he said. "Knowing these guys, you probably haven't had supper."

"That's so kind, Pat." She took a slice. "You're right. A girl could starve around these guys."

Niles refilled his mug. "Step four is story time, the front end. Use the information you gathered in step two to blend the program with their lifestyle, improving the way they travel."

Finished with a few bites of pizza, Becky put her hand back on my leg. I didn't object. In fact, I liked it. A lot.

"And step five: the close. This one separates the men from the boys." Niles looked around the table. "Never ask for the sale. Assume the sale. Never ask, 'Would you like to join?' Ask, '*How* would you like to join? Cash or check?'"

Niles sat back. "Follow the five steps, fail ninety percent of the time, and you make a boatload of money."

Sweets signaled for Pat, who brought the tab and, without hesitation, handed it to me.

The others were already putting on their jackets.

I pulled out the wad of cash that used to be the Alfa, peeled off a few twenties, and then noticed Becky watching. She smiled slowly as her gaze moved from the cash to my eyes.

The clouds had disappeared, and we headed up the mountain road in the Eldorado under a full moon. The cool breeze felt good, and in the backseat I felt comfortable and safe, with new friends and a fresh start ahead. Sweets stopped in front of the reception center and looked back at Niles, grinning.

"Why not?" Niles said. "Beautiful night for it."

"For what?" I asked.

"A ride down the mountain," said Sweets.

17

I followed the others to the illuminated area where the maintenance crew continued repairs on the alpine tracks.

"Evening, gents," Niles said. "Nice night for a ride."

He surveyed the neatly stacked sleds, hoisted one under his arm, and started up the mountain. "Pick one, Jake, and follow me."

I looked to Sweets and Becky, "Aren't you guys gonna do this?"

Sweets shook his head, "Nah. We're just gonna watch."

I grabbed a sled and followed Niles up the dimly lit path. I halted at the sound of footsteps approaching from behind us.

"Take that long coat off." Becky's voice nearly stopped my heart; I could hardly differentiate her silhouette against the grain of night. "It might get caught on the sled."

"Thanks, Beck." I handed her the coat as Niles yelled at me to step on it.

The narrow dirt path got steeper and steeper as we climbed. I was taken aback by how effortlessly Niles sprinted up the mountain.

"Almost there, recruit. You can do it."

After a long trek, we stood together at the top of the mountain. Niles grinned. "Tough climb, recruit?"

"Was this the only way up?"

He shook his head. "The chairlift is for paying customers, not grunts like us." He pointed to the second slide. "Lay your sled in there, but don't let go unless you want to walk down."

I started to feel my nerves through the adrenaline. The slides were fairly level here, but we'd passed areas where the chutes seemed almost vertical. "Is this safe?"

Niles put his sled on the track next to mine. "Do you want to live

50

forever? Two things you need to know. Push the stick forward, the wheels run free. Pull it back, the wheels come up and the pads on the bottom stop the sled. Piece of cake."

I didn't realize we were about to race until Niles settled on his sled. "On the count of three, push the stick forward. Remember: Jake, last one to the bottom's a pussy."

I grabbed the stick with both hands. Below, the silver glow of moonlight reflected off the white slide. Straight ahead, the speckled light from Pat's told me just how high we were.

Shit. After everything I went through to get here, this is how it ends.

"One, two, three, go-o-o-o ..." Niles's voice echoed through the trees.

I pushed the stick forward. The sled started slowly, but as the track steepened, it accelerated dramatically.

"Go for it, Jake! Feel the track!"

The wheels click-clacked over the creases between the ten-foot sections of the slide, the brakes made a shushing sound.

Niles was way ahead. I pushed the stick all the way forward, my head nestled just above my knees, and the sled rocketed down the mountain. It whipped around the bends so fast that I was pinned to it, until the track straightened out, where I began to freefall in a vertical descent.

I was getting the hang of it. After rounding one of the sweeping curves, I spotted Niles. *I got ya now.*

I pulled even with him on another level section, just long enough for me to witness the intense look on his face. This was more than just fun and games.

"You don't have what it takes, you puke!" Niles yelled as he leaned forward, urging the sled faster.

I did the same. The wheels sounded like a sewing machine. There were now no interruptions between the clicks and clacks—just one consistent *cliiickkk*. We were flying. I mastered the alpine slide on the first try. Niles would have to eat crow.

Out of the corner of my eye, I noticed Niles drop back out of view. As I looked forward, the shadows cast by the dim light made it nearly impossible to see the sharp curve in the track. All fell silent, the track vanished, and I was airborne.

After what seemed an eternity, my sled smashed to the ground and bounced down the mountain, sending me into a triple somersault. My body was a rag doll, a crash test dummy, tearing through shrubs before I skidded to a halt, flat on my back.

"Jake, you okay?" Becky's voice brought me back to my senses.

Slowly, and with hesitation, I moved various parts of my body. Everything still intact, I sat up to look back at the mountain. The track glowed triumphantly, as it was clearly the winner.

Niles, leaning back on his sled, howled, "For Christ's sake, Jake, why don't you watch where you're going?" Sweets joined him, and the howls got louder. I wasn't sure, but I thought Becky was laughing too. That hurt.

I was off the trail, in the woods, and the sled was nowhere to be found. I hoped at the very least I'd come across my pride, but the mountain had taken that too. I made my way on foot, and alone, through the trees that lined the bottom of the mountain. The gang faithfully awaited me, Niles and Sweets joined the crew under the glow of the work lights. As I limped toward them, I was welcomed with of a mixture of laughter and applause. My hip hurt, my shoulder was banged up, my back burned, and blood ran down the side of my face. Becky ran to me as the others shouted in unison, "Welcome to Jiminy Peak!"

18

I'd arrived at my new job, met the bosses, moved into a condo with a psycho Vietnam vet, and just about got killed. All in all, a great start.

Becky handed me my calfskin coat as I climbed from the backseat of Sweets's Eldorado. I took it without a word.

Niles was in the kitchen. "Bro," he called, "no puke recruit has ever survived a dump like that!"

"I could've been killed."

"But you weren't."

As far as I was concerned, this day was done. Exhausted, I headed to bed. When I rolled onto my left side, pain stabbed my shoulder; on my right, it seared through my ribs. Lying flat on my back, I took a deep breath, my entire body aching. It would be worse in the morning.

I don't know how long I'd been asleep when I heard someone call my name in the dark room. My eyes adjusted, and there she stood, wearing only black lingerie.

Maybe I died. "What's going on, Becky?"

I struggled to sit up as she sat next to me. "I came to see if you're okay. You could have been hurt real bad, Jakey. I'm so sorry."

She caressed my face, and I winced when her hand reached a bump on my forehead. She kissed it and rubbed my shoulder. "Does this hurt too?" I nodded.

Her lips moved to that bruise and then she stood, dropping the lingerie.

She was stunning, her skin smooth and glowing, her blond hair shimmering in the moonlight as she lifted the blanket and lay next to me. Resting her head on my chest, she caressed me, asking if it hurt as her hand moved. Each time I nodded, she kissed the spot.

53

Her body pressed against mine, and we kissed a slow, tender kiss as her hand moved farther south. "Does it hurt here?"

I shook my head and ran my hand along the small of her back. "What about Sweets?"

Her skin was as soft as silk. "He feels bad for you too."

That wasn't the question.

She rolled and straddled my body. "Tonight I belong to you, Jake. No one else exists. Just you and me."

She lowered her face to mine. The next kiss was deep and strong. "Let me take all the pain away from you," she whispered.

For the next few hours, I knew it was true. I had died. I was in heaven with an angel. Sweaty and exhausted, I put my head next to hers on the pillow and breathed in her perfume. Bliss.

When I woke, the sun was shining, the sky was blue, and the bed was empty.

Only her perfume lingered.

Niles was rustling around in the kitchen, so it was time to get up. When I tried, the night before hit hard. And the sight in the bathroom mirror was scary. The lump on my forehead looked like a unicorn horn, and the bruise on my shoulder was a monster. Down below, dried blood caked my knees, and both hips were seriously banged up. I looked like I'd been hit by a truck.

The hot shower loosened things up a little. While shaving, I half-turned to inspect the scratch marks running across both shoulders and laughed. *Those didn't come from the mountain.*

Back in the bedroom with a towel around my waist, I noticed my wad of cash stacked neatly on the bedside table. I didn't recall taking the money from my pants last night.

"Five minutes!" Niles yelled. "Don't piss off Batman and Robin on your first day."

I pulled a pair of pants and a shirt from the backpack—both creased across the middle—and put the money back in my pocket as I left the bedroom.

"Everything working, grunt? Need a wheelchair or what?"

"Just a little sore."

"Nothing like the touch of an angel to take the pain away."

He must be a light sleeper.

When Niles went next door to get Sweets, I hung back.

"What's wrong, soldier? Sometimes Becky has coffee and hot buns."

I already know she has hot buns.

Sweets appeared wearing an embroidered Mexican shirt with brown bellbottoms, a brown leather vest, and matching cowboy hat. He looked at me. "Hope your night ended up okay. You all right?"

I nodded.

Becky leaned in the open doorway, still in lingerie, and blew me a kiss. "Good luck, boys. See you soon."

"We walking this morning? Niles asked. Bunch of sorry grunts we are."

"Nah, let's take the bull," Sweets answered.

I didn't ask, but I didn't have to wait long for the answer. Mounted on the hood of the lime green Caddy was a pair of the largest bull horns I'd ever seen.

"You didn't notice last night? Too busy pulling the mountain out of your ass?"

"Got these in Texas," Sweets interjected. "Pretty horny car, huh?"

I laughed and climbed into the backseat. The roof was down, the air chilly, the sky blue, and the sun shining. Studded with evergreens and aged trees casting shadows of wisdom over their freshly fallen leaves, the valley was downright beautiful.

Sweets gunned the car in reverse, slammed the brakes, jammed it into drive, and fishtailed down the gravel road. When we passed the scene of my near demise, Niles high-fived him and looked in the rearview mirror. "Bet you didn't know you could fly, Jake."

"Need to work on that landing, buddy," Sweets added.

We were all laughing when the car skidded to a halt in front of the reception center, right on time for work. But with Sweets in his Tex-Mex getup, me in my calfskin coat, and Niles with his baseball cap pulled down over his shades, we looked like a band of hoods heading for a heist.

19

The place was bigger than I remembered. The guys sat at thirty-two-inch-round tables you'd expect to find at a middle-of-the-road restaurant. I followed Niles and Sweets to the far corner, toward Herbie and Charlie. Noticing my limp, Charlie looked from Niles to Sweets, shaking his head.

Herbie grinned as we helped ourselves to coffee. "Sleep well, Jake?"

"Yeah, pretty quiet night." I dragged myself to a seat and eased into it.

"All right guys!" Herbie yelled. "Eight o'clock. Let's get smart."

We all sat, but a table in the center remained empty. After being introduced, Herbie told me to say a few words.

I struggled to my feet. "I'm Jake—"

"Shut the fuck up, Jake," the others hollered.

Obviously, it was tradition. I sat.

"Step one, meet and greet," Herbie began. "You don't take this step seriously, you don't stand a chance."

A couple guys mumbled, "You only get one shot at a first impression."

Charlie took a drag from his pipe. "The UPs already have a pact. They're just waiting for you to screw up." He exhaled a cloud of blue smoke. "Get this right. Your opportunity to make money is driving here as we speak, planning to waste your time and cost us money." The guys were quiet. "I make money when you do! You don't make money, I don't need you!"

"We gonna be busy today, Chaz?" Niles asked.

Charlie ignored him. "Do this right, and you'll make more money than any lawyer or doctor." He'd whipped himself into a frenzy, spitting as he spoke. One string of spit bounced between his top and bottom lips during his tirade. It was pretty gross to witness first thing in the morning.

"All you have to do is learn five steps. Now take it seriously or get out!" He stared us down one at a time, daring each of us to challenge the alpha dog. "Get these girls ready," he told Herbie, and then he strolled out through the double doors.

The words hung in the air as thick as the pipe smoke until Niles broke the silence.

"No donuts today, Herbie?"

Even Herbie laughed. "Let's do this," he said. "Bobby O., what do you want to accomplish when you meet your UP?"

"Control, Herbie. Gotta get control immediately."

Herbie's grin reminded me of the grinch.

"And what exactly does 'control' mean, Bobby O.?"

"From the get-go, let them know we mean to do business, to sell them. Today."

"Eye contact?" Herbie prodded.

"Direct. Not threatening, never evasive. Like Charlie said, the UPs have already made a pact to not buy anything, just collect the gifts we use to lure them in here." Bobby O. was into it. "Right from the greeting, let them know this is serious business, that we're concerned about a problem they may not be aware of. Like doctors meeting patients for the first time, we need to convince them this is no joke."

"You summed it up right, Bobby O.," Herbie said. "Our owners have poured real money into this property. A lot is at stake here. We need to convert these UPs into cash."

He looked around the room, "Let's roleplay. Niles, you're the husband. Jake, you're his wife."

"Who the hell would marry anything as ugly as this grunt?"

The guys laughed; Herbie didn't. Niles stood and told me to follow. "Sit still and look pretty."

We sat at the round table in the center. Herbie gestured toward one of the other salesmen, "Carl, break the pact."

Carl sat between us, uneasy. Looking at me, he began, "Welcome to Jiminy Peak." Turning his head, he spoke to Niles. "We're happy you came here to learn how to vacation in resort accommodations instead of hotel rooms."

Herbie stopped him cold.

Niles leaned back in his chair. "Seating, my man. My wife and I should be side by side so you can maintain eye contact."

"I've been telling you this for weeks!" Herbie shouted. "Get the fuck out of here. You're fired!"

Carl left the room slowly, without a word.

"You don't have to like me"—Herbie scanned the crowd of us—"but you've got to learn the five steps."

Niles moved into the chair next to me and slipped his arm around my shoulders.

"Can we get our gifts now?"

The guys laughed. "Bobby O.," Herbie said, "show everyone how a real salesman breaks the pact."

Bobby O. sat directly across the table, making eye contact with Niles, with me, and then with Niles again. "John and Mary, today we're going to talk about the time and money your family spends on vacations. We can send you to the finest destinations, put you into luxury suites, villas, and chalets, all for a fraction of the cost of run-of-the-mill hotel rooms." He clasped his hands together. "Does that sound like something you and your family could use?"

Niles nodded.

Bobby O. leaned forward and asked again, "Does this sound like a program you and your loved ones could use?"

"Yes," Niles muttered.

Bobby O. was relentless. "Pardon me, John, what did you say?"

"Yes, that sounds good!" Niles hollered, committed in his response.

Satisfied, Bobby O. turned to me. "Mary, would you like to stay in top-notch accommodations for less money?"

I nodded. It wasn't good enough for Bobby O.

"Mary, do you and your family deserve the best accommodations on vacation?"

I looked at Niles, then back at Bobby O., "We do, but we can't afford them. We travel with our kids."

Bobby O. looked from me to Niles, then back to me. "John and Mary, today I will explain how time-sharing will work for you and your family. Once you see its value and realize it's one hundred percent affordable, is there any reason you wouldn't join?" He waited for an answer.

Niles turned to me. "That sounds fair, right, honey?" I nodded.

Bobby O. sat up straight, maintaining eye contact with both of us. "John and Mary, when I've done my job and you understand the value of the program and see how affordable it is, you will join today, correct?"

Niles looked at me, then at Bobby O. "Sounds fair."

Bobby O. wasn't satisfied. "John, does that mean yes?"

"If we like it and can afford it," Niles said, "we'll join."

"Same with you, Mary? If you like the program, you'll join today?"

"Yes," I said.

"Now let's have some fun and change the way you travel forever." Bobby O. shook hands with both of us, then leaned back in his chair as Herbie clapped.

I knew enough about sales to see that Bobby O. was a pro. His eye contact, words, body language—all smooth and effective.

"The sale's been made," Herbie said. "The UP has been pinned, the pact destroyed. They're committed to joining today if Bobby O. does his job. You'll do your job, right, big guy?"

"The product practically sells itself," Bobby O. said. "The only thing that kills a sale here is the B-back."

"What's that?" I asked.

"Exactly what it sounds like," Charlie's voice boomed. He had silently slipped into the back of the room. "The kiss of death. They want to go home and think about it." Noticing a distracted Sweets, he barked, "Sweets, what does that mean?"

Sweets had his head down, counting cash under the table. I reached into my pocket to count my own. Figuring the bill at Pat's last night and a few bucks on the toll roads, what remained of my $2,000 was $150 short.

"Let me rephrase the question. What exactly do we sell, Sweets?"

Holding his cash under the table, Sweets snapped to attention. "Time, Chaz. We're buying a steak, not the whole cow." He shot a glance at me and kissed the money, "Pay for only the time you want, then walk away."

Niles chuckled. "Or just go back to sleep."

I got it. Becky played me—took the money while I slept.

"Exactly," Charlie said. "Make sense, John and Mary?" A few guys nodded.

Charlie leaned forward and raised his voice, "Make sense, John and Mary?"

"Yes! That makes sense!" the room shouted in unison.

Satisfied, Charlie lit his pipe and turned to Herbie. "What if I don't want to go to the same place every year?"

"That's a great question, Charlie. The answer is RCI, Resort Condominiums International, whose thousands of members own time at resorts around the world. For a small fee, you can exchange your time with any of them. Want to trade Florida in the winter for Cape Cod in the summer? Your RCI representative will make it happen."

A delivery guy wheeled a few large boxes to the reception desk. Charlie sauntered over and opened one with a pocketknife, "Here they are, guys. The new premium. A genuine faux leather jacket. We'll give one to every qualified prospect who gives us ninety minutes."

The gang clapped.

"This little gem will bring in plenty of UPs so we can all make a boatload of money."

"About time, Charlie." Niles winked. "I'm out of clean socks and down to my last beer."

Herbie inspected the jacket, then passed it to Sweets, who let out a low whistle.

"Wow. Bet the plastic packaging cost more than this piece of shit."

The jacket made its way around the room, ending up with me. The rubbery brown coat was square, with no taper, and its oversize black buttons looked like relics from some long-lost checkers game. The crew started grumbling.

"Where'd you find this crap? The first guy we give this away to is gonna try to kill us."

Charlie held up his hand. "Bobby O., how do you see it?"

He took a moment to consider. "If it gets people in the door, Chaz, nothing else matters. If it brings in qualified UPs, I'll sell to them. We don't give them the gift until the pitch is done anyway. By then the sale's in the bag."

"Bingo, Bobby O. Once you're talking to a qualified UP, the rest is up to you. Just take the candy from the baby."

I raised my hand.

"What is it, pup?"

"What is a qualified UP, Charlie?"

A few guys snickered until Charlie's glare silenced them. "It's a good question, Jake. Let's hear one of you answer it."

"At least thirty years old," Sweets said, "but not over seventy."

Charlie nodded. "How old were you when you started making money, Sweets?"

"Fourteen when I hit the streets, sixteen when I bought my first car, twenty-one when I moved into my first house."

"We target married couples between thirty and seventy who are employed and own their homes. But make no mistake—everybody can be sold." Charlie had the spit thing going on again. "If they don't like to travel, change their minds. If they think they can't afford it, make them want it so bad they'll beg, borrow, and steal. Excuses are bullshit. If you don't take their money, it's because you suck."

I knew he was right.

When he paused for a breath, Bobby O. piped up. "When does the campaign kick in, Charlie? When do we start seeing the tours?"

Herbie took over. "We've mailed ten thousand invitations to prospects who live within two hours of the mountain. We expect two percent to respond. We'll book three shows a day, seven days a week. That gives you guys three shots a day to make real money."

Charlie started again. "We've paid for printing, mailing, telemarketing … Every prospect is a hundred-dollar bill. That means twenty thousand dollars a week. So convert these UPs into cash. Grab them by the throats, throw them to the ground, step on their necks. Make them fucking beg you to take their money."

"Any coming today?" Niles asked.

"Ten," Herbie said, "between now and two."

Niles groaned. "Two? Game seven starts at three."

"Are you shitting me, Niles?" Charlie looked like he might charge. "*This* is the game. Get your head out of your ass or get the fuck out of here!"

Niles seemed unconcerned with Charlie's fury. "Can I have Christmas and February 15 off?"

Charlie looked stunned, "What the hell is February 15?"

Niles smiled. "Your birthday, Chaz. I want to bake you a cake."

Starting with Sweets, a low rumble erupted into side-splitting laughter.

"What the fuck?" A piece of spit the size of Texas settled on his upper lip before he left the room.

20

A car had pulled up during the commotion, and a couple came through the door, an opened envelope in the man's hand. "Welcome to Jiminy Peak," the receptionist said with a smile. "I'm Annie. Are you here for our open house?"

Annie was good at her job. She explained that Jiminy Peak's owners had spent advertising dollars on gifts to bring potential members to the property, show them how beautiful the resort was, and introduce them to a representative who would explain the program's many benefits.

The woman held up the envelope. "This letter says we won a gift. It says we only need to be here ninety minutes and that we don't have to buy anything."

Annie smiled. "This is our form of advertisement. We hope you like what you see here at Jiminy Peak and spread the word to family and friends." She asked for two forms of ID so we could be sure they were the couple approved by the awards center. She had the pair fill out a short questionnaire on their travel habits and then directed them to the coffee and donuts.

"Who's up?" Annie asked as she delivered the form to Herbie.

"Bobby O. is first." Herbie scanned the sheet and gave it back to her, and she delivered it to Bobby O. Without so much as a glance at it, he went for the meet and greet.

"Welcome to Jiminy Peak, folks." Bobby O. extended his hand to the man, who had coffee in one hand, a donut in the other. After a chuckle, he passed the coffee to his wife. "I'm Jim Peterson," he said, "and this is Sandra."

Niles elbowed me, "Did you see that?"

"See what?"

"Always go to the guy first. It's an alpha thing. In three seconds, Bobby O. had control. He forced the guy to do what he wanted—shake hands—and the guy made his wife help. The guy would never introduce his wife to somebody dangerous, so this is her husband saying that Bobby O. is safe. He's okay. And it all happened in a few seconds."

Bobby O. led the couple to a round table near the window with a view of the mountain. After seating them together, facing him, he began the warm-up. In no time, he learned that Jim was a firefighter, Sandra a schoolteacher, and their two kids, fourteen-year-old Jessica and twelve-year-old Jason, loved the outdoors.

He swapped stories about his own two kids: sixteen-year-old Roberta and their unexpected gift from God, eight-year-old Peter.

"It's a crock," Niles said.

"Bobby O. doesn't have kids?"

"Sure he does. Bobby Jr. is nineteen, and Joey is seventeen."

The Petersons hailed from Springfield, and their lives revolved around family. Vacations were primarily day trips to ski in the winter, sometimes at Jiminy Peak. Sandra dreamed of taking the kids to Disney World during a February school break.

Bobby O. asked why they hadn't taken that trip yet. Sandra frowned and glanced at her husband.

"Awfully expensive at that time of year," Jim said.

Bobby O. leaned back in his chair and looked at them for a long moment. "If today I show you a way to take that trip, to stay in a suite at a resort that will blow your mind, for no more than the cost of a weekend at a New Hampshire motel, will you promise me you'll take your kids and go?"

Sandra looked to Jim. "Sure we will," he said.

She looked at Bobby O., who repeated the question. "Yes," she said. "Of course."

"You two agreed you wouldn't spend any money today, am I right?"

Sandra giggled. Her husband was silent.

"Isn't that the case, Jim? Didn't you two agree not to spend any money, no matter how great the program sounds?"

Jim shifted in his chair, looking uncomfortable. Bobby O. wanted an answer. "Yes or no, Jim?"

Jim said yes.

"I appreciate people who are honest, up-front." Bobby O. tightened the drag on his reel. "Don't you, Jim and Sandra?"

"Oh, yes," they said together.

"When we finish today, you will have seen this property and the plans for development. I'll explain how time-sharing works, plain and simple, and then I'll ask a few questions." Looking as intense as a laid-back country boy could, he continued. "I'll ask if you understand how easy it is to use this program, if you see how affordable a membership is, and if becoming a member would make some dreams come true for you and your kids." Jim and Sandra were focused. "Then I'll ask if you'd like to join. What I'll want from you is a yes or a no. Can you do that for me?"

Jim nodded. Sandra didn't budge.

Bobby O. pressed on. "Can the two of you promise to give me a straight answer? Either 'Yes, this is the best thing since apple pie,' or 'No, it's not for us.' Can you do that, Jim?"

"Yes."

"Can you do that, Sandra?"

"Yes," she echoed.

Bobby O. smiled as he shook Jim's hand and then Sandra's. "It's a beautiful day." He grinned. "Let's get some fresh air. I'll show you your resort and how to use your program."

He held the door for Sandra and Jim, then turned back to the sales staff and bowed.

21

He filled us in later. During the walk to the units, they chatted about their kids and the World Series. Bobby O. had lived in the area his whole life, so he knew every secret of the Berkshire Mountains. He told the Petersons about great fishing spots, hiking trails, and restaurants, putting in an extra plug for Pat's—free delivery for members.

Just before entering the model unit, he paused. "Imagine your vacations in accommodations like this—a level of quality your family will come to expect. And remember, whether here at Jiminy Peak or in Florida or anywhere else in the world, you'll spend no more than you would on a roadside motel."

With that, he swung the door open to the two-bedroom, two-bath suite, complete with living room, full kitchen, and a deck overlooking the mountain and the valley.

Sandra gasped as she took in the kitchen's state-of-the-art appliances. She opened cupboards to examine the dishes, drawers to see the cutlery. Then she hurried to the smaller bedroom. "Look, Jim. Twin beds. For Jessica and Jason."

Jim didn't say much, but Bobby O. could tell he liked what he saw. "Why don't you show Sandra the master suite?" he suggested, pointing down the hall. "And don't forget to take in the view from the deck."

"Honey, let's go see our room," Jim said.

Bobby O. trailed behind, but he heard every word. They loved it.

Jim turned and asked the question that is music to every salesman's ears: "So, Bobby O., what does it cost?"

"Don't worry about cost," he said calmly. "Like we agreed, Jim, if it would hurt your family's finances, I won't let you join."

They sat in Adirondack chairs on the deck as Bobby O. explained the annual maintenance fee, the VIP skiing rates for members even when they don't stay at the resort, and the small charge for maid service to keep the members supplied with fresh linens and towels.

Sandra almost fell off her chair. "We don't have to bring anything?"

Bobby O. smiled. "Just your toothbrush. And your desire to have fun."

"What does it cost?" Jim asked again.

"When it comes to owning a time-share, several factors need to be considered."

Jim frowned, wanting an answer.

"First, am I joining to use this specific property, or will I use my membership to travel the world?"

Jim waited.

"Take this unit. The developer has divided this condo into fifty-two separate deeds and titles, one for each week of the year. He'll sell fifty-one and set aside one for annual maintenance. The price of an interval, a week, is determined by the week you select."

Sandra was checking out the barbecue, already on her next vacation.

"Here at Jiminy, ski-season weeks are the most popular, and therefore the most expensive. If you swap your weeks for another destination, the same holds true. High season, when the resort expects an eighty percent occupancy rate, is coded red. Swing season, when the place will be fifty to seventy-nine percent full, is coded white. Off-season is blue."

"So if we own an off-season week," Jim said, "a blue week, we can forget about trading it for prime time anywhere else."

"Couldn't have put it better myself."

Sandra had gone back into the kitchen. "We have a washer and dryer!" she hollered. "We don't have to go home with a trunk full of dirty clothes!"

"So what's the cost of a unit like this during the third week in February," Jim asked, "when schools are on break?"

"Let's go back to the lodge, find out what's available, and I'll give you my recommendations."

Jim called to Sandra, who was in "the kids' room." Jim and Sandra were in love with the place, so Bobby O. knew he didn't have to sell the immediate surrounding area during the walk. Instead he focused on the many other resorts available through the program, paying special attention to the great properties near Disney World. The Petersons were sold, And Bobby O. knew it.

22

The pack of us made ourselves invisible through mundane tasks around the sales area while watching the master at work.

"Jim and Sandra," Bobby O. said, disrupting their walking daydream, "when you and the kids come back, Annie will be right here at the reception desk to make sure you have everything you need."

Annie gave them a warm smile. "Anything the staff can do to make you happy is our pleasure, Mr. and Mrs. Peterson. Remember: we work for you." The Petersons were already glowing.

Seated by the window, Bobby O. placed an eight-by-ten worksheet in the center of the round table. "Now I'll show you how easy it is. How would you like your names to appear on the membership?"

Jim looked as if he might throw up. "Wait a second, Bobby, we didn't say we were joining yet." He looked at his wife. "Did we?" She didn't answer.

"Jim, this is only a worksheet so I can show you my recommendations. If you're not completely satisfied, we rip it up." Jim stole another glance at his wife.

He twirled a pen around his hand with surprising finesse, "So whose name should appear on the membership?"

"I guess mine should go first," Jim said, and Sandra agreed.

Bobby O. confirmed for proper spelling, middle initials, and telephone number, and then sat back in his chair. "In the unit we just saw, the decks face east. You'll see the sunrise over the mountain in the morning, the lit ski slopes at night. Okay?" Jim and Sandra nodded enthusiastically.

He donned a pair of reading glasses and shuffled through a list of unit numbers and dates, some marked "SOLD" in bold red.

"Looks like you're in luck. The third week in February is available.

And the unit is ready. You won't mind coming back in just a few months, will you?"

"No!" Sandra jumped to her feet. "I mean, yes! I mean, that would be great!" Her cheeks flashed rosy hues as she took her seat again. "Would that be all right, honey?"

Jim looked at the worksheet as if it were a rattlesnake, and then at his wife. "Don't you want to know what it costs?"

Her jaw tightened as she looked across the table, "Please make it affordable, Bobby."

He wrote down the numbers. Purchase price $7,995, deposit $800, balance financed over five years at 16 percent. Monthly payments $160 …

He pushed the worksheet across the table and extended his hand to Jim. "Can I be the first to welcome Jiminy Peak's newest members?"

Bobby O. was more than a little surprised when Sandra offered her hand up to shake.

"Bobby, would you give my wife and I a few minutes to talk in private?"

Before leaving his chair, Bobby O. offered a reminder: "I promised a few things when we met. Most importantly, that you'd understand how to use your membership to its fullest potential. I'm confident you do." They both nodded. "I also promised that a membership would make your lives better. Now that I know a bit about you, I think it will give you and your family a lifetime of great memories." Their heads bobbled.

"I'll give you a few moments to discuss things among yourselves. He walked to the reception desk and made small talk with Annie, watching his couple the whole time.

I turned to Niles, handing him more napkins to fake fold. "Why don't we go talk to Bobby O.?"

"Kiss of death."

"Is he avoiding us?"

"Sure is," Niles centered a fork and knife on his napkin and slowly rolled it up, making a neat cutlery burrito. "UP sees you talking with another salesman, they remember that this is a sales pitch. All you've done to gain their trust goes out the door."

Bobby O. made his way back to the table.

"Here comes the verdict," Niles whispered, excited.

Everybody in the place was watching. Pretending to read a newspaper, diligently stirring a cup of black coffee, or carrying on a fake conversation, each salesman knew this was it; he'd arrived at *the close*.

When Bobby O. sat down and offered his hand, neither Jim nor Sandra accepted.

Instead, Jim started talking.

"Shit," Niles said, "He's gonna get the old B-back."

Jim had a lot to say. Every now and then, he glanced at his wife.

Pretending to work a crossword puzzle, Herbie looked up in time to see Bobby O. tear the worksheet in half. He had seen enough. He stood up and walked toward the back office.

Niles shrugged. "He's gonna give Charlie the bad news."

But then Bobby O. opened his binder and pulled out another worksheet.

"Does he have a deal or not?" I asked.

"Must have given a drop." Niles's brow climbed toward his hairline. "Lowered the price. Went to a white or blue week. But hey, a deal's a deal."

The worksheet in front of them, Jim and Sandra signed and then finally shook his hand. As Jim wrote out a check, Sandra walked around the table to give Bobby O. a hug.

He carried the check and the signed worksheet to the back office.

"I was sure you had them," we heard Herbie say. "I can't believe that son of a bitch went sideways on you. What was the objection?"

"One week wasn't enough."

"What the hell does that mean?"

"Her father died six months ago. Left her a decent chunk of change and told her to do something for the kids. So they bought two weeks—one to use here, one to swap for a place near Disney."

Charlie piped up. "Not bad. One UP, two sales."

"Bet they're going to love that faux leather jacket," Bobby said with a frown.

"What the hell do they expect for sixteen thousand?" Herbie muttered as he headed toward the office to process the paperwork.

The staff continued to feign disinterest as Bobby O. carried both the paperwork and the gift to the reception area.

After delivering a copy of the finalized documents, he then handed them their gift. With a glint in his eye he said, "Let me present the newest fabric from NASA. It's impervious to bugs, rain, meteors … Hell, go ahead and run a truck over it." He walked them to the door. Sandra gave him another hug and Jim shook his hand, hard.

He stood outside the doorway, waving as they drove down the mountain. As he came back into the building, the staff broke into applause.

"What did you get?" Niles yelled.

Bobby O. held up two fingers. "Red, February. Sixteen thousand cash." The applause grew louder.

"What did he make?" I asked.

Niles figured the math. "That's ten percent plus another two percent for cashing out in ten days. One thousand nine hundred and twenty bucks!"

Amazing.

Niles grinned. "Not bad for the time it took."

In two hours, Bobby O. had earned what most people work a month for. And I could do it too.

No other UPs showed, but that didn't dampen anybody's spirits. He had done what the preacher had preached and had hit the jackpot. Back slaps and high-fives were all around.

Charlie emerged from the back office looking smug. "Well, girls, looks like the simple steps work. Anyone have anything to say?"

Sweets jumped to his feet. "SPIF!" The rest of the guys took up the chant: "SPIF! SPIF! SPIF!"

Charlie looked to Herbie, who nodded. Cheers went up.

"What's a SPIF?" I asked.

"Just watch, little grunt."

Charlie took a crisp one-hundred-dollar bill from his pocket and handed it to Bobby O.

"Special promotional incentive funds," Niles clarified.

"SPIF." *Where has this business been my whole life?*

"When did you think you had the sale?" Charlie asked. "And when did you know you had the sale?"

We all took seats again, eager to listen. "Not to sound like a kiss-ass," Bobby O. said, "but the steps Herbie's been drilling into us really work."

Herbie smiled and looked over at Charlie, who quietly puffed on his pipe.

"The meet-and-greet was textbook," Bobby O. continued, "and the seating at the round table is crucial. All the steps are. It allowed me to speak to them as one, to break the pact." He turned to look at Charlie. "That's when I felt there was a good shot. And Herbie's right," he added, "a nod isn't good enough. You need a verbal commitment from both of them to make it count; anything else won't do. We live in a world of yes or no." The gang was psyched. Nobody wanted to leave.

"Once the pact was broken, I talked like they were already members. This is yours. Your resort, your staff, your unit, your program."

Numbers went racing through my head—numbers that meant dollars.

Charlie put his arm around Bobby O's shoulders. "So when did you know you had a deal?"

"Chaz, like you've always said, I knew I had a deal when they signed the worksheet, gave me the check, and left the property."

Charlie stood back and held his hands out toward Bobby O. "Ladies, I present to you a time-share salesman." The place erupted.

23

"Time to go to Pat's; it's game seven, maggots."

"Wait fifteen minutes," Charlie said, "in case more UPs show."

Niles reluctantly agreed, but Charlie took off to catch the pregame festivities. He was barely out of the building when a string of motorcycles roared up to the lodge.

Niles went to the window. "Four. On Harleys and wearing colors."

Through the doors they came, tattooed, long-haired, and *huge*.

"They got the envelope," Sweets groaned.

The one with the envelope approached Annie. "We want our four fox-leather jackets."

Annie buzzed Herbie, who told her to call Charlie at home. "I already did," she nervously whispered into the phone, "he's probably still driving."

Niles leaned against the office doorway. "Hey Herbie, this is target marketing, we have a biker gang here. Sweets is up next, and he wants nothing to do with it. You want me to handle them, cap?"

"You bet."

"I'm not gonna miss game seven over this, so I'll handle it my way. Okay Herbie?"

"Just take care of it, Niles."

Niles walked toward Annie to collect his UP. As he passed me, he whispered, "Watch this."

I was close enough to the desk to hear the meet-and-greet. "I'm Bruce Swish, and I'd like to welcome you to Jiminy Peak Mountain, where all your fantasies come true."

The bikers' faces could've made a grown man whimper.

"Come to the bar." Wrist bent, hand hanging like a wet dishtowel,

Bruce Swish reached out to the biggest biker. "We'll start our connection off on the right foot."

The goateed skinhead gave Bruce Swish a once-over. He wasn't about to touch him. When another biker laughed, the big guy turned. Chuckles shut up. "You wanna touch this?" Chuckles looked away.

Niles—rather, Mr. Swish—rested his hand on his cheek. "Let's get this party started, shall we?"

As Bruce Swish's swinging hips led the way to the bar, the sound system played Rod Stewart's "Da Ya Think I'm Sexy." Sweets upped the volume, and Niles squealed. "Don't you just luuuv the Rod?"

At the bar, he produced five large martini glasses. "This should help the mood a little." He used the soda gun to fill the glasses with ginger ale, garnishing each with a slice of orange. "Can't forget the cherry," he said, dropping one into each drink.

"As we say here at Pleasure Palace, bottoms up!"

He drained his glass, his head tilted back, eyes never leaving his guests. Chuckles drained his glass, too, but the others stood stock-still, drinks in hand.

Niles produced the cherry, clenched between his teeth, and crushed it. "Bottoms up, boys! The only way bottoms should be!"

Alpha Biker emptied his glass on the carpet. "Listen, fruitcake, just give us our fox leather jackets."

Niles frowned. "You've spilled your drinkie, and now you don't want to play?" The other guys set their drinks on the bar and stood back, folding their arms.

Herbie emerged from his office and joined us at the back of the sales center. "Bruce Swish is about to get his ass kicked," I told him.

"Don't underestimate Niles."

"But there are four of them." I looked around, taking inventory, the odds weren't in our favor. Bobby O. was gone, and I could tell Sweets was nervous. Annie would likely be more help than any of them.

"Give us four fox leather coats, you faggot," shouted Alpha Biker, "or there's gonna be trouble!"

Niles tapped his cheek with his index finger. "We seem to be in the midst of a dilemma. And for the life of me, I don't know how we ended up here. I was looking forward to a lovely afternoon."

The big guy took a step toward him, his fists clenched.

"Anyways," Niles continued, "the invitation clearly states one jacket per tour, providing you meet the qualifications, one of which is being married."

Niles pointed to Chuckles. "You are his wife, am I right?"

Chuckles didn't even grin. "I ain't nobody's bitch."

Charlie came through the door, unlit pipe in hand. "Chazzy," Niles called, "we have a misunderstanding over here. Perhaps you can help us sort it out."

As Charlie ambled toward the bar, Herbie muttered, "Target marketing."

"Chazzy, I tried to be nice like you taught me, but this bully spilled his drink on the floor on purpose and called me mean names, and well, now I just don't know what to do." With that, he put both hands over his face and began to sob.

Charlie patted Niles's shoulder in a 'there-there' manner, then looked at the bikers as he lit his pipe. "Good afternoon, gentlemen. How can I help?"

The big guy started. "I don't know what kind of freak show you're running here, but this faggot Swish should be in a cage."

"Swish?" Charlie asked.

Niles pulled his hands away from his eyes.

"Bruce Swish."

"Gentlemen," Charlie appeased, "life is too short. What can I do to make you happy?"

"Four fox leather coats," Alpha Biker demanded.

"Brucie"—Charlie was fully in it now—"why don't you go get four jackets for these fine men?" Niles pranced off to the reception desk, and the bikers followed, seeming pleased.

"Listen, you guys," Niles said. "you mustn't be strangers. Come see us again. I can show you all a good time." He handed four packages to the big guy and winked.

"Fuck you, faggot," said Alpha Biker.

The foursome left the building, started the bikes, and headed down the mountain. "I just don't know what went wrong," Niles said. "A tour like that should've been money in the bank!" Everybody in the place broke up.

"Let's go to Pat's," Herbie said. "First round's on me."

"Peachy!" Niles squealed.

"That guy had a point," Charlie said as we left. "Bruce Swish should be in a cage."

24

When Becky hurried out to the lime-green Caddy, Niles opened the door to let her into the backseat with me. She smiled as if nothing had happened between us. "How was your first twenty-four hours?"

"Not boring," I answered. Sweets grinned into the rearview mirror. At the bottom of the hill, Charlie, Herbie, and Annie were outside Pat's.

We all piled into the barroom and Niles threw his voice across the room. "Water for my men, beer for the horses, the bill for Charlie."

Bobby O. was inside with a couple of friends, so we pushed a few tables together. Pitchers of cold beer appeared, and wings were ordered for everyone. The game was scoreless in the second inning, and the group fell into two conversations, one about Bobby O.'s big deal, the other a debate over whether the Pirates' Willie Stargell would keep hitting the laces off the ball.

A loud roar of engines drove past Pat's. "A lot of bikers around here?" I asked.

Niles went to the window and silently watched as the roar faded, heading toward the reception area.

Sweets turned to Becky and Annie, pointing across the room, "Take your beers and go sit over there. Now."

"Friends of yours, Charlie?" Becky asked.

"Bruce Swish's pals." Charlie gestured toward Pat, who came to the table.

"Need more beer?"

Charlie shook his head, "You might want to stand near the phone. We're about to have company. And they're not here for the game."

Pat didn't ask any questions. He went back to the bar.

Thunder rolled back down the mountain, falling suddenly silent outside of the door. Niles left the window and returned to his chair.

"Six of them. Our original foursome and a couple more buddies."

Charlie lit his pipe. "Stay out of this, Herbie. I don't want you having a heart attack." He turned to Niles as a red ember grew from the center of his pipe. He lifted his freshly poured mug and downed it, burping out a cloud of white smoke, which almost concealed the light of mischief in his eyes. "Semper fi." A residual two puffs to accentuate the words were directed at Niles, whose eyes mirrored Charlie's.

"These ain't fox leather coats, you motherfuckers. They're fucking rubber." The biggest guy of the bunch charged Niles. "You're gonna pay, you faggot!"

Niles lurched up so fast that the tables, the beer pitchers, and the wings took flight. "That's Sergeant Faggot to you, maggot."

I was thrown to the floor, but not before I caught a glimpse of what mortification looks like on an alpha biker's face.

"Prepare to meet your maker." Niles lunged for him, dodging a right hook. Like a striking cobra, his left hand circled the guy's throat, squeezing his windpipe shut.

Alpha Biker froze, his eyes bulging, and Niles snap-kicked the bearded biker next to him in the nuts. Bearded biker doubled over; he barely got a groan in before Niles booted him in the face, knocking him upright. His body followed his eyes backwards, already unconscious as he met the beer-soaked floor.

On the other side of the room, Charlie took on one of the new additions, who had his fists up, seemingly unconcerned with his aged opponent. Charlie narrowly missed a right hook then hit the guy with two lightning-fast lefts and a right that would've put a horse to sleep.

Two down.

Chuckles closed in on Sweets, who backed all of his 120 pounds against a wall. Sweets squealed to the biker, who was nearly double his weight, "I'm gonna kill ya."

It was as if I had entered a slow-motion picture of my life, though I hardly recognized it as mine.

Niles still had the big guy by the windpipe, his eyes bulging out of their sockets.

"Remember: you can visit any time," he kissed Alpha Biker, deeply, on the mouth, before dropping him with a left hook.

Chuckles was about to go to town on Sweets when I snapped back into the present; I grabbed a pool cue and smashed his collarbone. The cue cracked in half, but it wasn't the only crack I heard.

Niles and Charlie were eerily composed as they walked toward the last two standing, who backed toward the door, then turned and ran. The dampened roar of exhausts disappeared down the mountain. The bar was void of noise, apart from the game. I realized we'd become the show: Jiminy Peak, 1: Bikers, 0.

The smattering of local customers had been stunned into silence. Becky and Annie sat undisturbed at their table. Chuckles moaned to nobody as his three comrades continued napping on the floor.

"Semper fi!" Niles's victory cry was well deserved.

Charlie put his pipe away and looked over at the bar. "Sorry," Pat said as he pulled the phone away from his face, "police are on the way."

Charlie put up a hand, assuring Pat he understood. He turned to Herbie. "Get yourself and the girls out of here. Somebody will have to bail us out."

Turning to Bobby O., Charlie said, "Beat it. Can't have my best salesman busted."

They all hustled out to the cars and headed up the mountain, knowing the cops would come from below.

"Pat, my good man," Niles said. "My soldiers and I will have a round of cold ones before we go."

Pat filled four mugs on the bar. Charlie, Niles, Sweets, and I each took one, raising our glasses as the sirens approached. The cruisers skidded to a halt outside, ambulances right behind them. The cops barreled through the doors and stopped dead in their tracks, absorbing the scene: four bikers down, four time-share salesmen drinking beer.

The EMTs loaded the bikers onto stretchers and carried them to the ambulances as the cops cuffed the four of us.

"All we wanted was our fox leather jackets," Chuckles said as his stretcher went by.

Charlie looked down at him. "That's *faux* leather jackets, you moron."

25

Aside from a couple of drunks sleeping it off, we had the cell to ourselves in the Pittsfield jail. The cops were decent—no love lost between them and the bikers—and Niles asked one of them who'd won the game.

"Pittsburgh, four to one. Stargell hit another, Series MVP."

Niles broke into song. "We are family. All my brothers and me ..."

We laughed and settled in, stuck for the night. The concrete floor wouldn't do anything good for my bruised body.

"So what do you think of your new career?" Niles asked.

I groaned, and the others laughed. A brush with death, a hooker, a barroom brawl, and jail—in my first twenty-four hours. But it was all good. I'd found a new life.

With no way to get comfortable, I sat up and leaned against the concrete wall. Flat on his back on a steel bench bolted to the floor, Niles studied the ceiling.

"What was the kiss about?" I asked.

Sweets came alive. "You kissed that filthy piece of shit on the mouth," he said. "Just as I was about to let one of them have it."

Charlie laughed. "Yeah, Sweets, you were set to move in for the kill."

Niles's gaze didn't leave the ceiling. "Some wounds never heal, Jake. For that guy, a bitch-kiss in front of his brothers left one."

"Imagine that conversation," Sweets said. "'What did you do after the fag kissed you on the mouth?' 'Well, I don't remember; the fag knocked me out with one shot!'"

We were all laughing. Except Niles. He draped his arm across his eyes. "Some wounds never heal," he said again.

I looked at Charlie, who shrugged. "What happens tomorrow, Chaz?"

"We go before the judge, make bail, go to work."

"Been in jail before?"

Charlie closed his eyes. "Once or twice, pup."

The cop woke us after what seemed like only a few minutes. "Seven o'clock," he hollered. "Time for breakfast and a visit with the judge."

When I sat up, I realized the others had been awake for a while. Niles handed me a plain donut and a paper cup full of water. "Good morning, Sleeping Beauty."

"I've got to piss like a racehorse," I said.

He nodded to the toilet in the corner. No stall, no seat, just a porcelain throne. With my donut in one hand and my johnson in the other, I took a leak that wouldn't quit, then felt better.

One of the drunks wasn't feeling so hot, though, throwing up like it came from his toes. When the retching stopped, he walked toward us with puke all over his shirt.

"Go sit in the corner," Niles said, and Mr. Puke did.

A cop told us to shut up and stand side by side, facing the wall. Then the key scraped in the lock, and the cell door clanged open. The cops cuffed Charlie to Niles, Niles to me, me to Sweets, Sweets to a drunk, the drunk to Mr. Puke, and we all paraded down the hallway.

Charlie stopped in front of the last cell, and Niles blew a kiss inside. When the chain gang moved on, I got a glimpse of the pathetic bikers. There were three on a bench with bandaged faces, Alpha Dog on the floor, alone, with his arm in a sling.

Some wounds never heal.

We clambered into a white van and sat on steel benches for the twenty-minute ride downtown. The driver honked twice at a closed garage door, it lifted, and the van entered the bowels of the courthouse. The cops ordered us out and herded us down a long hallway and into another cell.

"Judge will be with you soon," one cop said.

"Do we have to stay handcuffed to those two?" Sweets looked at the drunk and Mr. Puke. "They stink. I don't want the judge to get the wrong impression."

Everybody laughed, even the cops. They uncuffed them and locked the cell.

"Pirates rule!" Niles yelled. "If you see Willie, tell him congrats!" One cop grinned.

"Are you guys real pirates?" the drunk asked.

"Don't breathe on me," Niles said. "Sit far away or you'll see what kind of trouble real pirates cause."

The drunk sauntered over to the corner.

The clock on the gray wall said it was 8:50 when a new cop yelled, "Furano, Ditaccio, Niles, and Arril, you're up!"

Niles grinned at Charlie. "Just like work."

Down the corridor we went, into a less-than-impressive courtroom with sparsely occupied benches, a raised desk, a witness box, and two rectangular tables. A balding guy in a cheap suit sat at one. The cop told us to sit at the other.

"Hi, sweetie, we're here." Becky looked fine in tight jeans with a flannel shirt tied at the waist. Beside her, Herbie looked nervous. The clerk came through the side door.

"All rise for the Honorable Judge Whitmore!"

"Don't they look cute?" Becky whispered behind us.

Herbie shushed her.

The judge read our names, told us we were charged with assault and battery and disturbing the peace, and asked how we wanted to plead.

"Not guilty," said Charlie, and the rest of us did, too. The judge looked us over, and matter-of-factly said to the prosecutor, "bail set at $250 each?" The prosecutor simply nodded in agreement, and the trial was set for mid-January.

In the clerk's office, we signed the paperwork, Herbie produced ten one-hundred-dollar bills, and we were free to go.

Outside in the crisp fall morning, Becky started shadowboxing. "You guys were great," she yelled. "Niles, you are one badass. Charlie, you were still smoking your pipe when you knocked that guy out. And Jake, you saved my sweetie!"

She danced around, throwing lefts and rights, kicking imaginary bikers.

Sweets pouted. "What about me? I was gonna mop the place up with those guys."

Becky threw her arms around his neck. "Sweetie, you're my hero!"

Charlie cut the ceremony short. "Where's the car? Let's get our stuff from the station and go to work."

Herbie pointed to the lot, where the Caddy was parked in a handicapped space.

"For Christ's sake, Beck," Sweets said, "couldn't you find another spot?"

"Didn't want to be late for the show."

We piled in, drove to the station, and collected everything that had been confiscated the night before. I was counting my cash when Herbie walked over with his hand out. "Five hundred bucks. Half for you, half for your roomie."

Niles looked at me and shrugged. "I'll pay you back on payday."

I peeled off five hundreds and handed them to Herbie. My life's savings was disappearing fast.

26

By the time we made it to the lodge, the parking lot was crowded. Inside, Bobby O. returned to the same round table he'd used the day before, ready to pitch another tour. Three other reps sat with clients at round tables, and Annie looked relieved to see us. Herbie waved us over to the bar, where he was sipping coffee.

"Four couples waiting," he said. "One pair has been here since nine o'clock, so let's get to work. Niles, you're up. Sweets on point, Jake in the hole."

"Good luck, Jake," Niles said. "Break your cherry."

Annie handed each of us a survey sheet, an UP name printed neatly at the top.

"What am I supposed to do?" I asked Herbie. "I don't have a clue."

"Good thing they don't know that. Break the pact, find out what they need, show them the model, bring them back here to run the numbers. If you need help after that—and you will—come get me. Trial by fire, kid."

As I led Jeff and Martha Billings to a table, Bobby O. was writing up a worksheet, another sale under his belt. I felt strange as we sat, as if I might throw up. Jeff and Martha looked nervously at each other, then at me. At the next table, Niles held up his survey sheet, his eyes never leaving his UP. I got it. *Use the survey questions: How important are your family vacations? How frequently do you travel? What do you do for a living? How much do you earn? Where is your dream vacation? How much do you think it would cost?*

But I machine-gunned the questions, condensing the hour-long exercise into ten minutes. My only choice was to show the model. When I stood to lead my UP from the lodge, Niles looked surprised.

Herbie held up both hands, palms out, mouthing, "What the fuck are you doing?"

The walk to the unit was quiet, the tour of the model a disaster. "This is a bedroom," I said, "and this is a kitchen," as if showing them how earthlings live.

Stuck on stupid, I couldn't stop. Finally, after I explained the function of a refrigerator, we left the unit. On the way to the lodge, I tried to explain how they could use the program to go to Florida, Europe, or so many other places in the world.

Annie shook her head when we went back inside. Niles and Sweets were still working the front end. As we passed Niles's table, I heard him break the pact.

Shit. I forgot that, too.

Herbie was still at the bar. Charlie stood next to him, glaring.

I felt sick all over again. All I could do was show my UP the numbers and get fired. I wrote out the price, and asked Jeff and Martha Billings if they'd like to join.

They stared at the notepad. Finally, Mr. Billings said, "This has been interesting, James, and you've been great. Do you have a card? We'll talk it over and we'll be back."

Niles heard it, too. Herbie summoned me with an index finger. I excused myself and walked over to the two bosses, hoping to be put out of my misery. Charlie blew a cloud of smoke over my head. "Got them eating out of your hand, pup?"

"I screwed up. They're a good couple. They should've been a sale, but I suck."

Charlie put his pipe in the ashtray. "Come with me, pup. And don't say a word while I'm working."

Herbie looked as surprised as I was.

We joined Jeff and Martha Billings at the round table, and over the next two and a half hours, Charlie turned a botched sale into a deal. When Billings handed Charlie a signed check, I knew I'd witnessed a work of art.

On the bottom of the worksheet, in the spot marked "Representative," Charlie unceremoniously wrote my name, giving me my first sale in the time-share business. Then he went off to process the paperwork.

"Have you been doing this for a while, James?" asked Mr. Billings.

Given Charlie's warning, I didn't want to say a word. "Just started,"

I managed. "You're my first UP. I mean, clients." *I said UP?* "By the way, Mr. Billings, my name is Jake, Jake Arril."

"Well, Jake Arril, a salesman who succeeds on the first try is either lucky or good. Either way, I wish you the best in your new career. Your product will change the way people travel forever."

Charlie returned with Annie at his side, holding the paperwork. "Folks, Annie here will review everything we discussed. Welcome to the family. And enjoy your vacations." With that he turned to leave, signaling for me to follow.

"That was the most incredible thing I've ever seen, Charlie."

He didn't break his stride. "Didn't I tell you to shut the fuck up while I'm working?"

I decided not to answer.

Soon Mr. and Mrs. Billings drove down the mountain and the day came to a close. We'd had six UPs and two sales, Bobby O.'s for $4,995, an off-season white week, and mine for $7,995, a winter red week. Herbie and Charlie seemed pleased. Everyone in the place showered Charlie with compliments, and he didn't seem to mind.

One by one, the staff headed out as five o'clock approached. Annie winked and mouthed "congratulations" to me as she left.

"Popped your cherry," Niles said. "Drinks are on you."

"What's with the cherry?"

Sweets joined us, laughing. "Your first time."

Niles put his arm around me. "You're no longer a virgin."

"Congratulations, Jake. I had a feeling today was your day," Bobby O. echoed, and he meant it. I returned the compliment, but he shrugged it off.

"Hey pup, did you board your sale?" Charlie asked.

Niles explained. "Gotta write the details on the board. Never board the deal until the UP leaves the building, but don't forget about it, or bad things will happen."

I followed Niles into Charlie's office, where a chalkboard mounted on one wall was divided into columns. I filled in the date, the amount of the sale, and the salesman's initials—mine. I hesitated on the last column, which was labeled "TO."

Niles looked from Charlie to me. "Takeover. Who did the salesman turn the deal over to? Who closed it?"

Charlie puffed on his pipe. "Even if it was a lay down, the TO's name is boarded."

I wrote in "CF," then stood back and gazed at the board. Bobby O.'s two deals were on top, mine next. I'd made a sale. The board said so.

When I faced Charlie and Niles, we all knew what had happened. A baseball player never forgets his first hit, a fisherman his first catch, an actor his first role. And I would never forget this sale. More would come, some bigger and better, but this was the first. An unbreakable bond was formed at that moment between a salesman who'd realized his first deal and the witnesses to it.

I held out my hand to Charlie. Without taking it, he turned and left the room.

Niles shrugged. "Bad luck to shake," he said. "Too soon."

27

"Hooray!" Becky shouted, clapping and laughing as she opened the Caddy's door and Niles climbed into the backseat. Before I could follow, she threw her arms around me and kissed me on both cheeks. "Jakie, I'm so proud of you!"

Embarrassed, I mumbled, "Thanks," and climbed in.

"Congrats, little buddy," Sweets said. "Welcome to the club."

"These two are heading downtown for supplies," Niles said as the Caddy fishtailed out of the lot. "We should go. All we have left are yesterday's memories."

Riding with the roof down, the sky blue-green and the sun setting behind the mountains, I closed my eyes, exhausted and relieved. I'd taken my lumps and could still feel them, but I'd emerged from the arena victorious. I was a time-share salesman.

Niles lit a Marlboro. Becky turned on the radio, and Willie was singing again.

"Mama, don't let your babies grow up to be—"

"Time-share salesmen," Niles sang.

"Jakie, he's singing your song," Becky said.

At the grocery store on Elm Street in Pittsfield, Becky and Sweets went their own way while I wheeled a cart into the meat department behind Niles, who grabbed five packages of hamburger. "Don't worry, buddy, I'll reimburse you on payday."

Niles was broke, but what the heck? I'd just made $800 in a few hours, and tomorrow was another day. After stocking up on toilet paper, shaving gear, bread, and charcoal, I said good-bye to more of my disappearing bankroll at the cash register.

Sweets and Becky were waiting, so we made quick work of loading our supplies into the Caddy. "Need anything at the watering station?" Sweets asked as he backed out.

Niles did. We pulled into the package store, nestled two cases of beer into the trunk, and got back on our way. We hadn't gone far when I told Sweets to pull over and trotted to the front door of The 1880 Shoppe, which boasted of offering "Fine Clothing for the Distinctive Gentleman." It was locked. Niles rapped on the window.

The clerk inside shook his head and pointed to his watch. It was after six.

"Flash some cash," Niles said, so I waved the remains of my life's savings.

"What can I do for you gentlemen?" the clerk asked as he opened the door.

"What suits your fancy, sweetie?" Bruce Swish asked.

The clerk perked up. He clearly had no interest in Bruce Swish, who was gyrating away, but Bruce's pal was another story.

"I need a sport coat for work."

Becky had her doubts about my selection, but $300 later, I was the proud owner of a sport coat, lime green and yellow plaid on a beige background. Riding home under the twinkling stars with my friends, I felt good, safe. I'd acquired a salesman's mentality—one of optimism.

When Niles shook me awake at home, I wondered whether I'd broken something on the Alpine Slide. I unloaded the groceries, had a beer with him, and fell into my unmade bed.

The next morning, I woke in the same position, wearing yesterday's clothes. But I was excited about my new opportunities, chances to make big money. After a quick shower, I pulled on clean khakis, a blue dress shirt, and my new plaid sport coat. I paused in front of the mirror and quickly dismissed my second thoughts about the jacket.

Sweets was in the car, Niles on the porch. "Look good, shooter. Let's kick ass today. Yesterday is old news."

"You're a superstar, darling," Becky yelled from next door. "Do it again today!"

When we arrived at the lodge at eight sharp, Herbie and Charlie were by the bar, the staff at the round tables. Bobby O. and Niles headed for the java, and I followed, even though I didn't like coffee. *When in Rome ...*

I took a seat as Herbie began. "Congratulations to Bobby O.; Charlie has offered a fifty-dollar SPIF."

The reps clapped, and I got excited, thinking maybe I'd get a SPIF too.

Herbie moved on, speculating about the day's UPs and drilling the five steps. No mention of my success. When the meeting ended, he told me my deal had "kicked."

"What?"

"Buyers can cancel the contract for any reason within three days," Herbie snarled, "and they did. Sorry, kid. Dead deal." I was stunned.

"That's why Chaz didn't shake your hand," Niles said. "Never bank on a deal until after the cooling-off period. It's part of the game."

Jeff and Martha Billings had seemed happy. They had signed a contract and forked over a check. And they canceled the deal?

The coffee was lousy. I looked at my reflection in the mirror behind the bar. *How the hell am I gonna pay for this damn coat?*

28

"Want to work out?" Niles asked. The day at the lodge had been a bust. A couple of UPs, no deals. I didn't have my bike and hadn't taken a run since I arrived, so I agreed.

"Let's climb the mountain," Niles said.

Wearing sneakers, sweatpants, and a Natick sweatshirt, I followed him up the mountain until he pulled out two knives, flipping one to me. Its fourteen-inch blue-steel blade was honed razor sharp, its worn leather grip wrapped tightly with a strip of rawhide.

He crouched, index finger on his lips. The look on his face took me back to the chokehold on the biker's throat.

I crouched, too, following Niles's gaze into the woods.

He sprang up and hurled the steel blade with all his might. It found its mark thirty feet away, impaling the trunk of a pine tree five feet from the ground.

Back in a crouch, he bellowed, "Let's kill some gooks, Blue Dolphin!" He lurched to the tree, reclaimed his knife, and zigzagged down the mountain, screaming at the top of his lungs.

Blue Dolphin?

Niles crouched again and signaled for silence, then pointed forward.

This time, I followed.

He made his way down the slope, pausing behind a tree every ten feet or so to check on me. I moved carefully, holding the blade away from my body. When I finally caught up, I tried to hand the knife back. I didn't like this game, if it was a game.

Niles shook his head. "Never surrender your weapon, Blue Dolphin," he growled. "Make them pry it from your dead, clenched fist."

He was serious.

"Recon doesn't have a clue," he said. "The jungle is full of gooks. I can smell them."

He was on the move again, crawling down the mountain, using his elbows to move his body forward like a snake.

I figured it was better to head downhill toward the lodge. Niles kept turning back, giving me hand signals. The guy was out of his mind.

After a long time, still crawling, he reached a fallen pine tree. Peering over the moss-covered stump, he held up one hand.

I stopped. The sun had dropped behind the mountains. I couldn't see much.

Slowly, Niles half-stood, the knife cocked at his right ear.

I strained to see past him, not believing my eyes. Beside a creek bed stood a buck, its head raised, sniffing the air.

Niles let the knife fly. The world went into slow motion. I saw every revolution of the blade, from the time it left his hand, until it found the deer's left flank.

The animal jumped at the moment of impact, letting out a primal scream. It tried to run along the creek bed, but its back legs gave out.

Niles hurdled the fallen tree and reached the deer in seconds, as it struggled to escape on its two front legs. He knelt on its head, pinning it down, then pulled out the knife and buried the blade up to the handle in the animal's neck. It trembled, then lay still.

I was dumbfounded. Horrified. But deep inside, I marveled at his skill.

He rolled the deer over so its feet and stomach pointed downhill, and with the deftness of a surgeon, he slit the animal from its neck to its ass. Blood and guts obeyed the laws of gravity.

Niles rolled up his sweatshirt sleeves and reached into the cavity, pulling steaming organs onto the forest floor. The animal's lifeless eyes looked at me.

Niles was in up to his elbows, working the knife until he pulled out the heart. Smiling, he lifted it to his mouth and took a bite, blood running down his chin and onto his sweatshirt. Then he offered the bloody mess to me.

I wanted nothing to do with the ritual.

Niles discarded the rest of the heart as if it were a half-eaten sandwich and then walked toward me, his smile gone, his face, chest, arms, and knife covered in blood.

Aware of the knife in my own hand, I raised it as Niles approached.

In a flash, he dragged his empty hand across my forehead, smearing it with blood.

He looked at the knife in my hand and then sadly looked away. Niles hadn't meant to scare me. He motioned toward what was left of the buck and said, "Let's get this home; we won't need to buy groceries for a while."

29

Niles practically ran down the mountain with seventy pounds of dead deer on his back. At the dirt road, when we could see the condo lights, he looked back at me. "Mind helping a brother with a load?"

He shifted half the weight to me, and we marched home, the deer's head resting on his shoulder, its butt on mine.

"Let me have him," he said when we reached the front porch. "Go tear down a shower curtain, cover the dining room table, and pull it into the kitchen."

I followed orders, and soon Niles dropped the carcass onto the covered table with a thud. "See if we have any garbage bags." We didn't.

"Go next door and get some from Sweets." Niles stood over his kill, ready to butcher.

Becky opened the door wearing faded jeans and a tight beige sweater. I almost forgot why I was there. Her hand went to her mouth and her eyes widened. "What happened, Jake? Were you in a car wreck?"

I'd forgotten about the mud and the deer blood.

"You're bleeding," she said. "Let me help you."

"It's nothing, Beck. Just fooling around on the mountain with Niles." She folded her arms across her chest.

I mustered a smile. "Can you lend us some trash bags?"

She looked puzzled but turned and went into the kitchen, leaving the door open.

"How many do you need, honey?"

I stayed on the porch. "As many as you have."

She returned with an unopened box. "Is Niles dismembering a body?"

"Sort of."

She frowned. I thanked her and went back to the butcher.

Niles had already removed the deer's head and hooves and was hard at work peeling the hide from the meat, his bloody fingerprints all over an open can of Bud. "Any luck finding bags?"

I set the box down next to the Bud. "Is this legal? Don't you need a license or something?"

He put down the bloody knife and picked up the beer. "It's only a crime if we get caught." He took a gulp and belched. "We're gonna need the other shower curtain."

I fetched it and then went to the fridge for a beer, the eyes of the decapitated deer staring at me from the kitchen sink.

Niles ran his blade between the flesh and the hide, his movements effortless, clean, producing surprisingly little additional blood. Together we lifted the purplish, headless cadaver and moved it to the kitchen counter, next to its head and hooves. Evidence of the slaughter was everywhere. Head, body, skin, fur … I wondered if I'd ever eat in the kitchen again.

"Wrap the skin in the shower curtain," Niles said. "Dump it in the woods and bring the curtain back."

I was an accomplice for sure, getting rid of evidence.

By the time I got back, Niles had spread the second shower curtain on the table and had removed the front legs at the shoulders. With a serrated blade, he severed the rib cage.

He butchered for the next hour, producing roasts, steaks, loins, and stew meat. I packaged each cut in a trash bag, squeezed the air out, tied it shut, and stacked it in the freezer. Before long, nothing was left but a pile of bones and gristle, and a dozen empty Bud cans.

"That," Niles said proudly, "is how a marine gets his grub."

30

"What should we do with this?"

Niles took another beer from the fridge and stared at the bodiless antlered head in the sink. "Play a little game."

Another game.

He took the head and one hoof out to the back porch. I followed, figuring somebody ought to keep tabs.

He crept next door to Sweets's place. I stayed in our backyard.

Crouched under the living room window, dimly lit by the TV, Niles raised the deer's head above his own and tapped on the glass with the hoof.

No response from inside.

The hoof tapped harder. The antlered head moved side to side. Niles couldn't see what I saw.

Becky walked to the window and did a double take. Shrieking, she bolted out the front door and ran down the dark mountain road.

Niles doubled over, roaring. I thought it was pretty mean, but I laughed too. I couldn't help it.

Sweets drove up the road as Becky fled. We heard him skid to a stop.

He didn't knock. He pushed the front door open and charged in to find us drinking beer in the kitchen, me with the swath of blood on my forehead, Niles with blood all over his face, arms, and chest.

Sweets's jaw dropped. He took in the antlered head and the pile of bones. "You guys know anything about a deer trying to bust into my house?"

Niles belched. "Damnedest thing. We were sitting here minding our own business when this son of a bitch comes walking through the back door and tries to steal our beer."

He set the empty can on the table and reached for another. "Jake tackled him, and I cut his head off."

I just about choked.

Niles shrugged. "What else could we do?"

Sweets went to the fridge and opened a can as Becky came in, gaping at the mayhem. "What the fuck? Are you two devil worshipers?"

All three of us busted up. "The deer tried to steal their beer," Sweets explained.

We all laughed harder.

Becky turned and left, with a final word for Niles. "Asshole."

He looked at me. "Did we forget the asshole?" We all lost it again.

"I'd better go next door," Sweets said when he could breathe. "She's probably packing."

"Tell Becky we're sorry," I said.

"No need for you to apologize, Jake. This has Niles written all over it."

He headed for the door. "Don't think she won't get even, though. She always does. And she thought the damn creature was trying to break in."

Niles looked concerned. "Why would the buck break into your house, Sweets? You got beer?"

31

After dumping what was left of the buck in the woods, I found Niles in an armchair, watching the newly formed World Wrestling Federation on the new station ESPN. Wearing a white T-shirt with a beer in one hand, cigarette in the other, he said, "Friday Night Smackdown. Fuckin' fakes. I'd kick their asses in a street fight."

I sat on the sofa. "Where the hell did you learn all this shit, Niles?"

He went into his bedroom to get a bottle of Jack Daniels, took a slug, and held it out to me.

"No, thanks."

He glared. "You want to know who I am, you drink with me."

He frowned when he saw me wipe the bottle top. The liquid burned all the way to my gut. I passed the bottle back and he settled into the armchair again. "Here's my story, Jake. I come from a wealthy Boston family. My father was a surgeon, a Harvard grad. So when my time came, Harvard it was."

He took another swig. "My mother was a socialite. If the cause was halfway decent and the vodka was flowing, she did the fundraising."

He started to hand me the bottle but thought better of it. "In 1960, her cause was a young senator from Boston who wanted to become our commander-in-chief. Because of that and the Harvard ties, my family was invited to his inauguration. By then Mom was so into the pills and the drink, Dad took me instead of her. I doubt she knew she'd been invited, or even that JFK had won."

I accepted the bottle, drank, and handed it back.

"It was an honor to be there. And when Jack uncorked his speech, something in me changed; my eyes opened to something great." Niles tilted the bottle and gulped. "At least I thought so at the time." He looked sad, but he was getting drunk. "I felt like JFK was talking to me. His words blew me away."

Niles stood and raised the bottle. "'Let every nation know we shall pay any price, bear any burden, meet any hardship, support any friend, oppose any foe, to assure the survival and success of liberty.'"

Boston accents vary from neighborhood to neighborhood, but the Kennedys had their own. Niles nailed it, dragging his *r*'s and accenting his *a*'s, as if he were part of the family. "'Let us go forth to lead the land we love, asking His blessing and His help, but knowing that here on earth God's work must truly be our own.'"

I got up to get a beer but returned with a glass of water and a bag of chips.

"At the end, with Presidents Truman and Eisenhower, Vice Presidents Nixon and Johnson, and the whole world listening, he really uncorked it. 'And so, my fellow Americans, ask not what your country can do for you, but what you can do for your country.'"

Closing my eyes, I heard JFK himself. "'My fellow citizens of the world, ask not what America will do for you, but what we can do for the freedom of man.'" I damn near applauded.

Niles stood, walked to the door, and looked out at the darkness. "Then and there, I knew I was going to Vietnam. JFK's speech was a call to arms against communism in Southeast Asia. The president had spoken to me personally, and I vowed I'd do my part."

Leaning against the doorframe, Niles was quiet. When he finally turned, tears streamed down his face. "JFK spoke to me. He wanted my help for a noble cause."

Like a little boy lost, Niles wiped his face with both hands and sat in his chair.

"After graduation I enlisted, went through boot, and landed on a marine transport to Saigon. We were supposed to fact-gather and advise."

I reached for the bottle, didn't even think about wiping it.

"None of us ever recommended that the South go to war. Those people just wanted to tend their farms, grow their rice and their children. What did they care about communism or democracy? The people of that country didn't give a shit about politics." I took a long swallow.

"We advised, 'Let them work it out for themselves. We're not wanted or

99

needed here.' But someone decided to swap a handful of rice for a handful of bullets and the whole damn thing got out of control real quick."

Maybe it was the beer, the whiskey, or the story, but my stomach wasn't right.

"Some of us took leave and went into town. It was a shithole—rickshaws, yaks, mules, chickens, and little motorcycles screaming all over the place—but we wanted some action. Girls and drink. We were sitting in a little bar when a kid came through the door wanting to shine our boots."

I wasn't feeling so hot, but Niles kept talking.

"I went outside for a smoke, saw the kid run out and duck into an alley, and then the fucking world blew up. Four of my buddies, blown up by a kid with a shoeshine kit. Wasn't enough left of those guys to send home."

He leaned back and stared at the ceiling. "By the time I left, the fire was out of control. Didn't matter how it started. Troops were pouring out of transport planes in Saigon, fatigues clean, young faces full of piss and vinegar, ready to save the world."

He lit another cigarette. "But that world didn't want to be saved. So many of those kids came home in body bags. They never knew what hit them, never understood why they were there in the first place. You know what killed most of those GIs, Jake?" He didn't wait for an answer. "Booze. Drugs. Guilt. Even the guys who made it home left their souls in 'Nam. They came back alive, but dead. Goddamned 'Nam."

He stood again, seeming unable to stay in one place for long. "This whole theater—and it was a show—was about money. Our government spent two hundred billion, and it all ended up on the balance sheets of multinational corporations. Boeing. Colt. And let's not forget Monsanto, with its goddamned agent orange. US aircraft dumped twenty million gallons of that pesticide—named for the orange-striped fifty-gallon drums it came in—to kill foliage so the gooks wouldn't be able to hide. Then we realized that the fucking chemical caused cancer, and that the cancer would pass on to future generations, causing horrific birth defects and horrible diseases."

He started pacing. My stomach wasn't any better.

"Unfortunately, the wind couldn't tell the good guys from the bad guys, so they were all contaminated. Think about it, Jake; some soldiers killed their own kids before they were conceived. What kind of evil is that?"

Sergeant John Niles had talent, intellect, a good heart. And it had all been put through a meat grinder.

"Not one company in Vietnam, North or South, manufactured weapons. The rest of the world did. Some countries armed the North, some the South, some both. It was all about the balance sheets of big-buck corporations."

Niles was beginning to slur. "It took years of protests from the American people to shut the whole mess down. But for the fifty-six thousand US troops who died, and the hundreds of thousands who would never know another day's peace, it was too late."

He reached for the bottle, knocking it over, spilling what was left of the booze onto the floor. "I fucking hate my father for bringing me to Washington. I fucking hate myself for listening. I fucking hate Kennedy. I'm glad they shot the bastard. Wonder who made that gun?"

He finally sat down again. And passed out.

I went into the shower and turned the water on as hot as I could stand it, trying to wash the past few hours down the drain. Then I wiped the foggy mirror, looked at my reflection, and threw up. Three or four hurls later, my stomach was empty.

I went back to the living room and draped a blanket over Niles, dried blood still caked on his face and arms, snoring like a champ. This soldier had made it back alive, but not whole. Not even close.

Some wounds never heal.

32

The banging on the front door started at 7:55, five minutes to Herbie's meeting. I threw on clothes and grabbed my sport coat.

"Niles coming?" Sweets asked when I landed in the Caddy.

I shook my head. "I'll be surprised if he gets out of bed today."

Sweets backed out and put the car in drive. "Vietnam?" I nodded. "Did he tell you about his mother?"

Feeling like shit, I said, "No."

"Poor bastard makes it back from 'Nam, and three weeks later walks into the family home to find his mom hanging from the chandelier." I felt worse than shit. "A lot of baggage for one guy," Sweets said as we skidded to a stop.

The meeting had already started. Standing in front of the reps, Charlie looked at us and then at Herbie, who said, "Overage."

Sweets moaned. "C'mon. My watch says three minutes past. Traffic was a bitch." Some of the reps laughed. Herbie didn't.

"Fuck your watch," Charlie said. "The only time that matters is *my* time, got it?" Sweets shot me a rotten look as he sat at a round table, so I sat at another.

"UPs are driving here right now," Herbie said, "to pick up a gift and waste your time. And that's exactly what will happen if you're not one hundred percent ready. Murphy's law will bite you in the ass. If you're ready nine times out of ten, the tenth UP would've been the buyer."

"Bobby O., if you hadn't been ready this week, what would've happened?"

Bobby O. gave him the backup he was looking for. "It's a fact; Murphy will get you every time. A sale can be made or lost in the blink of an eye. You must be on your game. Always."

Herbie rattled on about the five steps, but I didn't listen. I couldn't stop thinking about Niles finding his mother hanging from the ceiling.

When the meeting wrapped up, I leaned over to Sweets. "Sorry, man. You want me to tell Charlie it was my fault?"

He headed for the coffee. "Fuck it. Charlie doesn't give a shit. Don't be late again, or I'll leave you behind."

Bobby O. was arranging his sales material when I walked up. "Morning, Jake. Ready to make some dough?"

"Sure, but tell me something. What's 'overage'?"

He frowned. "It's a bitch. You don't get a tour unless everybody else is busy. If you're next but someone decides to spin a tour, he gets yours. You're in limbo, at the mercy of the line."

"What?"

"The line is the pecking order, and it's based on a few things. Volume of sales, most recent deal, biggest deal. This business feeds the strongest first. I wrote the last deal yesterday, so I'm out first today."

"I still don't know what 'overage' is."

Sweets took over, "If I have an NQ, and your tour comes in to register, I spin the NQ because your UP looks better. When you're on overage, you can kill the whole day without getting out once."

"What's an NQ?"

Sweets and Bobby O explained, "Niles came up with that. In boot camp, when a recruit fell short, the drill instructor would call him an NQQ—a not-qualified quitter. Meant the guy couldn't shoot straight, wasn't qualified to back up another marine in a firefight."

I was having trouble connecting the dots.

Grinning, he continued, "Niles had an UP a while back that was unemployed, liked to camp out if they did go anywhere. After a while, he threw in the towel, gave them the gift, never bothered to show them the model unit. Charlie went ballistic, and in the middle of the screaming match, Niles yelled, 'Jesus Christ himself couldn't sell an NQ!'"

Sweets chuckled. "Niles was caught off guard. Charlie knew he meant 'not qualified.' We couldn't believe they both started laughing. And the term stuck."

I thanked them both and turned to go.

"Jake," Sweets called after me, "is Niles okay?" I shrugged and he nodded. He knew the story.

A few tours showed up at nine, registered with Annie, and went to round tables with reps. At the bar, Sweets pled his case to Charlie, who lit his pipe and shook his head.

Sweets stalked off to an empty table.

Charlie wiggled his index finger, summoning me to the bar. When I got there, he blew a cloud of smoke over my head. "You're not gonna make any money today, pup, so let's teach you something. Go through the steps with Sweets."

Expecting a tough warm-up, I walked over to the table and held out my hand.

"I'm Jake Arril. Welcome to Jiminy Peak. What's your name?"

Arms folded across his chest, Sweets said, "I'm fucking pissed off."

"Nice to meet you, Mr. Pissed Off. Any trouble finding the place?"

Charlie laughed. "Always use a first name, Jake. If the UP is older, ask if it's okay. You give them an advantage when you use Mr. or Mrs."

I took a seat across from Sweets. "May I call you Dick, Mr. Head?"

Charlie laughed harder. Even Sweets cracked a smile. "You can call me Fucked."

We all laughed, and just like that, everything was back to normal. This business is not for the thin-skinned.

In walked Niles, wearing all the evidence of a rough night: matted hair, wrinkled clothes, and bloodshot eyes. He was a mess, but grinning. Charlie headed him off at the reception desk, and Niles's grin disappeared. He turned and walked out of the building.

"He knows the unwritten law," Sweets said. "Never disrupt a room with working tours in progress."

The morning was busy—six tours during the first session—so even Sweets and I got out. As the round tables filled with reps and UPs, the room buzzed. Herbie's training was paying off. Bobby O. headed up to the units first, and soon we were all out of the building, on our way to see the vacation paradigm of the future.

33

We took our tours into the unit and eventually made our way back out to the deck. The air was chilly, the morning filled with blue sky and bright sunshine. We could hear the faint sound of Blondie's new song, "Heart of Glass," playing on Niles's portable radio as he squirted lighter fluid into a black kettle barbeque on the porch next door. Becky, barefoot, wearing a black silk robe, sipped coffee on a lawn chair. Niles tossed a lit match into the pit, and Becky shrieked as an eight-foot flame burst into the air.

"The coals should be ready soon," Niles told her. He rubbed his face and hair, checking for singes. "Survived 'Nam. Almost bought it from a barbecue."

"You guys need marshmallows?" I yelled.

"No," Becky called back, "but maybe the fire department."

As Bobby O. and his UPs took in the view, the wife looked over at Niles and Becky, and asked, "Are those people members?"

Bobby O. didn't hesitate. "Yup. They checked in today. This is the first time they've stayed at the resort."

The husband chuckled. "Well, I hope they don't burn the place down."

The wife smiled. "I'd like to talk to them, find out how they like the program."

Bobby O. looked taken aback. "Let me ask if they're settled enough for company." He yelled to Niles, "I know you guys just checked in, and I hate to bother new members, but can we join you for a few minutes?" Niles held up his beer and shouted back, "Sure. The more the merrier."

We walked down the steps of the deck and across the dirt, over to Niles and Becky. "Steve and Martha Hastings," Bobby O. said, "I'd like you to meet John and Becky Niles."

The men shook hands, and the women smiled, but the air was tense.

"Becky is John's daughter," Bobby O. blurted. "They joined last year, before the units were built. This is the first time they've seen the finished product."

Niles didn't miss a beat. Putting a fatherly arm around Becky, he pulled her close. "Rebecca is a student at U. Mass. Amherst down the road, so we can enjoy a little quiet time together and she doesn't miss any school."

Instantly, the tension evaporated. Becky caught on quickly. "Daddy moves around quite a bit with the military, so I don't get to see him as much as I'd like."

"What branch, John?" Steve asked.

"Marines, sir. Recruitment training. I might be in LA one month, Atlanta the next. Keeps me busy."

Martha dropped a bomb. "Is Mrs. Niles here?"

Niles froze. Becky didn't. "My mother is dead."

Martha dropped another one. "Oh, I'm sorry. How did she die?"

Niles squeezed Becky's shoulders. "Giving birth, twenty-one years ago. We bought this week to celebrate Rebecca's birthday."

The answer seemed to satisfy the inquisitive Martha, but Niles wasn't finished. "I was in the jungles of Vietnam at the time, serving my country. So every year, we celebrate with a vacation. Jiminy Peak is great; we're so happy we're members. We can't wait to see some of the other places the plan offers."

Niles smiled at Becky as a proud father would. Bobby O.'s mouth hung open.

"You got another one of those?" Steve pointed to Niles's beer.

"Sure do, Steve. And we're about to throw down some barbecue Jiminy Peak style. Can you stay a bit?"

Niles went inside to fetch the beer. Bobby O. put his hand over his eyes and walked away. Things were slipping out of control.

Martha said she'd have a beer too. "I don't normally drink alcohol this early, but what the heck? We're on vacation."

Niles returned with the beer and the meat, laying steaks and ribs over the glowing coals. Martha seemed to adopt Becky, and Steve was a former marine. Everyone was having a good time except Bobby O., who looked nervous.

Soon the other UPs, including mine, joined in the festivities. Drawn by the cold beer and the smell of cooking meat, they introduced themselves to Niles and his daughter, and every one of them decided to stay.

"Hope Charlie can make it!" Niles said, taking a swig of his beer. Bobby O. groaned.

"I don't remember anything like this in the five steps," I said to Sweets.

He half-laughed. "We're all gonna die. Worse than that, Niles is my fucking father-in- law."

We were screwed, breaking every rule in the book, but a good salesman knows how to adapt. With the ribs and steaks cooking, Niles walked over and spoke softly. "You guys need to run to the store. Get more beer, paper plates, and something to go with the meat. We don't want to look like a bunch of hillbillies."

"Charlie is gonna kill all of us," Sweets whispered, "and he's gonna kill you twice."

Niles smiled. "Fuck Charlie."

We headed out the front door of the unit to go get the car. "Be back in a minute," Sweets said to Bobby O. "Look after our tours."

"Going to get dynamite?" he asked. "Because we're gonna need it when the big guy gets wind of this."

We made quick business of rounding up potato salad, rolls, paper plates, and a case of beer at Pat's. Beating it back to the party, we passed the lodge just as the door opened. Out stepped Charlie.

He might not have noticed another car, but we were in the Caddy. He almost dropped his pipe. I corkscrewed around to look back as he watched us speed away.

"Fucking Murphy's law," Sweets said.

Skidding to a halt behind the unit, we hustled the supplies into the kitchen and went out to the porch, where Niles was giving a speech. Sweets mouthed "Charlie" to Bobby O., who made the sign of the cross.

Niles had the group's undivided attention. "After my first tour of 'Nam, I had a choice: stay and fight for my country or go home, where the love of my life was waiting."

He paused for a long look at his daughter. "Rebecca's mom." The women sighed. Martha patted Becky's leg.

"I decided to stay and fight," Niles continued. "I couldn't leave my brothers. We were fighting for our loved ones, for this great country, for democracy, freedom, the opportunity to chase the American dream."

A few guys nodded, but no one said a word.

"Between tours of duty, our great military would send us soldiers wherever we wanted to go. Some guys went home. Not me. I flew the most wonderful, beautiful woman in the world to Hawaii and met her there, to explain why I wouldn't come home right away, why I might not make it home at all."

The women dabbed their eyes. Even Becky sniffled.

"Under a banyan tree on the island of Maui, as the sun set, I asked Becky's mom to marry me. The next evening, we married under the stars on a secluded beach." There wasn't a dry eye on the porch.

"It was during those two weeks of love in paradise that God saw fit to bless us with Rebecca."

Charlie walked out of the unit as Niles blew his daughter a kiss. "Rebecca, you know I never set eyes on your mother again, but I see her every time you smile."

He had no idea Charlie was behind him. "So I guess now's as good a time as any to tell you. I've exchanged next year's vacation at Jiminy Peak for a week in Maui. Your mother loved it there, and you will too."

Becky put her hands to her mouth and squealed as the group clapped and cheered.

Charlie stepped forward.

As if he'd been waiting for this moment, Niles raised a hand and asked for quiet. "Ladies and gentlemen, let me introduce the man who made all this possible, Jiminy Peak's project director, Charlie Furano—The man who makes dreams come true!"

The applause was thunderous. Niles kissed Charlie on the cheek, and people actually stood. It was the funniest thing I'd ever seen. Or maybe the saddest.

Niles called for quiet again. "While you're standing, I'll ask Charlie to lead us in 'God Bless America.'" To Charlie he muttered, "Got 'em where I want 'em. Sing."

Charlie did. And so did everyone else. For the next few minutes, the patriotic strains echoed through Jericho Valley. As the last "home, sweet home" reverberated in the air, Niles yelled, "Let's eat!"

The women brought out the food, and the men crowded around Niles and Charlie, shaking hands and slapping backs. When everyone was busy filling plates, Charlie leaned into Niles. "If this doesn't work, you're dead."

"Charlie," Niles said with a smile, "you know I've been dead a long time now."

Niles walked away as Martha cornered Charlie. "That man is a hero. Thank you for taking care of him and his beautiful daughter."

"Sure thing," Charlie said.

"These are the best damn ribs I've ever had!" Steve hollered.

Niles caught my eye. "Pretty fresh," he called back. "You'd swear that meat was walking around in the woods twenty-four hours ago."

34

Eventually we led our well-fed tours back to the lodge, where Herbie and Charlie stood at the bar, executioners at the gallows awaiting the condemned. Bobby O. approached them wearing a lopsided grin, holding a worksheet and a check. One by one, the others did the same. I was the last rep still seated at a round table.

As Charlie and Herbie watched, I set my pen down on the completed worksheet and held out my hand. The husband looked at his wife, then at me, and shook. That made it a clean sweep. Six tours, six deals, three for two weeks. Seventy thousand dollars of new business. The Country Village at Jiminy Peak was officially on the map.

By the time my paperwork was done, only Sweets was still hanging around. "Where is everyone?" I asked.

He shrugged. "Fuckin' Charlie is gonna fire Niles."

"But we just made all those sales because of Niles."

"Think I don't know it?"

"We were supposed to have three shows with tours," I said as we left the lodge. "We only got one, and we kicked ass." *But somehow we lost.*

He shrugged again as we reached the condos.

"Congrats on your deal, Sweets."

He half-waved. "Good job yourself, Jake. You won't see a day like this often. Remember it."

Our spotless unit told me Becky had been there. And she wasn't the only one. The smell of pipe tobacco hung in the air. "Niles?" I called.

"In here, Private."

He was in his bedroom, packing a green duffel bag.

"That son of a bitch fired you?"

"Don't worry about me, Jake. I'll survive." I wasn't worried. I was pissed off.

"Charlie's a prick," he said, "but he's the head prick. He wants things done his way."

Niles and I had been together for what seemed like a lifetime. He'd become a friend. A real friend.

"Quite a show, wasn't it? I almost lost it during "America the Beautiful." Six for six. Tell people you were there. And that Sergeant Niles rallied the troops."

We grabbed a few beers and sat in the living room, where Niles offered a toast.

"Semper fi, little brother. Our paths will cross again."

I shook my head. "You made us all a lot of money today, especially that prick Charlie, and you got kicked in the ass. It's wrong."

"Jake, it's not about right or wrong. It's about rules. If anyone else pulled that stunt, it would've been a disaster."

"But it wasn't."

"Charlie's the commander. He expects his troops to follow orders, not think. I broke the rules, and this is the price."

"The price stinks."

"I'll be okay. You're just cutting your teeth, and these guys can teach you a lot. Learn the rules. Play the game. It will all work out," he said softly.

He suddenly perked up. "We've still got some sunlight. Wanna go up the mountain?"

I took a slug of beer and stared at him. "No way."

He laughed. "C'mon, let's get a pizza at Pat's. I gotta say good-bye, anyhow."

When we stopped next door, Becky looked concerned. "Should we all pack?"

"Just Niles so far," I told her. Soon all four of us were in the Caddy, but nobody said a word during the ride, Niles's last trip down the hill.

Charlie's car was parked outside Pat's. "You still want to go in?" I asked Niles.

"Why not? Maybe he'll spring for a round."

Sitting at a corner table with Herbie and Bobby O., Charlie waved us over. "Where you headed?" he asked.

"Don't have a clue," Niles said as we all got comfortable. "But, as you know, I'll be fine."

Charlie surprised me when he set five crisp C-notes on the table. "Here's a SPIF. Never saw a show like that. You are one crazy son of a bitch."

After a long quiet spell, Niles picked up the money and tucked it into his pocket.

"Thanks, Chaz. It'll tide me over 'til I find another foxhole."

Bobby O. laughed. "When you kissed Charlie, I thought I was gonna die." Herbie laughed, too. "I hear you sing real good, Charlie."

With that, the whole table roared. But Charlie sat quietly, cleaning out his pipe.

Pat came over to take orders. "Beer and wings for my troops," Niles said, and then he shook his hand. "Pat, my good man, I've been redeployed. Top-secret mission. Keep the troops fed and well-watered. We'll see each other again."

"Tab's on me tonight," Pat said.

Niles leaned back in his chair, smiling. "In that case, add a large pepperoni pizza, fold it in half, and wrap it to go. I'll have it on the trail."

Pat went off to the kitchen, and the table got quiet again, until Charlie broke the silence.

"How the hell did you come up with the barbecue?"

Niles grinned. "It just happened, Chaz. But what better way to get to know someone? It's primal. Animals only eat with animals they trust, you know."

"Niles, that's brilliant," Becky said. "Break bread with your neighbor."

Herbie looked at Charlie, who stoked his pipe. Niles turned to Becky. "Little daughter, you were great, especially with your dead mom."

"Me? A college student going to Hawaii to see where you and my mother got married? Damn, you can spin a yarn."

Everyone was laughing again as Charlie stood to say good night. Niles hugged him and kissed his cheek. "Semper fi, my captain. We'll meet again."

"Good-bye, Sergeant," Charlie answered. "Keep your ammo dry and your head down."

The pitchers of beer arrived, and Becky raised her glass. "To Daddy. We won't forget you."

We all toasted Niles, who drank to each of us. Herbie gave Niles a send-off hug and left.

Pat had doubled the wings order. "These are pretty good cold, too," he said. "Take the leftovers with you." He put the wrapped folded pizza on the table next to Niles and went back to the bar.

The table got quiet again, the mood sad, and soon we were ready to leave.

On the quick ride back, everyone was quiet. Outside the units, Becky hugged Niles for a long time, choking back tears. "You be safe out there."

"I'll give you a lift to the highway in the morning," Sweets said. "Seven o'clock okay?"

"See you then."

Inside, we each grabbed a beer and settled in the living room.

"Niles, what did you do when you came home from Vietnam?"

"I kept fighting. For my brothers. I joined the protests against the war." He sipped his beer. "The sixties were crazy, Jake. Flower power, hippies, drugs, music … I knew what was going on in 'Nam, and I did my best to end it. Funny thing, I saw more pain back home than I did over there."

I got up and went into the kitchen. We needed another round.

"Cops out of control, tear gassing marches, draft cards burning … I was in Washington when we tried to storm the White House. The fucking White House! Must've been a hundred thousand of us. It was a war zone."

He drained his beer, opened another. "No one inside the gates was listening as sixty thousand of our brothers and sisters were being slaughtered. In a fight that wasn't ours."

He fell quiet, and I knew he was talked out. "Niles, I'm sorry," I told him, "for all the things you had to do, for all the hurt you've been through."

He didn't respond. He was ready to nod off, and I was too.

After a restless night, I woke as the first rays of sunlight came through the window and got up to ride with Sweets and Niles to the highway. One of Niles's knives was on the kitchen table with a note:

Keep this close, Blue Dolphin. It will defend you and feed you. Use it with friend or foe. Thanks for your words.

113

I held the knife for a while, feeling its weight, and then went back to the bedroom to slip it under my mattress. It just felt right.

Sweets showed up at seven.

"He's gone," I said. "Must've left early this morning."

Sweets nodded and turned away. "Fucking Charlie," he muttered.

After he left, I stood under the hot shower, watching the water collect on the bathroom floor. I'd have to go buy a new shower curtain.

Goddamn Niles. *That is one crazy son of a bitch.*

35

"Watch yourself today," Sweets said as we climbed out of the Caddy. "If you question Charlie's decision to fire Niles, you'll be next."

Near the lodge's front entrance, a maintenance guy was assembling a barbecue. Inside, Annie was arranging trays of pastries on the bar. Charlie and Herbie stood off to the side. The other reps talked quietly at the round tables—not the kind of buzz you'd expect from the sales staff that pulled off yesterday's clean sweep.

"Yesterday is yesterday," Herbie said as he took his position. "It doesn't add up to much if we don't get results today."

He stared at each of us. "Charlie has made a few changes. We'll feed the morning UPs a continental breakfast. Burgers and dogs for the afternoon tours. Meet and greet, break the pact, feed them, head out on tour."

"Charlie's a fucking genius," Sweets muttered sarcastically.

"What was that?" Herbie snapped. "You guys have something to add?" We shook our heads.

Charlie walked over and stood next to Herbie. "It's my way or the highway," he said. "You guys think one sale makes you a hero? Or ten? Or a hundred?"

He glared, daring any one of us to challenge him. "I'm here to make a lot of money for a long time, not to get lucky here and there. Follow my steps or hit the road. Don't let the door hit you in the ass."

That ball of white spit was bouncing between his lips again. "And don't even think about eating any of this stuff unless you have an UP," he said. "This is for the workers, the guys making money."

The message was loud and clear: Produce or go home. Eat or be eaten. Live by the golden rule: he who has the gold rules.

By the time Charlie finished his, "my way or the highway" speech and stalked off to his office with Herbie, everybody's mood was down.

"Is it still okay to drink coffee?" Sweets muttered.

Outside, the maintenance guy was filling the newly assembled barbecue with charcoal.

"You're right," I told Sweets. "Charlie's a fuckin' genius."

"Won't be the same," he said. "Yesterday was about a lot more than food."

"What does that mean?"

"It was about the shill."

"What's a shill?"

"Man, you're green. In this case, Becky and Niles were shills … pretending to be something they're not—buyers, members—to convince the UPs that people actually enjoy the product."

Another lesson learned.

Once it was clear that there wouldn't be any tours for the nine o'clock show, we watched as Annie tossed the pastries into the trashcan, shaking her head, disgusted.

Bobby O. took off toward Charlie's office.

"Here come the fireworks," Sweets said. "When Bobby O. sees a wrong, he speaks his mind."

After a few minutes of yelling and a few minutes of silence, a door slammed.

Then a pissed-off Bobby O. reappeared and headed for the exit.

Sweets and I caught up with him at his car, "Don't tell me he had the balls to fire you, too," Sweets gasped.

Bobby O. was livid. "Firing Niles was bad enough. But throwing away food rather than letting the guys have it, well, that's just plain mean. Some of us have kids at home who would love those pastries."

"Did they toss you?"

Bobby O. took a deep breath. "No. I tossed them."

Sweets threw his head back and groaned. "First they ax a guy who makes the rest of us six for six, and now they lose the top rep in the place."

Bobby O. was a man of principle, still, there was no mistaking the look of disappointment on his face. He backed up his car, and before starting down the mountain, he slowly waved good-bye.

Watching the car disappear down the mountain, Sweets shook his head. "This whole damn thing is blowing up."

We went back into the lodge as Charlie was leaving, calm and composed.

Herbie was a nervous wreck at the bar, running his fingers through the hair he had left. "Christ. I'm sixty-five years old. Think I need this?"

The rest of the day was a bust. The two UPs who showed ate burgers and then left.

I was new to this game, but it didn't take an expert to see what was happening. A sales force is like a house of cards; remove the wrong one and it all falls down.

36

Days turned into weeks, weeks into months. Christmas came and went. Too much snow, not enough snow, gifts that made even the "fox leather" jackets look good. There was always an excuse for the poor tour production. The truth was, things were never the same between Herbie and Charlie after Niles was gone.

We got Bobby O. back, but he wasn't the same either. He went through the motions each day and then went home.

New recruits sat through training, worked the line, and got stuck paying the tab at Pat's. I remembered what it was like when I started, when I was the only one who had cash.

We all suffered through the mind-numbing eight o'clock meetings and the monotonous five steps, and did our best with the UPs who showed. I thought about quitting during that winter and spring, but I had no options. The developer must've seen something we sales reps never did, because in February he broke ground on two more clusters of units.

One morning, Herbie introduced the new RCI resort directory that showcased different destinations all over the world—New England, Florida, the Caribbean, and Europe—with black-and-white photos and contact numbers. It came with a vinyl album and a slide show, a three-minute audiovisual pitch. In a dark corner, Herbie turned on the projector and swung the arm on the record player, carefully placing the needle on the vinyl. At each loud beep, he turned the knob on the projector and advanced to the next slide.

Trumpets blared as the RCI logo appeared and a male voice introduced us to "Lucky Jim and his family!" Lucky Jim and his wife, their little boy, and their little girl were all smiles in a beautiful suite.

"As owners of time-share, they vacation in the best of accommodations! And when they check out, there's no bill!"

Beep!

"This is poor Phil and his family." Poor Phil was large and frowning. "Since they don't own time-share, they vacation in a claustrophobic room, paying lots of money to stay there!"

Poor Phil and his sad-looking family were packed into a crappy motel room, a middle-aged guy standing next to them with his hand out.

"What the fuck?" Sweets shouted. "You expect us to use this train wreck?" Everybody started laughing, even Herbie.

"Who produced this shit?" I asked.

The guys roared.

Herbie raised his hand for quiet. "Listen, we wouldn't have done it this way, but it's what we've got. Charlie wants it used, so starting today, we use it."

Looking at a staff that wasn't sold, he added, "A one-hundred-dollar SPIF goes to the first deal that uses the show."

It didn't last long. The slides were never in order, and nobody in the place could get them straight. Jim became Phil, Phil became Jim, hotel rooms were great, time-share units were crap. Anytime anybody showed the damn thing, it was a disaster, and so it was dropped.

Winter was long, spring longer. The Berkshire Mountains are no day at the beach during spring thaw. When the snow melts, mud flows.

We were all excited when Memorial Day finally approached, hoping for a busy three-day weekend. Everyone was broke.

Saturday was beautiful, the morning sun warm. I put on my sport jacket for the first time in a while, then called out to my new roommate, Eddie, telling him it was time to go. He'd taken the front bedroom, the larger one. I hadn't even thought about taking it when Niles moved out. It didn't seem right.

"We better get tours today," Eddie said. "If I don't send my wife some cash, she's gonna dump my sorry ass."

Eddie was an okay guy in his early thirties, a car salesman from Boston with two kids. "If I don't make some money, I'm gonna leave myself," I told him.

We headed to the lodge with Sweets—Eddie in the backseat, me in front (seniority has its perks)—and arrived at eight o'clock sharp. Herbie didn't look happy.

"Listen up," he said. "I've got bad news and worse news." Everybody groaned.

"The marketing department thought we'd be closed over the weekend. Didn't start booking UPs until last night. Tours will be light." The group groan turned to silence.

Herbie shrugged. "Help yourself to the pastries." Charlie was nowhere to be seen.

"Anybody got something to say?" Herbie asked.

Sweets shifted to one side of his ass and ripped a fart that would've made any man proud.

I started laughing. Herbie didn't, so I laughed harder.

Sweets turned to me. "Jake, that's the smartest thing you've said in a long time!" The whole place broke up. I laughed so hard my sides hurt.

Herbie threw up his hands and left. As the laughter died down and the guys dug into the pastries, Sweets said, "C'mon. Let's check out the new units."

Bobby O. piled into the Caddy with us. "That was the best-timed fart in history, Jake."

I pointed at Sweets, who was watching in the rearview mirror. "Pizza and beer at Pat's last night," he said. "They're lucky I don't shit on the whole damn crew."

At the construction site, each of us sank an inch into black mud. Sweets, wearing ostrich-skin boots, complained the loudest. A foot-wide plank led to one of the new two-story units. Inside, we were all wowed.

The first floor featured a living room, kitchen, large bedroom with bath, and a laundry room with half-bath. The two upstairs bedrooms shared a bathroom. The vaulted ceilings made the place look huge. "I could live here for real," I said. "Forget about vacation."

As we took in the view of the valley from one of the second-floor bedrooms, Bobby O. said, "Uh-oh." And there was Charlie, marching toward the units.

"I'm in no mood for his bullshit," Sweets said. "He's done fuck all about delivering UPs."

"You think Herbie ratted us out?" I asked. Sweets nodded. "That prick."

We were in the kitchen by the time Charlie walked through the front door. "Nice units we're building for phase two," he said to me. "Shame you won't be here."

Sweets started to protest. Charlie ignored him. Still looking at me, he said, "You're done. Pack up."

He pissed me off, and frankly, I didn't like the guy. "Come outside, motherfucker, I'm gonna kick your ass."

I opened the kitchen slider and stepped out, prepared to make good on my promise. Nobody told me the back porch hadn't been built yet.

Stepping into thin air, I dropped three feet and landed with a thud on my back. Scrambling to get up, I slipped and fell into the mud again, face-first this time. When I managed to get to my knees, Charlie smiled down at me.

"Look at the young pup," he said, "playing in the mud."

When he left, Sweets and Bobby O. pulled me up into the kitchen. "Very impressive, killer," Sweets said. "You're one hell of a mud wrestler."

"Are you nuts?" Bobby O. asked. "Charlie used to box. He'd have killed you!"

"But I'd have given him one good shot," I said, pulling mud from my face and hair. "And that would've been worth it."

"Get cleaned up and grab your things," Sweets said. "I'll give you a lift. I'm outta here, too. Who needs this bullshit?"

"What am I supposed to do now," I asked, "with no money and no place to stay?"

"If I didn't have family here, I'd head to Cape Cod," Bobby O. said. "My buddy needs sales reps at a resort in Provincetown. Want me to tell him you're coming?"

"Tell him I'll get there today."

"Shortest unemployment I've ever seen," Sweets said. "What's it been, four minutes?"

"Should I put in a word for you, Sweets?" Bobby O. asked.

Sweets shook his head. "Me and Beck will head back to Texas. Good deals on boots this time of year."

Bobby O. shook Sweets's hand and hugged him good-bye. He shook my hand too. Giving me a once over, he passed on the mud-hug.

Back at the units, Sweets called, "Beck, start packing. We're on the road again."

"Yahoo!" she hollered. "Good-bye, rednecks!"

Thirty minutes later, Sweets lowered the Caddy's roof and backed up.

"Hold it!" I yelled. "I forgot something."

I hopped out without waiting for Becky to open the door, ran inside, and came back with Niles' knife.

"Don't ask me to stop at the lodge," Sweets said. "I've seen enough of the jail in these woods." We all laughed as we passed the lodge for the last time. No one wanted to stop.

The mountains gave way to flat terrain, and the majestic trees got smaller as we traveled east. A couple of hours later, at the other end of the state, Sweets pulled over.

"Route 495, Jake. Two hours to Provincetown—and your new destiny."

They got out with me. We all hugged and promised to stay in touch. I had a feeling we'd meet up again.

The Caddy pulled away as I hoisted the backpack onto my shoulder. Then I stuck out my thumb.

SECTION III |

| Provincetown

The Sand Castle

37

The holiday weekend traffic was brisk. By noon, I'd made it to Plymouth. Hot and hungry, I jammed my jacket into my backpack and wished I'd ordered a folded pizza for the journey, like Niles. I stopped thinking about pizza when a Volkswagen Beetle pulled over, stopped thinking altogether when I got a look at the driver. "I'm only going as far as Provincetown," she said.

"That ought to do it." The next stop after Provincetown was London, with nothing but the Atlantic in between. I tossed my stuff in the backseat and got in, realizing why they called it a bug.

"I'm Jake."

"Nice to meet you, Jake. I'm Mandy." Smiling, she moved the stick shift through the gears, and the lawn mower engine did its best. "Been waiting long?"

I shook my head. "Ten minutes. Heading to a new job."

She checked the rearview mirror as a truck bore down on the back bumper. The little bug tried to accelerate, but the truck driver laid on the horn as he passed, and then again when Mandy gave him the finger. "What a dickhead," she said. "Over the bridge, there's a whole different mindset. Know what I mean?"

I'd only been to the cape a few times, on day trips with my family, but I agreed. "Everything about Cape Cod is mellow. Light blue sky, soothing gray fog, scrub pines, sand. I think those soft tones make people relax."

"Exactly. Have you spent much time in P-town?"

I knew better than to bluff on that question. "Never been there. Truth is, this will be my first chance to spend real time on the cape."

"You straight?" She caught me off guard. "It's none of my business. And I don't care. But you don't look gay."

"I'm not. Straight as they come."

"Interesting way to put it, Jake."

Realizing what I'd said, I took in her blond ponytail and the killer body under her fitted blouse and blue jeans.

"What about you?" I asked. "You straight?"

"Bingo!" she yelled, scaring the shit out of me. She laughed when I jumped, then pointed ahead. "Bingo. There's the bridge."

And there it was, one of the two sister bridges onto Cape Cod.

"When I was a kid, my dad would run a contest between me and my brother. First one to see the bridge had to shout, 'Bingo!'"

"You won today." We circled the rotary and drove up the Sagamore Bridge, the panoramic view breathtaking.

"Wonder how high we are."

"A hundred and thirty feet."

I stared at her. "How do you know that?"

"Been coming over this bridge my whole life. Talk is a twelve-foot fence is going up to stop the suicides."

Below us, a tanker was making its way through the canal. "What a way to go."

Mandy nodded. "Of the fifty or sixty people who've jumped, way more came from the mainland than from the Cape. Probably doesn't mean anything, but it's an interesting stat."

"With my luck, I'd land on the deck of a freighter."

She laughed. "That would screw up your lunch, wouldn't it?"

We came down from the height of the bridge and eased onto Route 6, heading to Provincetown. "Want me to be your tour guide?" she asked.

I looked around the tiny car. "Is there a choice?"

She slapped my leg. "For the price of admission, you get what you get."

I raised both hands in surrender. "Okay. Okay. I'll take it."

The next hour flew by. She told me about the Kennedy Compound in Hyannis Port, the T-shirt emporiums in Dennis, and the famous nighttime beach parties in Chatham, home to the "real" Cape Cod money. Next we made our way through the outer cape, where small clam shanties lined the road. Tall sand dunes tapered down to the cold blue Atlantic through Eastham, Wellfleet, and Truro. Cape Cod Bay lay to the west.

As we left Truro, approaching Provincetown, the tall dunes moved in, bordering the road. And then came a sight to behold. To the west, the bay glistened like a blue carpet sprinkled with diamonds. The sweeping arm of the land clutched the village of Provincetown. Mandy pulled over, and we got out to take in the view—that sweeping arm of Cape Cod holding a defiant fist to the open ocean.

"Am I seeing things," I asked, "or is that fist clutching a monument?"

Mandy stood close. "The Provincetown Monument. Gay men dominate this town. P-town holds the penis tight." I couldn't tear my eyes from the hand holding the penis.

Mandy moved closer. "This little stretch of sand is big enough for all of us. We just have to share."

She took hold of my hips and pulled me close. "Sweetie, I don't know the answer to the question you asked on the bridge. I'm trying to figure it out."

I hugged her. "If you figure out you want to be with a guy, keep me in mind."

We got back into the bug, and in no time we were at the Sandcastle Resort. She stopped in front of the Reception Center.

I wanted to stay with her to at least buy her lunch, but I had no money. Zero. So I hugged her again and said good-bye.

"Hope I see you soon," she whispered.

Shouldering the backpack, I asked, "How will I find you?"

She winked and blew me a kiss. "This is a small place. You can find anything you want pretty easily."

38

At the end of the long hallway beyond the Welcome sign, three stories of units overlooked a huge swimming pool. Music mingled with children's laughter as they played in the water. Inside Reception, chairs lined the walls of a simple room and an attractive girl read behind the desk.

"Welcome to the Sandcastle," she said as she set down her book. "I'm Kelli with an *i*. How can I help you?"

"Jake Arril. I'm here to see Bruce."

She checked me out from head to toe. "You'll find him at the pool bar. Look for a bamboo hat and reflector sunglasses."

I thanked her and turned to leave. "New talent?" she asked.

"Excuse me?"

"Taking a sales job?"

"Hope so."

"Good. We need some fine-looking talent around here."

I thanked her again and headed toward the pool, where the deck chairs were full, the barbecue smoking, and the music loud. A teenager bounced off the diving board, landing flat on his back with a thwack. The crowd cheered as the poor guy struggled to the side, where his buddies helped him and his beet-red back out of the water.

Bruce wasn't hard to find in the thatch-roofed bar, as he was the only guy wearing a wide-rimmed bamboo hat and reflector glasses.

"Stop!" he shouted.

I wasn't sure he meant me, but I stopped anyway.

He swiveled on the bar stool.

I looked around, then faced him again. He was in lotus position, with a Marine Corps patch on the right thigh of his cut-off blue jeans and a T-shirt that read, "Beam Me Up, Scotty. No Intelligent Life Down Here."

In front of him on the bar sat a can of beer and a cigarette burning in an ashtray. "You have a purple aura," he said.

He looked me over, his eyes serious. "You're a hungry bluefish, but you can be a great white shark. You've traveled far but have a distance to go before your journey will end. How can I help?"

"I have no money," I heard myself say. "I need a job and a place to stay."

Without missing a beat, he reached into his pocket. At the same moment, the phone rang. The bartender answered, listened, and hung up again.

Bruce forked over a crisp hundred-dollar bill, then pointed beyond me. "Stay in that second-floor unit tonight."

"Excuse me, boss," said the bartender. "You've got one."

Bruce grinned. "Your UP is waiting."

I jammed the hundred into my pocket, thanked the madman, and turned to go, but then thought better of it. "Where do I pitch? Do you have a model? What are the prices?"

Bruce shrugged. "I gave you what you desired. Now go get me what I need."

39

"That was fast," said Kelli with an *i*. "Welcome aboard."

"Can I leave my backpack with you? It's everything I own."

She nodded. "The models are 201 and 203, oceanfront, second-floor. Studio sells for about five, the two-bedroom, eight." She handed me a yellow notepad and a couple of worksheets.

On the way back to Reception, I'd noticed that some of the first-floor units contained only a round table and a few chairs, so my problems were solved. *A place to pitch. Models. Prices.*

"You're the best," I told her. "I'll hug you later."

"I'll be looking for more than a hug, sweetie."

I was trying to come up with a response when she looked past me. "All finished, Mr. Thomas? Now that didn't hurt, did it?" She took his paperwork. "Jake, this is Mr. Bill Thomas. You guys get along now, and have fun."

I shook his hand. "Bill, I'm Jake Arril. Who's that pretty girl over there? She chasing you?"

"That's Edna," Bill said. "She's been chasing me for fifty-two years now."

"Don't you listen to that old buzzard," Edna said. "It's the other way around. And I'm pretty picky about who catches me!"

We all laughed. "Come with me," I told them. "Let's see what kind of trouble we can get into."

I led them to a first-floor unit and looked over at the bar before sliding the door closed. Bruce was staring in our direction, grinning in his reflector sunglasses. Bill and Edna were a great couple—a retired corporate executive and a proud mom with four grandkids. Once I explained the general overview of the program, I took them upstairs.

"You're going to love the units," I said.

Not sure where I was going, I wove through lounge chairs and poolside partiers, hoping Bill and Edna wouldn't land in the pool or get killed by an errant football. I happened upon the stairway. The second-story units faced the ocean, not the pool. Unit 203 was an ordinary hotel room with a linoleum floor, a top-burner electric stove, a bathroom, and a small table set for two. A couple of easy chairs faced a TV on a six-drawer cabinet. Sliding glass doors led to the deck.

"There's no place to sleep," Edna said. I panicked. She was right.

Bill reached for a cord on the far side of the room and pulled a bed down from the wall. "A Murphy bed, hon."

I'd never heard of a Murphy bed. Edna clapped.

"You had me going, Jake. You're a good actor." They both laughed, and I did too. But I was the only one sweating.

When we made our way out to the deck, I knew at once what I was selling: Western exposure—Provincetown to the right, Truro's sand dunes to the left, nothing but a sandy beach and Cape Cod Bay straight ahead. No one said a word as we settled in lounge chairs, drinking in the view.

Bill finally broke the silence. "Must be spectacular sunsets." I nodded, seeing no reason to speak.

"The lights from Provincetown must be pretty at night," Edna added.

I was sold too. Jiminy Peak could have its oversize units. I'd take this any day of the week. But I was supposed to sell, not buy. "Let's take a look at the two-bedroom," I suggested. Reluctantly, they followed me out to the hallway. As we walked, I pointed toward the pool. "Those lucky members will have all of this for a lifetime."

"About that," Edna said, "what happens when the owner passes away?"

"The title transfers to family members. See those kids playing by the pool? After a lifetime of fun, they'll pass it on to their kids. Pretty cool, don't you think?"

She nodded, then looked at Bill.

The two-bedroom was nothing more than two studios, double doors between them. A half wall separated the kitchen from what passed as a living room, with a pair of easy chairs, a TV on top of a chest of drawers, and a table set for six. Against the wall was a sleeper sofa; beside it, the door to a simple bath. Beyond the doors we found two double beds, another bathroom, and a second TV.

I took Bill and Edna out to the deck, and again we sank into lounge chairs, hypnotized. "You know," I said, "every time I look at this view, it's like the first time."

"What does it cost to join, Jake?" Bill asked, holding Edna's hand.

Time to close the deal. "Let's go downstairs and I'll show you the options."

The pool area wasn't so crowded when we passed. Off to the side, a steel drum band was setting up, and the crowd had drifted over to watch. Back at the round table, Bill and Edna continued to hold hands as I explained that pricing hinged on the size of the unit and the time of year they wanted to enjoy.

After I covered all the bases, I said, "Bill, Edna, what would make your family the happiest?"

"What would make *you* happy?" Bill asked his wife of fifty-two years.

"Well, I'd love to bring the grandchildren here for a week during the summer."

My heart leapt into my throat.

Bill patted Edna's hand affectionately. She kept talking. "But it would be nice if you and I could spend time here in September, when it's not so hot and busy."

Bill didn't hesitate. "Jake, how about a two-bedroom on the water for a week in July, and a studio on the water for two weeks in September?"

Somehow I kept my cool. "Let me write up the order, and then I'll check inventory." Filling out the worksheet, I hoped for the best with pricing, penciling in $7,995 for the two-bedroom, $4,995 per week for the studio. When I started to fill in the 10 percent deposit, Bill stopped me. "I'll write you a check," he said, "for the full amount." *Seventeen thousand nine hundred eighty-five dollars!*

I turned the worksheet toward them, and Edna signed first.

"Which weeks would you prefer?" I asked.

Edna looked at Bill. "I don't think the kids care," she said, "but I'd prefer the middle two weeks in September."

Bill set down the pen and looked up. "September 15 marks fifty-three years since she begged me to marry her!"

Edna slapped his arm as I made a beeline for the offices.

Kelli's jaw dropped when she saw the worksheet. She jumped to her feet like a cheerleader, arms above her head, down at her sides, then up again, spelling "yay." She was clapping when I carried the worksheet through the door to Administration.

I waited at the counter for one of two middle-aged women behind it to help me. The first to leave her desk was fortyish and chubby, with short dark hair and a genuine smile.

"You have no unit numbers," she said as she looked over the worksheet, "and no weeks."

"Where do I find out what's available?" I asked.

The second woman sporting a gray crewcut looked up at me with a no-nonsense glare. "Check the book." The first woman pointed to a green book on the counter.

It didn't take long to figure out the system. Each page had a unit number on top, weeks one through fifty-two listed below. An empty line next to a week number meant that unit was available. I wrote "Bill and Edna Thomas" next to the first week in July on an oceanfront two-bedroom page, and again next to the second and third weeks in September for an oceanfront studio.

"I'm Jan," the first one offered.

Relieved, I handed Jan the worksheet and she headed back to her desk. "Who does the paperwork?" I asked.

"Christ, hasn't Bruce trained you?" the other secretary growled. "You do!"

I panicked. "I don't know how. I'll screw it up."

She grudgingly stood from her desk and sauntered toward the counter. Her paunchy frame leaned forward and peered over her spectacles. Her short, spiked hair resembled the quills of an angry porcupine. "Just how long have you been working here?"

The clock on the wall read 5:25. "I got here at two," I told her.

"This is ridiculous," she said, "even by Bruce's standards."

"It's an eighteen-thousand-dollar deal," Jan said from her desk. "Cash. No financing."

Attila the Hun's mood improved immediately.

"Oh," she said. "I'm Robby. Who are you?"

133

I told her and asked again about the paperwork. "A mule could do it," she said. "One page. Unit and week numbers. Pay your maintenance fees. You break it, you bought it. Think you can handle that?"

Robby was taking no prisoners. It was her way or the highway.

Jan brought the paperwork back. "Remember: the contract is in triplicate. If they don't lean on the pen, the signatures won't come through. White and pink copies are ours, yellow is theirs. And make sure they get a directory. Got it?"

I got it, and I even remembered to tell Bill and Edna to lean on the pen.

When I walked them out to the parking lot, Bill said, "Jake, aren't we supposed to get a barbecue grill for coming here today?"

Who knew? "Be right back," I said, and I ran toward Kelli.

She was waiting, holding a parcel in brown cardboard. "One grill," she said.

I grabbed it and ran back to Bill and Edna. "Hope you think of us every time you use it."

Edna hugged me, and Bill shook my hand. "Thank you, Jake. We'll see you in July with our grandkids."

"It's been a pleasure," I said.

The steel drum band began to play as I went back to Administration, triumphant.

"Piece of cake, right?" Robby asked.

"Piece of cake."

Kelli opened the door. "Good night. I'm heading out."

I opened my arms, "I really appreciate your help, Kelli."

She gave me a bear hug, lifting me a foot off the ground. "Just what this place needs," she said as she set me down. "Good-looking new blood."

Jan was waiting at the counter, pleased with the clear signatures on the copies.

"Where's the check?" she asked.

"Fuck."

Frantic, I ran down the hallway to the parking lot. Bill and Edna were gone.

When I got back to the office, Robby read my face. "Pender ..." she said.

134

I'd just done the unimaginable. I sighed and went across the hall to get my backpack. Reception was locked, and Kelli was gone.

I headed for the bar, hoping Bruce would let me in to get my stuff. He wasn't there. But Bill and Edna were! Bill waved me over. "Let us buy you a drink, Jake."

I asked the bartender for a beer.

"When the band started playing," Edna said, "we couldn't resist staying for a while."

The bartender put the beer in front of me, and I downed half of it.

"Thirsty?" Bill asked.

Smiling at him, I nodded. After a few seconds of silence, I sheepishly asked, "By the way, do you have a check?"

He looked stunned. "My God, I've been having such a good time, I forgot!"

Edna laughed, reached into her purse and produced a checkbook. Bill filled it out and handed it over.

I polished off the Bud. "Enjoy the band and the sunset. They're all yours now. Welcome to the Castle."

Back in Administration, I held up the check without a word.

"Full down! Cash out!" Robby said.

"Good work, Jake." Jan smiled as she took the check. "No one has hit the ground running like you have."

"Any chance my screwup can stay between us?" Robby gave me a thumbs-up and Jan zipped her lips.

Kelli climbed out of her car as I reached the door. "My God," she said, "I forgot about your backpack. And you need a key to the unit you're staying in tonight. And before I forget again, Bruce wants to meet you at Rose's."

Just like that, it came together. My stuff. A room. A big deal out of my first tour.

Bruce told me to figure it out, and I did.

Shouldering the pack, key #227 in hand, I stood looking at Kelli. "You really helped me out today. I want you to know how much I appreciate it."

Seeming a little embarrassed, perhaps unfamiliar with genuine gratitude, she gave me a quick peck on the cheek and walked back to her car.

"Where is Rose's?" I called after her.

"Ten-minute walk down Commercial Street," she yelled, "on the left."

Studio 227 was identical to the model unit. I pulled the bed down from the wall and unpacked, slid the knife under the mattress, and tossed the plastic bag holding my muddied sport coat and clothes in the corner. Then I took a shower, letting the hot water beat down on me, thinking about the events of the day.

"Look at me now, Charlie!" I shouted. "Fuck you!"

40

The sun was starting to set as I left the unit in a blue polo shirt and jeans. Little kids were playing their own game on the courts, smashing tennis balls into each other, shrieking and giggling whenever one of them got hit. Next to the courts, outside a single-story L-shaped building, seven or eight people were enjoying the evening, some relaxed in deck chairs, others milling around near a smoking barbecue. I hadn't eaten all day, and whatever they were grilling smelled awfully good.

"Hey, are you the new shooter?" shouted a middle-aged guy holding a beer.

No one else was around, and the others were looking at me too. "Excuse me?"

The guy offered his hand. "Dick Akers, sales." He waved back toward the group. "This is the rest of the staff."

We shook. "Jake Arril. Just came from the Berkshires. Jiminy Peak."

A girl in her twenties groaned. "Charlie."

A thin, curly-headed kid introduced himself as Boone. "You didn't bring that son of a bitch along, did ya?"

I laughed. "If I never see him or Herbie again, it'll be too soon."

The group chorused, "Herbie!"

Dick Akers explained that some of them had dealt with Charlie in the car business, and a few had been to Jiminy.

"Is Niles still there?" Boone asked. I shook my head. "A Charlie casualty."

The girl who'd groaned told me she was Reggie. "Niles. Any day now that crooked-toothed maniac will show up here." I stared at her. "I love Niles," she added. "He's one twisted bastard, but I love him."

"Nice sale today," Akers said. "Haven't seen one of those in a while."

They'd all heard the news. "Just lucky," I told them. "You know how it goes. Right place, right time."

A tall, lanky guy introduced himself as Jim. "I'd rather be lucky than good, but I'll take it any way I can get it."

"Believe me," Reggie piped in, putting her arm around Jim, "he's more lucky than good." The whole gang laughed.

"They're our happy couple," Akers said. He nodded his head toward the cooler. "Help yourself to a beer." I explained that I was supposed to meet Bruce at Rose's.

"No sweat. We'll be seeing a lot of each other. They'll move you to the Barracks tomorrow."

"The Barracks?"

He swept his hand toward the L-shaped building. "She's not pretty, but the price is right, and you can't beat the commute."

I waved, walked the twenty yards to Commercial Street, and in ten minutes stood in front of a hand-painted wooden sign engraved with a red rose. Inside, soft music played as diners enjoyed meals in a quaint setting. Beyond them, large bay windows and glass-paned doors framed a deck overlooking the bay and the most spectacular sunset I'd ever seen.

"Welcome to Rose's." The bartender wore a white shirt and black tie. "Need anything?" he asked.

Bruce sat alone in the dim light at the bar, wearing khakis, a dress shirt, and a Red Sox cap, a green bottle of beer in front of him. "I'll have one of those," I said.

Bruce pulled out a high-backed stool, we shook, and he took a drag from his cigarette. "You are a great white shark. I know one when I see one."

"You heard about my deal?"

He snickered. "Everyone knows of Jake Arril's first tour. Everyone."

"Word travels fast around here." He saluted as we both drank.

"That Kelli is a doll. I couldn't have pulled it off without her help. Is she hooked up?"

He grinned. "Kelvin." I set the beer back on the bar. "His real name is Kelvin."

My jaw dropped. "Kelli's a guy?"

"Do your homework, Jake. This is one place where you really *can't* judge a book by its cover."

138

I'd never met a transvestite. At least I didn't think I had.

Bruce was still grinning. "Girls in Admin any help?"

"Don't tell me they're guys." He shook his head. "The big one, Robby, she's tough," I said. "And it seems like Jan won't do anything without Robby's approval."

He nodded. "That's marriage. Alpha and Beta."

"They're married," I heard myself say. "This will take some getting used to."

He snickered again. "You haven't seen anything yet, Jake."

I took a gulp of my beer and after a moment asked, "What's the commission structure, Bruce?"

He grabbed a napkin and pulled a pen from his shirt pocket. "Red weeks pay ten percent, white weeks fifteen percent, blue weeks twenty percent. For a cash sale, add two percent."

He kept scribbling. "Three business days is the cooling-off period. With ten percent down, you get paid on the fourth day."

"So, if I write a deal a day, after three days I'll get a check every day?"

He nodded. "Our developers own the three biggest hotels in Provincetown. You can cash your check at any of them, 24-7."

I leaned back on the stool. "Doesn't get any better than that. Wonder how much I made today."

Bruce drew a line under his final number. "Just like a shark," he said. "Eat first, wonder what it was later."

My eyes almost popped out of my head when he handed me the napkin. "I made two thousand six hundred sixty?"

"Not bad for a few hours work." He stood and put a fifty-dollar bill on the bar. "Take care of my friend, Aaron," he said to the bartender. "What's left is yours."

"Off to see the wife and kids?" Aaron asked.

Bruce nodded and patted my shoulder. "A great white with a purple aura. Can you beat that?"

He was almost out the door when I called after him. "Bruce, what time tomorrow?"

He didn't look back. "Nine-thirty roll call. Anything before that should be illegal."

41

As Aaron polished a wineglass, I asked whether it would be okay to walk out on the deck, where a sliver of orange was left on the horizon. "Make yourself at home, Jake," he said. "I mean that. We have great chefs here—breakfast, lunch, and dinner—and six suites upstairs that overlook the bay."

I made my way through the dining room, where a few couples were enjoying dinner and soft strains of classical music. I walked through the french doors to the deck just as the last of the sun sank below the sea. Two couples sat at a candlelit table, their conversation hushed. The breeze off the water was cool.

The bent arm of the shoreline swung out into the bay, and the faint sounds of a party carried on the breeze. Multicolored lights from the shops, clubs, and eateries made the place look like a jewel floating alone on the black sea.

The aromas reminded me I was hungry. I went back to the bar and asked Aaron where I should eat.

"Jake, if you live to be one hundred and eat every meal out, you'll never be disappointed in this town."

I downed what was left of my beer.

"For a single guy like you, I'd recommend the wharf. Try the takeout at Mojo's and eat on the pier. Best seat in P-town."

I thanked him and headed for the door. "Don't forget your change," he called.

The fifty was still on the bar. "You heard the man," I told him. "That's yours."

He flashed a smile. "Remember, Jake: Consider Rose's your home."

Quaint houses lined Commercial Street, a narrow road with cars parked on both sides. Other cars managed to pass, none seeming to be in any hurry. Even the bicycles coasted slowly. Near the center of town, the small houses turned into restaurants with hand-carved wooden signs: Cirro & Sal's, The Boathouse, The Garden … I was tempted to stop at each, to go in and find out what smelled so damn good.

Soon I was in the heart of town, at the party. The center was packed. Arm-in-arm walked guys with guys, girls with girls, guys with girls, families with kids, older couples, teenagers—a carnival of people surrounded by a menagerie of shops and restaurants on the edge of the sea.

At the Lobster Pot, the bay window was actually a fish tank, and in it sat Oscar the Lobster. Three feet long and twenty-six pounds, according to the plaque, he was roughly one hundred years old. When I crouched down to look Oscar in the eyes, he wiggled his tentacles and crept to a back corner of the tank.

Heading toward the wharf, I passed tattoo parlors, glass blowers, cotton candy stands, and pizza-and-beer joints. And there it was. Mojo's. The crowd and the smells told me Aaron had steered me right. I wanted one of everything on the menu. A few minutes later, holding a cardboard box filled with a burger, onion rings, clam chowder, fried clams, and a chocolate shake, I was as happy as I could remember.

When I finally found an empty wooden bench, I burned my mouth with the first few onion rings, but my only concern was what to eat next: juicy burger, sweet fried clams, or delicious chowder. I couldn't get it down fast enough.

Pausing for a gulp of the shake, I noticed three commercial fishermen who'd stopped unloading their catch to laugh at my frenzied feeding. Realizing I was the center of attention, I lowered the shake. One of them called out in a language I didn't understand. I rubbed my stomach. They laughed and went back to work.

So did I. As the food disappeared, I ate slower, beyond full but unwilling to stop until the box was empty and the last drop of chocolate shake was gone. Then I leaned back on the bench, watched the three-man crew pack fish into wooden crates on the wharf, and thought about the day: the trip, the deal, the commission, Bruce.

Everything about Provincetown screamed, "Stay awake! Don't miss a thing!" Even so, my wobbly legs told me to call it a day. As I paused on a corner at the center of town, two bikers walked by, sporting black boots, studded jackets, and pink Speedos, exposing their asses under the leggings of their leather chaps. The thought of Niles and the Berkshire Bikers made me grin, Jiminy Peak was a world away.

The vibrant atmosphere was contagious. Bars and nightclubs turned up the music and the whole town came alive. From a two-story Victorian with open double-doors, strobe lights flashed and a sound system blasted Queen's new hit, "Another One Bites the Dust." Catching a second wind, I walked past the bouncer and into the club.

It took a few seconds for my eyes to adjust to the darkness. The only light came from the strobes and the colored bulbs reflecting off a huge disco ball hanging from the ceiling. Waiters in hot pants and button-down shirts tied in mid-chest knots carried trays of drinks to tables scattered around a packed dance floor. The guys working the bar wore the same hot pants but were bare-chested. I wandered over and found an empty stool.

"What'll it be, lover?" asked a frisky bartender.

Lover? I didn't mean to frown, but I guess I did. "Just a beer, whatever's cheap."

"Attitude!" the bartender shouted. "Attitude from the breeder." A five-dollar tip made us friends again.

I was still stuffed, so the beer sat on the bar as I studied the crowd. This was a carefree zone, with everybody blending into one on the dance floor. The sound system was great, crisp and loud, blasting the Thompson Twins' "Hold Me Now."

For the second time that day, it seemed like another guy wearing sunglasses was staring at me. He looked to be about my age, at a table by himself with a cocktail, shades on in the darkness. I picked up the Bud and took a gulp. When a new song cleared the speakers, he was on the dance floor. Alone. Head back. Body moving slowly, warming up. The guy could dance.

Two beautiful girls, hand in hand, joined him as the beat picked up. He swapped between the two, the two with each other, the three together. They put on quite a show, and the dance floor filled. The song was half over when I heard my name. And there was Mandy.

She was dancing with a beautiful blond, waving for me to join them. I took another swig of beer and did. "See, Jake, you *can* find anything you want here!" she yelled over the music. "Say hi to Jenn."

Mandy's friend took my hand and spun around until she was tight against me, her back to my chest. She pulled my arms around her waist and reached out to Mandy. And just like that, we were all friends, dancing.

After a few more songs, the guy in the glasses and the two girls showed up next to us.

"C'mon, Jake!" Mandy yelled. "Join us for a drink."

The guy in the glasses put his arm around my shoulder. "I've got a front-row table," he said. "Why don't you three join us?"

Mandy and Jenn nodded, and the other girls smiled, so the six of us settled in the front row. The guy held out his hand. "Peter V. D. Farnsworth. Nice to meet you." Introductions were made all around.

"What are you drinking?" Farnsworth asked.

"Beer," I told him.

He shook his head. "Nah. Vodka and cranberry." He opened his arms to the girls. "Am I right?"

They agreed enthusiastically as the waiter appeared. "The local elixir!" Peter proclaimed.

"Let me guess, Peter," the waiter said. "Cape Codders. And keep them coming." He giggled when Peter blew him a kiss.

The party didn't stop, and neither did the drinks. After a few, I got a second wind—or maybe a third—and didn't even notice the taste of vodka anymore. We all danced together—guys, girls, it didn't matter—and the music played on.

Farnsworth and I were alone at the table, waiting for another round, when he said, "Nice touch today. First UP on the track and you crush it. Gonna make the rest of us look bad."

I leaned back in the chair. "How the hell does everyone know?"

He smiled. "I'm a rep at the Castle. Trust me, everyone knows Jake Arril is in town."

So he *had* been looking at me from behind those sunglasses. Mandy was right; this was a small place.

"Do I want to know what 'V. D.' stands for?" I asked.

Peter laughed. "It's not what you think. My father bestowed the family name on me instead of my big brother," he said.

"What's the name?"

"Van Dyke. I'm Peter Van Dyke Farnsworth."

"That's a mouthful. What'd your brother end up with?"

He sipped his new drink. "Calvin Bartlett Farnsworth the third."

"He got the short end of the stick."

We were both laughing when the girls returned from the dance floor, bringing a fifth girl along to join the party. When a ship's bell rang out from the bar, the waiters gleefully took over the dance floor.

Farnsworth leaned toward me. "Here's dessert."

Everyone who worked at the place was part of the choreography for the Village People hit "Y.M.C.A." Before long, the whole house joined in. The party wrapped up at 1:00 a.m., with thunderous applause.

By the time we settled up, I was pretty tired, but I was more troubled by a dull ache in my stomach. Good thing Bruce gave me the hundred-dollar bill, because Peter didn't have nearly enough to cover the tab.

"C'mon, Jake," Mandy said. "My car is in the lot by the wharf."

A lift to the Sandcastle sounded good; the ache in my stomach was getting worse. In the back of the VW, I realized just how tired I was. It had been a long, long day. I was ready for bed, and for work tomorrow.

As Mandy paid five dollars to the lot lady and turned onto Commercial Street, the pain in my gut got worse. I started to think a hospital might be in order.

When we passed Rose's, I knew we were close to the Sandcastle. Just before the entrance, Mandy pulled into the driveway of a waterfront house and turned to the backseat. "This is Jenn's place," she said. I was about to double over from the pain. "Come on up, and we'll smoke a joint." An alien had taken over my lower intestine. Or I was going to have a baby. But the prospect of a joint with those two spurred me on, and soon we were upstairs, in Jenn's bedroom.

I was out on the balcony, where the moonlight made the bay look as if it were covered with tiny diamonds, when the pain dropped like an Aspen avalanche. *Probably the clams.*

In the bedroom, the girls were holding and kissing each other. Mandy held out her hand for me to join them.

Gurgling. Rumbling. And then a shift of the planets in the lower region of my stomach.

Jenn rested her head on Mandy's shoulder.

"Rain check," I managed.

"I can't believe he's gay," Mandy said as I ran for the stairs.

"It's all right, honey," Jenn answered. "We have each other."

The pressure reached no-return status as I beelined for the Sandcastle. A few guys still sitting by the barbecue at the Barracks called out, but a monstrous gurgle led to the inevitable.

Only divine intervention allowed me to scramble up the stairs, moving like a constipated duck with a cork up its ass. My hands shook as I opened the door, hobbled to the bathroom, battled my belt, and dropped my grateful ass onto the toilet seat. Thank God what happened next wasn't witnessed by another man or beast.

Relieved, I turned off the faucet. Pausing to see the exhausted reflection in the mirror, I grinned. *Welcome to Provincetown.*

42

Still on Jiminy Peak time, I went out on the balcony at 7:30 a.m. in boxer shorts, to a cloudless blue sky and near-blinding sunlight reflecting off the bay. A man cleaning the pool pretended to get mad as kids pulled on the hose he was using. He'd turn suddenly and growl, sending them off squealing.

I showered and dressed, thinking Bruce was a genius to schedule the meeting at nine thirty. Remembering my likely move to the Barracks, I packed and took the knife from under the mattress. Before leaving the unit, I looked in the mirror and shook my head, recalling last night's events. "Rain check?"

There was no sign of life at the Barracks, but the kids were on the tennis courts again, playing kill the other kid, having a blast. Reception was empty, but in the sales pit, I found Kelli—or Kelvin—making coffee. "Well, if it isn't the superstar!" she said. "Survive your first night?"

"Just barely, Kells."

Her face changed. "Bruce told you, didn't he?"

"What?"

She planted her hands on her hips. "That fucking freak can't keep his mouth shut." Her voice dropped half an octave. "Maybe I should mention a few things about him."

She sighed, and then her voice climbed back up the scale. "Let's keep it our secret, okay?"

I nodded. "Our secret, Kells."

The masculine voice returned. "My name is Kelli. Got it, Jake?"

"Our secret, Kelli."

"How about a cup of coffee?"

"Black, Kelli. Thanks."

She gave me the coffee and went back to Reception, seeming happy.

The pit was furnished with living room chairs, a few sofas, a couple of round tables and the sales board. I was glad to see someone had boarded my sale. The windows looked out on the parking lot, and a few bodies from the Barracks were headed toward the office. With thirty minutes to go until the meeting, I decided to take a walk. I discovered an indoor pool and a Chinese restaurant serving breakfast, lunch, and dinner with a full bar seven days a week. A fifty-cent shuttle bus ran from the resort to the outer beaches and downtown every fifteen minutes from 8:00 a.m. until midnight.

At 9:20 a.m., I walked back through Reception. "Thanks for boarding my deal, Kelli," I said.

She beamed. "Wouldn't want to jinx your first, Jake. Especially that one."

Seven or eight people had gathered in the pit, including Akers, Jim, Reggie, and Boone. On the sofa sat Farnsworth, still wearing his Ray Charles sunglasses. It was the first time I'd seen him without a smile.

"So, Peter," Akers said, "what did you do last night? Go to the library?" The others laughed.

"Did you get any, Farns?" asked a guy in khakis, a polo shirt, and docksiders. "Or should I say, 'How many?'"

Farnsworth didn't respond. He didn't answer when I sat next to him and said good morning, either. I wasn't sure he was awake until he mumbled, "Roses."

"Did you say something?" I asked.

"Roses," he repeated, looking straight ahead.

"I'm not following."

He turned to me, the smile back on his face. "Vodka and cranberry make your poop smell like roses."

"Huh, didn't notice."

Bruce came through the door wearing cut-off jeans, a Mickey Mouse T-shirt, sneakers, and his reflector glasses.

Akers moaned. "Christ, Bruce, every time you wear that shirt, all I write is Mickeys."

"That's all you ever write, Akers," said the guy in the polo shirt. "I swear to God you must ask for loose change at the close."

"Piss off, Brown. Without your trust fund, you'd starve."

Bruce opened the meeting with an enthusiastic welcome to me, and the whole staff gave one clap—just one—all at the same time. *Better than the "Fuck you, shut up, sit down" at Jiminy Peak. But that was pretty funny too.*

"How many today?" Boone asked.

Bruce shrugged. "No clue."

And that was the meeting.

Bruce left the room, and everybody else started talking—except Farnsworth. He sat still, in another world.

"A Mickey is a pender, right?" I asked.

He sprang from the sofa like a cat, did a forward flip, and landed perfectly on his feet. "Flippin' right," he said. "Let's get some air."

As we left the room, the polo-shirt guy was doing his best to charm Kelli. Farnsworth let out a low whistle. He knew a secret.

At the pool bar, Bruce was reading the newspaper, but only the comics. "Anything we should be concerned about in the world, Brucie?" Farnsworth asked.

Bruce snickered.

Akers arrived with the polo shirt guy, who extended his hand to me. "John Brown, from Dover, Mass."

That said it all. The town next to blue-collar Natick, Dover was strictly white-collar. I didn't give a damn—I was proud of my roots—but the dickhead had gone out of his way to bring it to my attention.

"We need more UPs, Bruce," Akers said. "It's Memorial Day. Soon it'll be July 4, then summer will be gone."

Bruce acted as if Akers wasn't there.

"With Jake on board, there are eight of us," he continued, "and fifty tours a week doesn't cut it."

The bartender snapped open a beer for Bruce as Akers walked away mumbling. The rest of us took stools. "Can't wait to break out my '65 Vette," Brown said, "and tow my sailboat down here."

Bruce snickered again. "Must be a goddamned small sailboat."

Farnsworth and I laughed, but Brown took offense. "They race four-seventy sloops in the Olympics!"

Bruce sipped his beer. "Summer or winter?" Farnsworth and I cracked up.

Brown got off his stool and headed for Reception. "I've got better things to do than talk with you peasants. I'm working on some pussy."

Farnsworth let out that low whistle again. I covered my eyes.

"Hope you get it," Bruce muttered. "You deserve it."

43

Brown looked triumphant, his arm around Kelli's waist as she popped out to the pool deck and held up three fingers. "Time to feed," Bruce said. "You're first, Jake. Tell Akers he's second, Farnsworth third. Hunt, my boys!"

I went to the sales pit to gather my tools: a resort directory, a lined yellow pad, a pen, and worksheets. A neatly attired thirtysomething read a book on a sofa. "Good luck," he said.

"Excuse me?"

He held out his hand. "Warren Finch. Just wished you luck with the tour." He was reading the Bible.

"Put in a good word upstairs, will you?" I asked.

"Will do, but *he* hasn't been listening to me lately."

Farnsworth introduced himself to what looked like a good prospect, almost a carbon copy of Bill and Edna Thomas. Brown leaned over Kelli's desk as the two giggled like schoolkids. Her smile faded as she handed me the UP sheet.

"Wish me luck, Kelli."

"You're gonna need it," she said under her breath. "Their kid is a little prick."

I met Mike and Jean Daley, a middle-aged couple from Braintree, who introduced a pudgy twelve-year-old simply as their son. He looked sullen, with dried-up chocolate caked in the corners of his mouth. "What's your name, big guy?" I asked.

"I'm hungry," the kid spat. "You got anything to eat around here?" The parents looked embarrassed.

"Nice to meet you, Hungry," I said. "Never met anyone with that name before."

The kid frowned and folded his arms across his chest. I winked at Mike and Jean, who looked relieved. "Let's head out," I told them. "Maybe we'll find a burger on a barbecue for Mr. Hungry."

The kid wasn't impressed. "My name is Mikey, not Mr. Hungry. And I hate hamburgers. I want a hot dog, chips, and a Coke." The parents looked more embarrassed.

"You'll get a hot dog if you're good," I told the brat. "If not, you'll get a fish guts sandwich."

Mikey looked to his parents for help but found none. Jean winked, Mike smiled, and I knew we had a deal. Control the uncontrollable. The rest will follow.

We walked out to the deck, where Jean and Mike were obviously impressed. Already the deck chairs were filling with people slathering on suntan lotion as happy kids squealed in the pool. It wasn't yet ten thirty, but the tiki bar was full, and the barbecue was smoking. I headed straight for it, hoping to calm the little beast.

"What'll you have?" asked the teenager working.

He tossed the dog on the grill, and while we waited, I pointed out the pool, the tiki bar, the units, the members having fun. When I finally had a grilled hot dog on a paper plate, with chips and a can of Coke, I turned to Mikey, who frowned again.

I looked at his parents, and Jean took the plate. "Catsup, mustard, relish, and onions," she said. Finding it all on a table next to the grill, she heaped each item on the dog, and then we headed for an available sales room.

Inside, there were only three chairs. I pulled a plastic chair in from the deck, put it at the table and motioned for Kid Brat to sit. The little bastard stood defiantly, arms folded again, shaking his head.

"What now?" I asked.

"I wanna sit in one of those chairs," he said, pointing.

Jean started to get up but stopped when I held up my hand. "Mikey, you've got three seconds to sit down and eat that hot dog," I said, "or I swear to God it's gone and all that's left is fish guts."

Jean muffled a chuckle. Mikey took the plate of food and sat on the floor behind his parents.

With the situation under control, I started the pitch. Mike and Jean, a mailman and housewife, had married late and had a kid later. It was clear that the twelve-year-old bully ran the Daley household and that his parents were worn out. It was also clear that it was their own fault. They didn't seem able to say no. I sure didn't want them to learn the word that day.

Mike stared toward the tiki bar, and Jean couldn't tear her eyes from the pool. Behind them, Kid Brat poured the chips on the carpet. I didn't say a word. Halfway through the pitch, the hot dog found its way to the rug, catsup, mustard, onions, and relish all over the place, knowing it was only a matter of time for the Coke. I still didn't say a word. I was working.

Mikey didn't disappoint. As I told the Daleys how to access other vacation destinations, the half-empty can tipped over, and the kid watched the Coke soak into the carpet. The pitch was going well until I completely forgot what I was saying.

Mikey was eating the carpet. He'd pinch a swatch of rug—steeped in catsup, mustard, onions, relish, and Coke—rip it out, and swallow it. Soon the eating machine was using both hands. The hole in the rug was the size of a dinner plate.

Somehow, I wrapped up the presentation and stood, telling the brat it was time to look for ice cream. He didn't need to be told twice.

The Daleys made it clear that the studio was a no-go—the prospect of a week in one room with Mikey no doubt as appealing as a life sentence at Alcatraz—so we went to the suite. We passed Farnsworth and his couple on the stairs. Farnsworth was laughing, and the lady was wearing his glasses—a good sign.

Mike and Jean loved the suite, so we went downstairs to talk money. Their son had opened every drawer and cabinet in search of food—and been dismayed at not finding any ice cream. But he didn't fuss for long. As soon as we all took our seats, he started eating the carpet again.

Worksheet signed and check in hand—I remembered this time—I headed to the office to choose a unit and a week that would make the Daleys happy.

"Got a quick study here," Jan said as she looked over the paperwork. "He's a keeper." Robby's eyes didn't move from her desktop, but she gave me a thumbs-up.

Farnsworth strolled in with his own worksheet and check, claiming his paperwork should be handled first because of his "seniority." "Jake's is already done," Jan told him.

Farnsworth laughed. "I'd have been in here first if I hadn't stopped for a cold one."

When I got back to the Daleys, they were standing on either side of Kid Brat, looking mortified. The kid looked ready to puke.

"I don't know how else to put this," Mike said, "but our son ate your rug."

I acted surprised. "No worries. These units will be redone at the end of the summer."

They were visibly relieved. We walked to the lobby and shook hands, then Mikey whispered to his mother. Blushing, she asked for a restroom.

Jean and I made small talk while Mikey and his dad went to the can. A few minutes later, we were all in the parking lot, where I shook hands with Mike and Jean again, then ruffled their son's hair.

Christ. That little bastard must've shit a sweater.

44

Brown and Kelli were still swooning when I went into the pit to board my deal: $7,995.

Right behind me, Farnsworth boarded his: $4,995. "First round is on you, buddy," he said.

The math made me happy. I'd made another $960, bringing my total to $3,700 in less than twenty-four hours. Farnsworth slapped me on the back.

"Let's go see our fearless leader. He's good for a cold one after a deal."

We were almost out the door when Warren Finch called out from the couch. "Gotta believe, man," he said, pointing to his Bible. "Gotta believe."

I wondered if God had let the little bastard eat the rug for the sake of the deal.

Kelli dropped Brown's hand. "Hold on, Jake. I have a message for you."

Farnsworth stopped dead in his tracks. "Uh-oh."

Kelli frowned. "I took a call from Bill Thomas. You know, Bill and Edna, from yesterday?"

The deal must've kicked.

"I was nice to them, Jake," Kelli continued. "Real, real nice." She was stalling. "They wanted to talk to you, but I explained that you were with new members and couldn't be interrupted. They were fine with that."

I just wanted to know if the deal had kicked.

She smirked. "They made an appointment with you for Saturday ... to bring in friends who want to buy the same package they did!"

Farnsworth let out a low whistle.

"I've already booked the rooms," Kelli added, "complimentary, for the Thomases and their *two* couples."

Brown folded his arms across his chest. "You didn't tell me that, Kelli. Christ, that's another five grand in commissions."

Farnsworth chimed in: "Someone has to pay for the beer."

He turned for the door, and Brown followed him, asking, "Where are you going?"

Kelli grinned when I thanked her. "See, Jake," she said in her low voice, "I was nice. You gonna be nice to me?"

"Brown is all yours," I told her. "In my mind, he's just a dick."

She giggled. "That's all I'm after."

When I caught up with Farnsworth and Bruce—and Brown—the bartender put a cold brew in front of me. "You're the big man on campus, Jake," he said. "Keep it going."

"He's four for two," Farnsworth said. "He just got a referral for the weekend."

From behind his mirrored glasses, Bruce snickered. "Great white shark."

"Some things are more important than money," said Brown, who hadn't even gotten out on tour. "I have a date tonight."

Farnsworth sipped his beer.

"Good for you," Bruce said.

"Am I supposed to move to the Barracks today?" I asked.

Bruce leaned back on his barstool and reached into his pocket. "Number four. Welcome home."

"Glad to be here," I told him as I took the key.

"We're roomies," Farnsworth said. "That unit's next to mine." I was happy to hear it. Farnsworth was a bud, a pal.

We thanked Bruce, collected my pack from the pit, and headed to my new digs with Brown in tow.

"Welcome to the Barracks," Farnsworth announced when we arrived. "The end for most. The beginning for a few."

I never got to ask what he meant. Inside my room stood a six-foot-four woman dressed in a white nurse's uniform, complete with a cap on top of her stringy black-and-gray hair. She held the front leg of the bed three feet off the floor with one hand as she mopped underneath with the other. "Be a minute, sweetie," she said, her smile revealing a solitary front tooth. "Tidying up a bit."

I dropped my pack and went back outside. "Used to be a Baptist minister by the name of Tom," Farnsworth said. "Now Tomola's a maid and a part-time midwife."

"Tranny," Brown added. "Transsexual. Unhappy with your sex, surgeons change it."

Ignoring him, I asked, "Is it okay to leave my stuff in the room?"

"If you can trust anyone in this town," Peter said, "it's Tomola."

We stopped at Rose's for a beer, sitting on the deck in the blazing afternoon sun. "How about a game of pool later?" Brown asked.

Farnsworth frowned. The day was perfect—blue sky, warm sun, the bay flat as a mirror. Why go inside to play pool? But when the waitress asked if we wanted another round, Brown reached into his pocket for cash.

"No thanks," he said, "just the check."

We were almost out the door when someone called my name, then Farnsworth's. Aaron was polishing glasses again. Seeing the two of us together, he grinned. "God help us all. This town just got nuttier."

"Save me a drink," Farnsworth told him. "I'll pick it up on my way home."

"Vodka and cranberry," Aaron said. "It'll be waiting."

The street was an explosion of color—pinks, blues, yellows—the quaint houses surrounded by colorful gardens I hadn't noticed the night before. A lunch crowd filled tables outside bistros, and the air was rich with aromas. We ducked into the Salty Dawg, a dark pub with a wooden bar, a dozen empty stools, and an older, ponytailed bartender wearing a red bandanna. From the jukebox, Pat Benatar belted "Hit Me with Your Best Shot." The only other patrons were five guys standing around the pool table.

Farnsworth got a quick vodka and cranberry. I asked for a beer. We sat at the bar while Brown stood a couple feet behind us and watched the crowd of five guys at the pool table. One holding a pool cue was about five foot ten and bald, and judging by the size of his biceps, he spent the majority of his time training at the gym. He watched his opponent miss an easy shot near a corner pocket. The other guys burst out laughing. "Show him how it's done, champ," one said to the bald guy.

He did. He lasered the cue ball into the eight ball, burying it in the side pocket. The guys erupted. Brown walked back toward us. "Hope these fucking guys don't plan to stay long."

The bald guy's head shot up and glared in Brown's direction. He set the pool stick on the table and whispered to some of his buddies, who turned and walked, slowly, toward Brown.

Brown was trying to flag down the bartender, who moved to the far end of the bar and was busy wiping down a clean table.

Farnsworth, peering over Brown's shoulder, put down his drink. "I think you just made some friends."

Four of them approached, three in front of the bald guy, like linemen blocking for a running back, as Brown finally turned and took in the situation. "No problem, I'll handle this."

"Do you know what time it is?" asked the biggest of the bunch.

Brown smiled before he answered. "No, what time is it?"

"Time for you to leave or go to sleep."

Brown stepped to the side, waving his arms, hissing like a pissed-off cat, then half-turned and raised his front leg, bent at the knee.

"He knows karate, too," Farnsworth said as he sipped his drink.

The punch landed smack in the middle of Brown's face. The sound hurt. People three bars away must've heard it. He never felt the back of his head slam into the wooden floor, he was out cold.

With the bald guy in the middle, his eyes met mine.

I took a sip of my half-empty beer. "The guy's a dick; he had it coming."

The bald guy nodded, and they walked out.

"Hope Brown's better at sailing than he is at karate," Farnsworth said.

The bartender shook his ponytail. "That was the stupidest thing I've ever seen, and I've worked here thirty-five years. Who the hell picks a fight with Marvin Hagler?"

Farnsworth let out a low whistle as I covered my face with my hands. Marvelous Marvin Hagler had just finished a ten-round draw against Vito Antuofermo for the middleweight championship of the world. The Provincetown Inn was training headquarters for his upcoming title shot, and Marvelous could be seen on the beach each day before sunup, running ten miles barefoot in the Cape dunes.

It all happened so fast that Farnsworth had barely finished his drink—and that's fast. Pat Benatar was just wrapping it up, and we all burst out laughing when she wailed, "Hit me with your best shot."

Regaining consciousness, Brown sat up, and slowly got to his feet. He walked over to the bar and asked, "What happened?"

The bartender smirked. "I think you had too much to drink."

Brown reached into his pocket, pulled out a fistful of cash and placed it on the bar. Turning to walk out he said, "I think I'm going to head back for a nap."

The bartender brought us another round and then poured himself a shot. "Yup," he said, lifting the shot glass, "stupidest thing I ever saw."

45

At the four corners in the center of town, a cop tried to direct throngs of tourists, cyclists, and motorists moving at a crawl. "Check this guy out," Farnsworth said. "He's great."

In the middle of the intersection, the cop blew a whistle every few seconds, spinning around in 360s, his arms waving wildly. He had to know it was a lost cause, but he was having a great time in the middle of the boisterous mob, trading high-fives and laughs with people passing by. His valiant effort to keep everyone safe was just one more spectacle for the crowd to enjoy. Everyone laughed when he bent over and blew the whistle backward through his legs to direct pedestrians across the street. And when a driver going nowhere honked, the crowd cheered as he flipped him the finger.

Farnsworth paused at the Lobster Pot's window-turned-fish-tank. "Have you seen the size of this lobster?" Oscar pointed his long antennae and edged toward him, but when I got closer to the glass, he retreated to the back of the tank.

"He doesn't like you," Farnsworth said.

"Maybe he's gay and he knows I'm not."

"So he thinks I am?"

I shrugged. "Maybe it's your sunglasses."

We walked on toward the pier, the action nonstop. A shirtless musclebound juggler wearing skin-tight black hot pants and cowboy boots tossed flaming batons in the air, while another performer walked a tightrope strung between two lampposts.

Farnsworth threw his head back and howled. "The pink tutu is cute, and the bleached white hair is a nice touch, but the matching pink underarms are priceless!"

"I like the pink eyebrows and the silver glitter mascara."

He nodded.

The crowd applauded enthusiastically as the tightrope walker finished his act, waving to his audience.

"Look, Mommy," shouted a little girl, "he has bunny rabbits under his arms!"

The applause for the small girl was even louder.

"You hungry?" Farnsworth asked as we neared a takeout window. "This place has great tube steaks."

A robust woman leaned from the window, her open blouse exposing her large breasts. "Is it me you come to see, sweetie?" she asked Farnsworth. "Or do you really love Momma's cookin'?"

"I'd be here even if the food wasn't great, Momma, 'cause you are pure eye candy." Peter let out his low whistle. "Nothing like dessert before dinner."

"How many?" she asked. He held up two fingers.

At almost 5:00 p.m., the breeze was cool, and a few clouds gathered to the west. Across the street, a steady stream of male couples poured through the double doors of the Crown & Anchor.

Farnsworth came away from the window holding two foot-long hot dogs covered with mustard, catsup, relish, onions, and cheese, wrapped in napkins. "Momma's tube steak," he said, holding one out, "stacked and racked."

The Crown & Anchor bouncers stopped only the occasional straight couple or family, engaged in brief conversation, and turned them away.

The dog was surprisingly heavy. As I took my first bite, a shirtless twentysomething male with pierced nipples walking by yelled, "Ouch! That hurt."

Farnsworth laughed so hard he nearly choked. "Are you uncomfortable with the gays?"

I wiped my mouth with the napkin. "To be honest, this is a new world for me. The looks, the passes, the comments—it'll take some getting used to."

"Think of them as women you're not interested in," Farnsworth suggested. "Remember: a pass is a compliment. The guy likes the way you look. No big deal."

I pointed across the street. "What's up over there? The bouncers won't let anyone in who's not gay?"

"Tea dance," Farnsworth said, "a gay mixer, and it gets crazy. We can get in if you want to check it out; they won't question two guys."

"What kind of crazy?"

Farnsworth finished his hot dog, spun around, and threw his balled-up napkin into a trashcan. "Rumor has it they do a hamster dance."

"Do I want to know the details?"

"Rumor comes from a Crown & Anchor regular."

I told him to spill.

"Well, as the party whips up and the drugs and booze flow, they bring out a two-foot clear plastic tube. In front of a chanting crowd, one guy puts an end of the tube in his ass. Another guy slips a hamster through the other end, then sticks that end of the tube in *his* ass."

My jaw dropped. "A fuckin' *hamster?*"

Farnsworth pursed his lips. "Heard it straight from a doctor in town."

I didn't get it.

"They need the doctor's services when the hamster doesn't make it," Farnsworth explained.

"You're shitting me."

He laughed again, and this time he did choke. I slapped his back until he held up his hand. "You want to check it out?"

"Pass." I walked toward the pier. "Christ, a fuckin' hamster dies in someone's ass and a doctor digs it out?"

"Imagine the business card: 'Specializing in rodent removal from anal cavities.'"

We passed open-air displays of scrimshaw jewelry, etched sea glass, and fake tattoos. "Why do they do it in the first place?" I asked.

"Giving it way too much thought, amigo. But I figure the little bugger must tickle when he slams around trying to find a way out."

I shuddered in the cold air. "So what kills it? I mean, it must die if the doctor has to remove it, right?"

Farnsworth shrugged. "Bad air? Sphincter spasm? I doubt they do an autopsy."

I knew I looked sick, and he grinned from ear to ear. A minute later we erupted, laughing until we cried, turning ourselves into one more spectacle on the wharf. People may come to Provincetown to see the show, but some of us join the cast.

Arms around each other's shoulders, we walked on through the blur of sights, smells, and sounds, until I heard my name.

Mandy took her arm from Jenn's waist to hug me. "He's really cute, Jake," she whispered. "Hope it works out for you." I pulled back but fumbled for words. She put her hand on my mouth, softly. "Have you and your friend been to the end? To hear the sounds?" I shook my head. Things were pretty mixed-up. "Why don't the four of us watch the sunset and listen to the most beautiful sounds in the world?"

Farnsworth was already walking in that direction with Jenn, so Mandy took my arm, and we followed. The evening was beautiful, and I was happy in this wild place, with newfound friends and—finally—money.

We strolled past commercial fishing boats, and the sweet smells of fresh codfish, haddock, and mussels wafted over us as Portuguese crewmen unloaded their catches. P-town's lights glowed behind us as the sun fell slowly into the sea. At the end of the pier, we watched as the last rays washed the sky in orange, yellow, red, and purple.

"Not tonight," Farnsworth whispered.

"What does that mean?" Jenn asked.

He cleared his throat. "At times, when the sun drops into the water, a green flash appears. Legend says it only happens in P-town and Key West. It's good luck to see it."

"Have you ever seen it?" I asked.

He shrugged. "Can't say for sure."

"Why not?" Jenn prodded.

"One night in Key West, I swore I saw something, but I was seeing a lot of things that night."

Red and green buoys marked the channel, and the lighthouse's powerful white beam swept across the water, occasionally catching a returning boat in its glow. The vessel's rigging chimed in the soft breeze. I held Mandy close, my arm around her shoulder, her arm around my waist. Farnsworth and Jenn huddled, too, and soon we were surrounded by the mellow tones of a trumpet.

"Listen, Jake," Mandy whispered. "This moves me."

We drifted toward the haunting music. Silhouetted against a fishing boat's lights, a dark figure swayed in the breeze—a thin guy in his early twenties wearing tinted sunglasses, ever so slowly raising and lowering the trumpet. I held Mandy and drank everything in.

Everything.

The scent in the air told us Farnsworth and Jenn were smoking a joint, and we moved closer to share it. When the song ended, he packed up his trumpet and joined us.

"Where the hell does a skinny white kid learn to play the blues like that?" Farnsworth asked.

He accepted the joint. "Around," he said with a slight twang. "You know. Just around."

Jenn spoke up. "That's a New Orleans accent if I ever heard one."

He passed the joint back to Farnsworth. "N'orleans," he said. "We call home N'orleans."

Jenn repeated "N'orleans" as she took the joint from Farnsworth.

"What's your name?" I asked the kid.

He leaned down for his trumpet case and wore a sad expression when he looked up. "Doesn't matter," he said, "any more than the cry of the world or the tears from your heart."

With that, he walked away and vanished, just as he had appeared, a silhouette in the dim light cast by the fishing boats.

Thick fog had rolled in, and the air got chillier as the four of us strolled back toward town, side by side, each with an arm around the other. Mandy rested her head on my shoulder.

"I like your new friend," she told me. "He's handsome and charming. You two make a good pair."

"He's a friend who works at the Sandcastle, Mandy. And I'm not gay."

"Is he?"

Before I could answer, Farnsworth looked over at us. "We make a pretty good-looking sandwich."

Mandy giggled. "What kind of sandwich?"

Farnsworth laughed. "White bread, lean meat, no deckle."

"What's deckle?" Jenn asked.

"It's Jewish," Mandy told her. "No fat."

Jenn looked less than impressed, and the mood started to go south, so I changed the subject. "That joint gave me the munchies. Want to get something to eat?" Both girls perked up.

"A hot slice of pepperoni from George's," Jenn said.

"With a cold beer," Mandy added.

We walked on under the yellow glow of the streetlights. Music cranked from the open doors of the Crown & Anchor as we passed. Soon we stood in front of the sign: "George's Pizza, Since 1973". For the moment, everything was back to normal. Whatever that meant.

46

Only a few customers were scattered around the dozen tables inside, and the girl behind the counter looked pissed off. I smiled when I ordered a large pepperoni, half with green peppers, but she didn't thaw.

Mandy and Jenn went to the washroom, and Farnsworth headed to an empty table with a pitcher of beer and four mugs. "Man," he said, "the help isn't happy tonight."

He stared toward the counter as he poured. "Pretty slow for a long weekend. And they're calling for rain tomorrow. A lot of people probably headed off-Cape. If you're not into the bar scene, there's not much to do when the weather doesn't cooperate."

"What do people do here in the winter?" I asked.

He laughed. "Drink or head south. Me, I do both." The girls reappeared.

"What's so funny?" Mandy asked.

"Farnsworth says the best thing to do here in the winter is leave."

Jenn agreed. "Key West."

Mandy sipped her beer. "Most of the business owners here have shops and bars in Key West. Around mid-November, they follow the birds, migrate to warmer lands."

"They all say, 'Let's get the flock outa here,'" Farnsworth added.

We were laughing when the frumpy waitress delivered our pizza. "C'mon, things can't be that bad," Farnsworth told her. "Have a slice."

She planted her hands on her hips. "How would you know? And no thanks, I don't eat that shit."

The shocked look on Farnsworth's face made the rest of us burst out laughing. The frump went back to the counter as we all reached for a slice of the bubbling pie. Dropping hers on a paper plate, Mandy cried, "Hot,

hot, hot!" She grabbed her beer with one hand, fanned her mouth with the other.

Farnsworth tilted his head and pursed his lips, producing a perfect smoke ring that hovered. "This ought to be interesting," he mumbled, looking toward the two newcomers entering the place.

Brown wore his stupid grin as he grabbed a chair and sat at our table, reaching for a slice. "Great minds think alike," he said.

He took a bite, and a chunk of the volcanic cheese slapped against his lower lip, reaching all the way to his chin. He jumped up and knocked over the chair, yelping as he tried to peel the lava from his face.

We were laughing again—everyone except Kelli, who looked nervously at Farnsworth, me, and finally the girls. Brown dunked a napkin into the pitcher, applied it to his burning face, and motioned for Kelli to grab a chair. She didn't move. Brown fetched one for her, holding the dripping napkin to his face, and introduced himself and Kelli to the girls.

Kelli sat, nodding coldly toward Mandy and Jenn, who returned the favor.

Farnsworth signaled the waitress for more glasses, but she pretended not to see him. I offered Kelli a slice, but she declined. Brown pasted more beer-soaked napkins to his nuked face, which was starting to blister. In ten seconds, the warm-and-fuzzy mood had shifted to ice-cold.

After a few uncomfortable moments of silence, Kelli excused herself and headed toward the washrooms. I watched, curious about which door she'd open. After a quick glance back at the table, she went into the ladies' room.

Brown whimpered, his mound of beer-soaked napkins piled up next to the pitcher, his left eye swelling from his earlier encounter with Marvelous. I tried to stifle a laugh. "What's so funny?" he whined.

The table fell painfully quiet when Farnsworth left to get more beer. He got back with another pitcher and two more glasses just as Kelli returned from her mission. With Mandy and Jenn visibly unimpressed, he yawned and stretched. "Man, am I pooped."

The girls stood on cue. Farnsworth dug into his pocket for cash, but Brown insisted on picking up the tab. Farnsworth graciously accepted, folded half the pizza between two paper plates, saluted Kelli and Brown, and, with the girls, marched toward the door.

I stood up, grabbed a few napkins, and winked at Kelly. "Thanks for the pie, Brown. See you in the morning." I walked toward the open door, where Farnsworth and the girls waited.

Brown poured Kelli a beer from the half-empty pitcher he'd been using to dip napkins, then said, "What the hell," and downed the rest. He belched, turned his battered face to Kelli, and managed a grin.

"C'mon, lover," she said. "Let's get out of here."

Brown brightened as she took his hand and led him to the door, passing the waitress along the way.

"Thanks for comin' in; glad you had such a good time," she snarled. Brown smiled at her. Kelli used her free hand to flip the bird.

47

Outside, we quickly finished off the slices Farnsworth had rescued. The air was cold, and the heavy fog hung like a shroud over the town. Farnsworth kept his arm wrapped around Jenn, and I held Mandy tight, until we got to the car. Jenn opened the passenger door and tilted the seat forward, claiming the front.

"Where to?" Mandy asked, holding her hand out to Jenn. Jenn took it, then turned to the backseat. "Want to collect on that rain check, Jake?"

"Not much on the calendar tonight," I said.

When Mandy pulled in at Jenn's place, the girls and I went straight to the house, but Farnsworth stood in the sandy driveway, seeming uncertain, until Jenn called his name and he trotted to join us. In the living room, two sofas were separated by a coffee table, a fireplace to the side, and a door in the small kitchen that led to a waterfront deck.

"Get comfortable, boys," Jenn said. "Sweetie, why don't you put on some music?"

At that point, I wasn't entirely sure who "sweetie" was, but Mandy searched through a record cabinet and pulled out an album, looking triumphant.

Farnsworth rolled a joint, and a popping cork told us Jenn was opening a bottle of wine.

"A fire would be nice, Jake," she called. "Wood's on the side of the house."

Happy to do something, I went outside to gather firewood from the covered pile.

When I got back, I recognized the soft, almost haunting music we'd heard on the pier. Mandy took a few logs, her eyes locked with mine. As we leaned down to stack, she gave me a little kiss. On the lips. She dropped the wood and, with her mouth half-open, kissed me again, long and hard, pausing only to breathe heavily in my ear.

I glanced away long enough to see Jenn and Farnsworth locked in each other's arms on the sofa, then looked back at Mandy. "Do you want a fire?" I asked.

She smiled. "It's already lit."

I jammed crumpled-up newspaper under the wood and struck a match. As soon as the paper ignited, the wood crackled.

Everything is perfect.

Mandy took my hand, and we walked to the empty sofa.

"This music," I said, "it's the same melody we heard on the pier, right?" she grinned.

We toasted with two of the four glasses of red wine on the coffee table. "Welcome to P-town, Jake," she whispered, then she put both glasses back on the table and stroked my face softly, leaning toward me until our lips locked.

"Who is this?" I asked. "I mean, the music."

"Miles Davis. 'Blue in Green.' Beautiful, huh?" I looked into her eyes. "Absolutely beautiful."

On the opposite sofa, Farnsworth handed the joint to Jenn. After a toke, she stood and walked to Mandy, blowing the smoke into her waiting mouth, finishing with a gentle kiss, and following that with a deeper, longer one.

Farnsworth watched as Jenn began undressing Mandy, slowly unbuttoning her blouse as Mandy cooed and kissed her neck. Soon the girls were naked, hugging and kissing.

Farnsworth's grin told me he'd been in these waters before, but it was uncharted territory for me. I took a long, deep swallow of my wine.

As the girls headed for the stairway, Mandy glanced over her shoulder and wiggled a finger at me. I looked at Farnsworth. She nodded for him to follow as well. "Only one bedroom up there," I said.

Farnsworth stood. "How many do we need?"

I whispered to him, "You're not interested in guys, right?"

He grinned again. "The only gays I'm interested in are women. It's my mission in life to convert them back. Too much prime inventory taken out of circulation."

Satisfied with the answer, I followed him to the staircase. He looked back at me as we climbed. "How do you know there's only one bedroom?"

I shook my head. "Story for another day."

The candles provided enough light to tell us the action had already begun, but not who was who, or who was doing what. We both got undressed and climbed in on opposite sides of the bed. I stroked the back closest to me and heard a sigh. Then a hand gently probed my face, sliding two fingers into my mouth. Slowly, two sets of lips found each other, and after a deep kiss, I felt a gasp on my neck.

"Told you I'd find you, sweetie," Mandy whispered.

For the next few hours, a symphony of coos, aahs, and heavy breathing played out from a tangle of bodies. At times, I tried to guess who was next to me, under me, or on top. It was all good.

Long after the candles burned out, I reached down to stroke the leg resting on mine.

"Girls," I said into the darkness, "I hope one of you is in need of a big-time shave."

Farnsworth pulled the leg away. "Sorry, Captain," he said. "Don't know how that got way over there."

48

When morning came, Jenn's head rested on the left side of my chest, Mandy's on the right, their arms hugging me and each other. Farnsworth was nowhere to be found.

Careful not to wake the girls, I untangled us and got out of bed, pulling my clothes on as I looked through the glass doors at a gray, rainy day. Before leaving, I kissed each of them. Mandy's eyes fluttered open.

"Morning, sweetie. See you soon," she said, then she scooted over to hug Jenn, who sighed in her sleep.

After a short walk to the Barracks, I found my clothes hanging neatly in the closet.

Even my muddied sport coat had been cleaned. *Tomola. What a sweetheart.*

The clock read 6:15 a.m., three hours until work, and the freshly made bed looked inviting, but I opted for a shower. I stood under the warm water for a long time, and the sound of running water from Farnsworth's room told me he'd made the same decision.

He was standing in the hallway when I opened the door. "Breakfast?" he asked.

"Where to?"

He pointed to the Chinese restaurant. "Gotta try the lo mein omelet." I hoped he was kidding.

A cute Chinese girl greeted us. "Why you no call me, Peter?"

"Pretty busy with family, honey," he answered sheepishly, "but I will soon. We'll go back to our beach." She frowned.

Four chairs surrounded each round table, and the laminated menu balanced between a napkin holder and a glass container full of sugar. Eggs, bacon, sausage, pancakes—breakfast fare from any small-town American diner. The waitress had shoulder-length brown hair and turquoise eyes.

"Let me guess, boys. A salesman's breakfast. A pot of coffee to go with your cigarettes?"

Farnsworth lit a thin cigarette and reached over to the next table for an ashtray. "You've got it, Donna. How's Doug?"

She glanced at a waiter across the room. "Not happy. We're not making any money. I wish you'd get him into sales."

"Meet Jake," Farnsworth offered. "He's new here."

"You're the superstar," she said. "Congratulations."

"Man, this is a small town."

"You have no idea," Farnsworth said. "Half the things I do I learn from other people."

Across the room, Akers was reading a newspaper, sipping coffee. He frowned when I caught his eye, pointing at the rain-spattered windows. I shrugged and turned to see Brown come through the door.

"Great," I muttered. "Now we'll get a blow-by-blow of his date with Kelli."

"Blow-by-blow is right," Farnsworth said.

I choked on my coffee as Brown joined us, signaling Donna with an imaginary mug raised to his lips.

"Looking good," Farnsworth said.

Brown touched his blackened, swollen eye, and then his red, blistered chin. "Even looking like this, I did better than you guys last night. Best head ever. She could suck the chrome off a trailer hitch."

Farnsworth took a drag from his cigarette. "Quiet night. Got a good night's sleep."

Brown threw his head back, laughing. "I knew it. They were lesbos. Why'd you guys even try?"

He looked from Farnsworth to me. "What do I know?" I said. "I just got here."

Brown beamed. "Don't worry, kid. I met Kelli's friends last night at the A-House. I'll hook you up."

"You're the man," Farnsworth said.

In came Bruce, wearing his reflector glasses, a baby tucked under his arm like a football. The little kid was wearing a stained Cape Cod sweatshirt and a diaper.

"Babysitting today, boss?" Farnsworth asked.

Bruce scowled. "Until Mom gets groceries."

Akers called out, and Bruce turned, sending spray from the piss-soaked diaper all over Brown's face and halfway down his shirt. He reeled back, spilling an entire cup of hot coffee into his crotch.

"For Christ's sake, Bruce," he yelped. "You just hosed me with Sam's piss. Why don't you change his goddamn diaper?"

Brown looked at Peter, at me, and then at his shirt. "I gotta change. See you later ... for fuck's sake."

Bruce grinned. "You two owe me one."

"Damn," Farnsworth said. "We were just about to hear the details of his date."

Bruce and the kid headed for the door. Akers made a beeline for them.

"He's gonna bitch about the UPs," Farnsworth said, "or lack of them. Akers doesn't get it. Things don't heat up here until the Fourth of July. Most of these reps will be blown out when the real hitters show up in a month."

I got it.

"It's simple math," he continued. "Mail more invitations to tour when the property shows best and when you have a staff that can actually sell."

A few moments later, Akers flung the door open and stormed over to our table. He sat in the seat where Brown had been and, reaching under his ass, complained the chair was wet. "Another wasted day," he said. "Goddamn Bruce with his 'hurry up and wait' attitude. I'm going broke waiting for Ups."

After reaching under his ass again, he sniffed his hand. "Christ, what's on this chair? Smells like piss." He got up and stalked off.

We were still laughing when a waiter in his early twenties came to the table and offered me his hand.

"Name's Doug," he said. Farnsworth introduced us. "I know who you are. You've made more money in two days than I'll make all summer."

"Why don't you join the sales team?" Farnsworth asked. "Now's the time. In a month, the spots will be filled. Live on what Donna earns and make it happen this summer."

I agreed.

"We'll help you with the basics," Farnsworth added.

"You mean it? You guys would help me? You think I could sell this stuff?"

"Are you afraid of people?" I asked.

He looked surprised. "I'm not afraid of anything."

"There you have it," Farnsworth said. "Want us to talk to Bruce?"

Doug thought for a moment. "Yeah, what the fuck do I have to lose?"

Farnsworth stuck out his hand. "Welcome to the tribe."

Doug pumped his hand. "You think Bruce will give me a shot?"

"With us taking you under our wings, why not?" Farnsworth said.

Doug thanked us, and from across the room Donna blew us a kiss.

Back at the Barracks, lightning flashed and thunder rumbled. "Wow, Farnsworth, check it out. Tomola put my clothes away, and she even dry-cleaned my sport coat. Should I leave her a tip?"

Farnsworth shook his head. "She does that only for people she likes. She wouldn't accept it. All she wants is for people to be nice."

"Pretty cool," I said.

"Some of the guys won't let her into their rooms. They think she's a freak." Another bolt of lightning sliced through the sky as the heavens rumbled again.

"What the heck do you do here when it rains?" I asked.

"We could drink," Farnsworth said as he finished rolling a joint at the table. "Or maybe drink."

It wasn't even 8:30 a.m.

"Let's get out of here. My men are thirsty," he said.

As we approached the sales pit, Farnsworth called out to the property manager. Jimmy McGann had run the day-to-day operations at the Sandcastle for years and knew every inch of the property.

"What's up, buddy?" Farnsworth asked.

Jimmy smiled. "Owners of the restaurant are complaining. Liquor disappeared from the basement. Again."

Farnsworth looked genuinely concerned. "What kind of booze?"

Still smiling, Jimmy said, "Rum. A case."

Farnsworth shook his head as Jimmy handed him a small paper bag. He pocketed it, then forked over some cash.

"Just about to head back to the house," Jimmy said. "Wanna take a ride?"

Farnsworth looked at his wrist, though he wasn't wearing a watch. "We're pretty busy, but for you, we'll go. Have to be back for a 9:30 a.m."

We got into Jimmy's faded green two-door car and sped down Route 6 toward Truro. In the backseat, I could feel the engine's power, and Jimmy answered my question before I asked. "1969 Oldsmobile Cutlass four-four-two with a four fifty-five four-speed." Farnsworth turned in the passenger bucket seat. "Ragtop. Nice, huh?"

It sure was. The car growled as Jimmy shifted through the gears. Farnsworth reached into his pocket and proudly produced a joint.

After a few drags, he handed it to Jimmy, who took a few hits and passed it back to me.

It was early, but I took a hit before passing the joint back to Farnsworth

Jimmy downshifted and turned right onto a dirt road, fishtailing and accelerating on the trail before taking a sharp turn and slamming on the brakes in front of an old cottage. Farnsworth got out and tilted the front seat forward. "Jimmy's place," he said.

A stone fireplace in the living room faced a large window overlooking the bay. The cottage was perched on top of a two-hundred-foot sand dune, surrounded by nothing but more dunes and water. "Wow, what a view," I said.

Jimmy smiled. "Belongs to The Sandcastle's owners, but they let me stay here. No neighbors. Just the birds, deer, raccoons, squirrels, and me."

"And the skunk," Farnsworth added, handing the still-burning joint to Jimmy. "Don't forget the goddamned skunk."

Jimmy took the joint. "A mother of a skunk," he said, his Boston accent coming through. "Doesn't bother me, but really has it in for Farns."

Farnsworth frowned. "I don't know what I did to it, but every time I'm here, the damn thing shows up and aims its tail at me. Almost got me a couple of times."

I checked out the porch on the other side of the dated kitchen door, settling into an old rocking chair. The roof kept me dry as I took in the scrub pine, beach grass, sand, and sea. Chickadees peeped, flitting from tree to tree.

The peaceful scene erupted as a lightning flash split the sky and thunder boomed, then crackled.

"Did that one get ya, Jake?" Jimmy yelled from the kitchen.

Farnsworth was laughing when I rushed back inside.

"Man, that was close!" I said, refusing the joint.

"We're on the highest dune in Truro," Jimmy said. "Trees get zapped, and the house has been hit a few times. Half of it burned down after one strike; the owners had to rebuild. Good for me. It's the warmest part of the house. The fireplace is the only heat I have, and man, it gets cold here during the winter."

We went to the car to go back to the Castle. "Got a few cold ones in the back," Jimmy said.

Farnsworth turned and nodded toward the cooler. When I handed him a can of beer, he snapped it open and took a long swallow.

"Ah," he said, "breakfast of champions."

We parted ways in the Castle parking lot. "Catch ya later," Jimmy said. "If you wanna come over tonight, we'll throw some stripers on the barbecue."

"They're in?" Farnsworth asked. "I didn't know they were running."

"Schoolies, but a shitload of 'em," Jimmy yelled over his shoulder. He then disappeared through a door next to the restaurant.

"What's a striper?" I asked.

Farnsworth looked surprised. "You've never had charcoaled striped bass?" I shook my head. "Best fish in the ocean. Wrapped in foil with nothing but butter and a few lemon wedges, seven minutes on the coals. Pure heaven with a few cold ones."

He finished the cold one he was holding with a resounding burp. "We'll get fresh asparagus, and I'll whip up hollandaise sauce. Sound good?"

It didn't. When my mom made asparagus, it smelled like piss. And I'd never heard of hollandaise. "What's a schoolie?" I asked.

Farnsworth threw the empty can into the trash. "Small bass, twenty inches or so. They're the first to migrate from the spawning grounds in the Chesapeake. The big ones don't get here until summer and fall. Those bruisers can be forty or fifty pounds."

We went into Farnsworth's room, and I spotted the box of Bacardi while he gargled, masking the beer.

"Looks like the missing booze mystery is solved," I said.

"It's their own fault. Everyone else charges two fifty for a rum and coke. These guys charge three fifty. I'm controlling their profits on behalf of all customers."

I laughed. "You're the Robin Hood of the Castle? And the liquor in the basement is your Sherwood Forest?"

"Exactly." Farnsworth looked serious. "I don't do it for me. I do it for the people."

49

Brown cooed with Kelli until she stopped us on our way to the meeting.

"Boys, my friend here tells me you want to hook up with my friends!" She patted her hands together. "What a surprise! We can have a party!"

"Why are you surprised, Kelli?" Farnsworth asked. "Look at us. We're handsome, single, and love to mingle!"

Farnsworth looked from Kelli to Brown, who said, "Yeah, why the surprise? You don't think these guys are fags, do ya?"

Kelli's smile evaporated. I winked at her and went into the pit.

The gang was all there, Akers holding a gripe session and Warren Lynch reading the Bible. "There's always hope for the believers," he said.

"Believe me," I answered, "I believe."

Farnsworth plopped into a chair—his sunglasses made sense now—and I settled in to the one next to him as Brown walked toward us. "Don't know why she was surprised you guys wanted to get hooked up."

Farnsworth let out a low whistle, and I shrugged as Bruce walked in wearing his reflector glasses. I wondered whether he was stoned too.

"Might be a good day to OPC," he said. "I can't control the weather." Then he left for the tiki bar, where plenty of people had already bellied up. A little rain wouldn't dampen their vacations.

Akers groaned. "OPC. Christ, I'm fifty-five years old."

"What's OPC?" I asked Farnsworth.

"Depends on who you ask. 'Off-property contact' or 'obnoxious people chasing.' You find people downtown—on the beaches, in the restaurants, wherever—and offer a twenty-dollar gas voucher in return for an hour and a half of their time. Then you bring them here and sell them." He leaned back. "It's kind of illegal. You can get arrested for solicitation, which happens to be the same charge as prostitution."

He stared up at the ceiling. "Hotel owners hate it. If their guests join the Castle, they won't need a hotel again. But the upside is, the clients are already here; they like P-town. And an OPC sale pays an extra ten percent. You double your commission."

That was all I needed to hear. I stood, ready to go.

"The developers budget about thirty percent for marketing," Farnsworth explained, "so they pass ten percent back to Sales as a bonus."

He was still talking as Kelli handed me the OPC cards. "Did you have fun last night?" I asked.

She giggled. "You're right. He is a little prick."

I groaned and took the cards—four-by-four-inch black-and-whites offering free gas for attending a ninety-minute presentation. The back of the card listed the qualifications: age, income, and all the rest.

"Have you ever done this?" I asked Farnsworth.

"Last winter, in Key West, for a resort in Marathon. And it worked. Anyone leaving Key West drives right by the resort heading back to Miami. We gave a free lunch or dinner to each tour."

"If you're downtown handing out cards, how can you sell at the resort?"

Farnsworth took off his glasses. "You don't. OPC-ing is a separate job. You put your name on the card and get paid for each qualified tour."

I was amazed. "How much?"

"Fifty bucks a pop."

"What's the most you ever made in a week?"

He smiled. "Got paid on thirty-five tours one week." The math left me even more amazed.

"You made seventeen fifty in one week handing out invitations for free meals?"

Glasses back on, Farnsworth stood. "Yup."

This business was full of surprises. And each one meant more money.

Farnsworth headed for the bar, and I was right behind him. Bruce was in his usual chair, an open bottle in front of him, cigarette burning between his fingers. "Sharks. Hungry sharks," he said as we approached.

"Farnsworth explained the OPC thing," I said, "and I wouldn't mind trying it out. But if I'm downtown, I'll mess up the rotation. How does that work?"

Bruce snickered. "A hungry white shark is always looking to feed. I'll

179

take you off the line. Go downtown, set bait, and come back and see what you caught."

I thought it over. "Do I get my own tour if I'm here? And what if more than one comes in at a time?"

He shrugged. "Up to you. If the first UP doesn't break the pact, spin it." The sun peeked through the clouds as he continued. "Doesn't cost us anything. They don't stay ninety minutes, we don't give them the free gas. If it's a good shot and someone else sells it, you make ten percent."

This far out in the ocean, one town can be rainy, the next beautiful. As Bruce laid out the possibilities, the clouds drifted away, leaving a cool but sunny day.

"What about you?" he asked Farnsworth. "You game?"

"It's worth a shot," Farnsworth said. "Not much is gonna happen here today."

Bruce stood. "C'mon, I'll show you a trick."

Farnsworth jogged to Reception to pick up OPC cards and caught up with us at the bus stop. A few minutes later, we were downtown. With the rain over and the sun making an appearance, people were walking the streets. But they weren't *people* to me, or even tourists. They were UPs, and I needed to filter out the NQs.

We split up to solicit different couples. "Hey folks," I heard myself say. "We're having an open house. For a bit of your time, we'll give you twenty dollars' worth of gas."

Some took the cards; others declined. After a while, the three of us met up on a corner in the center of town. "How's it going?" Bruce asked. "Any takers?"

I nodded. "Don't know where the pitch came from, but 'open house' gets their attention. The close is twenty bucks' worth of gas."

"Open house," Farnsworth repeated. "I like it."

Farnsworth had ten cards left; I had nine. Bruce looked up at the returning rain clouds and said, "Follow my lead. This could be the perfect opportunity."

At a large puddle left by the morning rain, he got down on all fours and started barking, stopping only to lap up the water.

Farnsworth howled, slapping his knee and snorting. My jaw dropped. In no time, a huge crowd had gathered to watch the human dog.

Farnsworth and I sized up the UPs and moved in. Five minutes later, Bruce stood, shrugged, and walked away.

Some people actually clapped.

"Did it work?" he asked when we caught up with him.

It had. We'd passed out all the cards. As if on cue, the sky darkened, and the rain began.

"Proves there's a God," Bruce said. "They'll all start heading off-Cape now. Every one of those cards will drive by the Castle during the next few hours. Good work, my sharks."

A few minutes later, the bus dropped us off and we headed to the pit. We'd been gone about forty-five minutes. In Reception, Bruce told Kelli to round up the troops. She looked curious—it wasn't like Bruce to call a midday meeting—but in no time, the staff was assembled.

"Fifty OPC cards were just handed to the most qualified UPs in P-town," he announced. "We should have tours for the rest of the day."

The troops cheered, and Bruce explained that he'd reset the line—me first, Farnsworth next.

Then he called out to Kelli. "Do you know how to handle an OPC tour? They're more skeptical than letter UPs; you've got to handle them with kid gloves."

She looked hurt. "You act like this is my first day. Don't worry. I'll handle it."

Not twenty minutes later, the first car pulled in, headlights on, windshield wipers working. A middle-aged couple rushed in out of the rain, the man holding the OPC card.

They were one of mine.

Soon I was on tour with my first OPC. The big stakes had doubled, and the day proved to be phenomenal. Thirty UPs reached Kelli, and twenty-five toured, resulting in a staggering thirteen sales: eight summer two-bedrooms, five studios. The total volume was over $85,000.

The last tour walked in at 7:00 p.m. and bought at 9:15 p.m. Every rep was still there. The air was electric. Just about everybody had a sale, and four of us had multiples, including Farnsworth and me. He bagged a two-bedroom and a studio; I landed a couple of two-bedrooms, both for cash.

After the paperwork was done, we gathered at the bar, where our fearless leader sat in his chair, smoke drifting up from the ashtray, a Cheshire cat grin on his face.

"Drinks on the house!" he told the bartender, and the staff erupted.

Farnsworth and I were the happiest in the bunch. We navigated away from the excitement and back-slapping but stayed under the tiki bar as the rain continued. He put his arm around my shoulders. "It'll take a few days just to figure out how much we made."

I laughed. "You know what's funny? We didn't put our names on the cards. We don't even know which of us brought in what."

"What do you want to do? This was all your idea, buddy. It's up to you."

I thought it over. "Our sales are our sales," I said. "The ten percent on the rest we split fifty-fifty, okay?"

He lifted me off my feet and yelled my name. Soon the whole staff was chanting, "Jake! Jake! Jake!"

From my spot in the air, I noticed Kelli standing alone in the entrance to Reception. I asked Farnsworth to put me down and called to her, signaling that she should join us. She squealed as she ran through the rain to the protection of the tiki bar. I hugged her.

"You did a great job today, Kelli. Thanks." Tears welled up in her eyes.

Bruce excused himself, instructing the bartender to shut the party down at $500.

He paused and met my eyes before he shook his head and left.

"Jimmy's here," Farnsworth said a few minutes later. "Wanna go cook up the fish?"

"Why not?" I said. "Got nothing else to do."

Arms around each other's shoulders, we made our way to the parking lot.

50

Jimmy let the Oldsmobile Cutlass idle in front of the Barracks while Farnsworth ran inside "to get a few things." He returned with two bottles of Bacardi rum.

"Surprise, surprise ..." Jimmy muttered.

Farnsworth looked hurt, then laughed. "Robin Hood. Treats for the merry men."

"More like Robber Hood," Jimmy said as we pulled out.

Farnsworth dug through his pockets, finally producing the brown paper bag, and rolled a joint—a big one.

"Good job today, you guys." Jimmy said. "Heard about it from the big guys. Biggest day ever at the Castle."

Farnsworth lit the finished product and took a few hits. "Jake and I cleaned up."

Jimmy took the joint. "I heard you made some money. Now can you pay me back?"

"You bet," Farnsworth said as he exhaled. "And if you need extra, just ask."

Jimmy looked surprised. "How much did you make? I mean, you owe me seven hundred bucks."

"I don't even know." Farnsworth passed the joint back to me. "Do you know how much I made today?"

I took a toke and coughed, shaking my head. The pot was strong.

"Beer's in the cooler." Jimmy told me.

I grabbed one for each of us. Farnsworth opened Jimmy's beer, then his own. After a few sips, I could talk again. "We'll figure it out when we get to your place, Jimmy, but I'll need paper and a pencil."

He looked like he thought we might be putting him on. "Are you shittin' me? You made that much?"

Farnsworth nodded as we pulled into the driveway. We ran inside to get out of the rain, and Farnsworth went straight to the kitchen.

"Only two bottles of Coke. Ya got more someplace, Jimmy?"

"Yeah, there's a case in the closet."

After searching through a drawer under the kitchen counter, Jimmy handed me a sheet of loose leaf and a stub of a pencil.

Farnsworth took a few glasses from the cupboard, poured three strong rum and colas, and raised his. "To my new friend Jake and the biggest money day of my life!" After a gulp, he added, "By far!"

Jimmy broke into a huge smile. "I've never seen Farnsworth act like this. How much did you guys make?"

I divided the paper into two columns, one labeled "F," the other "J."

"What was your volume?" I asked Farnsworth.

He sipped his drink. "Thirteen thousand dollars."

I explained as I wrote. "Eight thousand at ten percent is eight hundred, five thousand at fifteen percent is seven fifty, for a total of fifteen hundred fifty dollars."

Jimmy patted his friend on the back. "Takes me almost three weeks to make that much."

"Add to that thirteen hundred for the OPC commission," I continued, "and it comes to two thousand eight hundred fifty."

Jimmy jumped up, knocking his chair over. "Are you kidding? That's half a summer's pay for me!"

I was still scribbling. "There's more?" he asked.

I took a big gulp of my drink. "Total volume was eighty-five thousand, give or take. Subtract our combined volume of twenty-nine thousand, and that leaves fifty-six thousand of OPC-generated volume. Ten percent of that is fifty-six hundred, which we split fifty-fifty, giving you a grand total of five thousand five hundred fifty dollars!"

Farnsworth raised his glass, Jimmy gaped at me, and I leaned over to work on the J column.

When I looked up, they were staring at it:

$1600 + 1600 + 2800 + 320 = $6,320.

"Aw, shucks, you beat me," Farnsworth said. "What's the three hundred twenty?"

"Cash deals."

"How do you get cash deals all the time?"

"I don't tell them about financing. If they ask, I tell them the interest rate is too high."

"Smart." Jimmy said. "Everyone wins."

"Everyone wins. You make more money, and the developers have a better cash flow."

Farnsworth looked confused. "Cash flow?"

"Think about it." Jimmy stood up to pace the room. "The costs—gifts, commissions, secretaries—add up to about fifty percent—cash that goes out the door with every sale. With only a ten percent down payment, thousands of dollars go out-of-pocket on every deal. If today's whole volume was financed, the developers would get only about eight thousand in cash, the rest on paper."

"What's paper?" I asked.

"The promissory note," Jimmy said. "It's paper, not cash. In the long run, the developers make more as long as the paper performs."

We weren't entirely clear.

"'Performs' means they make the payments."

I nodded. "Ahh, gotcha."

"I guess we should help them with cash flow," Farnsworth said.

I polished off my drink. "Yup, let's help them pay us more!"

We all laughed. Farnsworth refilled the three empty glasses, and Jimmy went out to the porch and the grill.

Farnsworth pulled a plate heaped with striped bass fillets from the fridge. "Nice touch today, Jake. Thanks. I can use the money."

I tilted my refilled glass toward him. "I hear you, compadre. I was broke when I got here on Saturday. And I mean *broke*."

He found the aluminum foil, then returned to the fridge for a stick of butter, a carton of eggs, and a bunch of asparagus. "Time-share," he said. "Nothing like it. Rags to riches overnight."

I agreed. Getting fired from Jiminy Peak was the best thing that could've happened to me.

"Grill's lit," Jimmy said. "Coals will be ready in ten minutes." Looking at Farnsworth, he added, "Need any help, bud?"

"Yeah." Farnsworth pulled the bag from his pocket. "Roll one, will ya?"

"No problemo," Jimmy said.

Farnsworth placed slivers of butter into the slits of the firm white fish resting on the foil. He squeezed fresh lemon over the fillets and wrapped them loosely.

"Delectable." he said. I walked closer to watch.

"Now the veggies." He cracked five eggs on the side of a bowl. "Let's hold it together, girls."

Jimmy turned on the radio. "Hollandaise over asparagus, striped bass, booze, and buds," he said. "Not bad."

I saluted him as Kool and the Gang's new song "Celebration," began.

Farnsworth separated the eggs, gingerly rolling each yellow orb around in his hand before placing the yolk gently in the steel bowl.

"Ever made this, buddy?" I shook my head. I'd never even tasted it. "It's all timing. Blow it and you end up with scrambled eggs. Melt the butter slowly, add cayenne, fresh lemon juice, a pinch of salt, and then pour it over the whisked egg yolks on top of a steaming pot of water, stirring the whole time. I use low heat; it's more forgiving. It'll take about ten minutes, so now we steam the asparagus and pour another drink."

His timing was perfect. The music blared, "Celebrate good times, come on!"

Farnsworth used a wooden spoon as a microphone as we all sang the chorus over and over. When the song ended, Jimmy lit another joint.

Farnsworth put the asparagus in the boiling water, then took the fish out to the grill.

Joining the table, Jimmy handed the joint to me. "What you guys did today is incredible. Bruce must be happy. He's been under some pressure."

I nodded. "There's been some griping about the number of UPs."

"The developers aren't stupid. They won't spend money on tours 'til Bruce gets a staff that can sell. He's gotta get more fresh blood, Jake, like you."

I didn't want to get into anything serious, just wanted to enjoy the moment.

"Ten minutes 'til blastoff!" Farnsworth announced.

"Where'd you learn to cook?" I asked.

"Sally." He moved the pot of asparagus away from the boiling water.

I looked at Jimmy, who mouthed, "His mother."

Farnsworth whisked the yolks like a madman, then ran outside to flip the fish. "Timing." he yelled. "It's everything."

"He's a great cook," Jimmy said.

Farnsworth ran back in, put the bowl on top of the boiling water, added the butter with the other ingredients, and whisked the mixture gently. "C'mon, baby, come to Daddy."

"Weird," Jimmy added, "but great."

A few minutes later, we sat down to a perfectly grilled striped bass, with crunchy asparagus swimming in Hollandaise sauce. Maybe it was because of the monster sales, maybe the rum or the pot, or maybe all of it combined, but I couldn't remember eating a better supper.

After a quick cleanup, Jimmy said, "I don't have the luxury of a nine thirty start tomorrow, boys. My day begins at seven, so if you want a lift back to the Barracks, we should go now. Otherwise, you can bunk here."

"I'm tired, too," I said. "Let's head back." Farnsworth saluted. "Right on, Skipper."

It was still raining as we piled into the car. When we got close to the Castle, Farnsworth leaned over to Jimmy. "Mind dropping me downtown?"

"No problem."

In the center of town, Farnsworth turned to me. "C'mon, buddy," he said, jutting his head at the crowded sidewalk. "There'll be plenty of time to sleep when we're dead."

51

Dolly Parton's "9 to 5" greeted us as we hustled through the open doors of the Atlantic House, and there was Dolly herself, belting it out live on stage. This Dolly, though, was six feet tall.

When my eyes adjusted to the darkness and I caught up with Farnsworth at the bar, he handed me a red drink, raised his own glass, and took a gulp. "Cape Codder, buuuddy!"

The crowd howled as female impersonators recreated the likes of Cher, Dionne Warwick, and Joan Rivers, with a cameo appearance from Marilyn Monroe. Cher and Joan Rivers wrapped up "I Got You Babe"—a duet that brought down the house—and the lights came up for intermission. Cher walked toward us, licking her upper lip as only Cher can.

"Who's your good-looking friend, Peter?"

Dark shades back on, Farnsworth introduced us. As we shook hands, she spun halfway around, ending up in my lap, running her gloved hand down the side of my face. "How'd you like to be my Sonny tonight, you gorgeous thing?"

Farnsworth came to the rescue. "Hey Cher, he's my Sonny."

She pouted. "Shut up, Peter. We both know you're not queer. Too bad, I might add."

She removed herself from my lap, but not before dragging her hand across it. When I flinched, they both laughed.

Behind Cher, Warren Lynch from the Castle walked arm-in-arm with a guy sporting bright yellow hair. He dropped one hand until he found his friend's ass, and his friend returned the favor.

Farnsworth was conversing with Marilyn Monroe; she was stunning in a white dress, her hair falling in delicate curls. My drink was still half full, but I chugged it and signaled the shirtless bartender for another round. He spun in his hot pants and sent a kiss my way.

"Meet Norma Jean," Farnsworth said.

The booze, the pot, or whatever kicked in as I took Marilyn's hand. I got lost in her beauty, knowing she was not always a she. New drinks kept showing up, as did Joan Rivers, Dionne, and again, Cher.

Farnsworth was a people magnet. He knew everybody and they knew him. He followed me when I excused myself and went to the washroom.

"How're you doing, buddy?" he asked as we stood side by side at the urinals.

"Pretty wild, bro. This is crazy. Did you see Warren Lynch?"

He rolled his eyes as he zipped his fly. "The guy has a wife and two kids. That's gotta be confusing."

I nodded, too tired to get into it.

"We're invited to the after-party in the basement," he said. "Wanna go?"

"I need to call it a night. I'm beat."

"Come here." In a vacant stall, he pulled out a bag of white powder and dipped the top of a Bic pen inside.

"What's this?"

"Crystal." He held the pen top under my nose. "C'mon, sniff. It'll wake you up, keep you going."

The surge was immediate. All thoughts of sleep vanished.

Farnsworth took a few sniffs of the powder. "Still tired?"

I shook my head. "You kidding? Let's party."

We left the stall just as Marilyn walked to the urinal and lifted her skirt.

"Give me some vitamin C, will you, honey?" she said. "Gonna be a long night downstairs."

Farnsworth held the bag under her nose as she took a few big whiffs, standing at the urinal. *Not something you see every day. Then again, maybe it is in this town.*

Marilyn smoothed her dress and checked her makeup in the mirror. The three of us left the washroom as two big, bald, bearded bikers went into a stall. Farnsworth whistled.

Back at the bar, high and drunk, I couldn't stop talking. I'd figured out the secret to the universe! Farnsworth laughed—and so did I, just because.

Later, as Farnsworth poured another drink down my throat, he nodded toward a corner of the club. There was Kelli, crying, Brown moving at her as if he might hit her. After a few minutes, he flipped her the bird, yelled into her face, and stormed out.

"Looks like the honeymoon's over," Farnsworth said.

"Poor bastard," I mumbled.

"Which one?"

"Both," I said. "I meant Brown, but he deserved it. He's a dick."

The air in the basement was thick with the smell of pot. White lines of powder waited on almost every table as the music blared and disco balls lit up men, women, and anything in between. It was a zoo. The rest of the night was a blur.

In the early morning, while I stood in a corner with my back against the wall, Farnsworth showed up. "Had enough?"

I couldn't manage an answer. As he ducked under my arm and helped me to the door, I mumbled something about sleep.

He shook his head. "Four hours 'til the sales meeting. Might be tough to get up. C'mon, we'll get some coffee."

52

◈

Waking to find myself curled up in a restaurant booth, I groaned and reached for the coffee. Then I thought better of it. Sunshine streamed in through a window overlooking the bay. I was at Rose's.

"You want a bottle of tequila with a straw?" asked a cute waitress.

"Turn off the sun, please. And I'd like a transfusion."

She laughed. "I'm Susan, Jake. Your buddies told me not to wake you. They're on the deck."

I did my best to walk upright through the double doors. The sun glistening on the water hurt my eyes. I spotted a pitcher of water and ice on a table where Farnsworth sat with a new friend. Without looking at either of them, I carried the pitcher to the rail and poured it over my head.

Absorbing the cold shock, I looked out at the bay and then turned to the table. The water dripped down my neck and shoulders. Unable to take my eyes off of Farnsworth's new friend, I almost forgot my pain.

"The dead awaken," Farnsworth said. "This is Camille."

I wiped my face with a cloth napkin. Farnsworth kept talking, but his words got lost. Camille sat in front of me, her dark, lush hair cropped just above her shoulder. A halter top and faded denim shorts complemented her athletic figure. Her olive complexion showed she wore little makeup. A natural beauty.

Camille flashed a mischievous grin. "Good nap, Jake?"

I stared at her as I sat, then managed to look at Farnsworth. "Where did Camille come from? I mean, how long was I asleep?"

She giggled.

"Well, buddy," Farnsworth said, "I thought we could use some coffee after the party. It was too early for the bus, so we went to a little shop that opens early for the fishermen. I went to the washroom to clean up, and that's where we met." Camille giggled again.

"You were holding court," Farnsworth continued, "telling the fishermen that they don't know how to fish, that real fishermen work in Alaska. Forty-foot seas, boats sinking, people dying …"

I groaned.

"I didn't think we should stick around, so we hopped the first bus and came here."

A monster headache was building.

"None of them spoke English—not that it mattered to you. Must've been something, fishing the Bering."

I turned to Camille. "You met in the bathroom? Are you a …?"

Farnsworth threw his head back and laughed as I groped for words. "She pees sittin' down."

I gingerly took a bite of toast. Susan came to the table to ask whether I wanted anything. When I shook my head, she gave Farnsworth the tab.

"Can I put this on my account?" he asked, "on account of I have no money?"

"For you, Farnsworth, no problem."

He blew her a kiss, then stood. "Time to head back to the Castle. The general is expecting his troops in an hour, and I don't know about you two, but I need a shower."

Camille slung a knitted white duffel bag over her shoulder, and the three of us walked out to Commercial Street.

"What brings you to P-town?" I asked.

She wasn't long on words, and I liked that. From New York City, a struggling dancer who needed a break, she had boarded a bus to come to the end of the world.

As we unlocked our doors at the Barracks, Camille hesitated, then followed Farnsworth into his room. In mine, I wondered if I'd ever get to sleep in the bed. I stood under the hot shower, listening to the running water and the giggling on the other side of the wall.

Lucky dog.

I walked out of the bathroom with a towel around my waist and nearly jumped out of my skin. Tomola stood in front of the large window in her white nurse's outfit, checking me out from head to toe.

"Thought you might need fresh towels."

"Thanks, Tomola. Just leave them on the dresser."

She set the towels down and started to open the door, but then stopped. "You're really cute, Jake. And just so you know, I'm still a virgin."

She was standing between me and the door. No way could I out-muscle her, so I'd have to take my chances with the window. "Tomola, I like you. And if I was put together that way, you betcha. Thanks for the compliment; I'm hoping for the next life." I winked at her. I hated to be another rejection story; I really did like her.

She smiled sadly and left. From the window, I watched her cross the parking lot back to the Castle, then I closed the blinds and sat on the bed. My head was throbbing.

Way too much drama.

Suddenly I realized I hadn't seen the knife Niles gave me since moving into the Barracks. Not finding it in any of the drawers, I wondered if it had been stolen, but then found it in my backpack. I slid it under the mattress and took a quick inventory of the room, making a mental note to upgrade my wardrobe sometime soon.

I was on my way to the sales pit when Farnsworth called out. "Wait up, Jake. What's the hurry?"

He grinned as he caught up with me. "Have a good shower, buddy?"

I frowned. "Not as good as yours."

"You should've come over."

I stared at him.

"She likes you. Really likes you."

"Do you mean—"

He let out his trademark whistle. "She's a wildcat. And I mean *wild*."

53

Busy at her desk, Kelli greeted us with a cheery "good morning," without a trace of last night's distress.

Akers started to clap when I walked into the pit, and the rest of the staff joined in—everyone but Brown. The sales board told the story from the day before. The only one that had blanked was Brown.

I gave the reps an "aw shucks" wave and settled into a chair beside Farnsworth.

Bruce didn't look happy. "Good news and bad," he said. "What do you want to hear first?"

Most wanted the bad.

"No tours today," he announced. The staff groaned.

"What's the good news?" Warren asked.

"Your wife didn't see you last night," I muttered.

Farnsworth chuckled. "With canary boy."

Bruce smiled. "If we get the tours, we make money. We proved it."

Brown squirmed in his chair as Bruce called out the names of the reps he wanted to see in his office. He was on the list.

When the meeting broke, a few lingered to say good-bye, knowing what was coming. Brown just sat, his black eye yellowing, his chin blister almost gone, looking as if he might cry.

"First I get beat up," he said. "Then I find out my girlfriend's not a girl. Now I'm gonna get fired."

He was pathetic. It was all I could do to not bust up.

"Does this mean I'm a fag?" he asked as he stood. "An unemployed, beat-up fag?"

"Well, you are beat up," Farnsworth answered solemnly. "Let's see what happens with Bruce. As for the rest, that's up to you."

194

All bets were off. I doubled over, howling.

"Fuck me," Brown muttered as he left.

"I'll pass," Farnsworth said, and I laughed so hard I thought I might throw up.

Akers was holding court. "I hope Bruce does fire those guys. We don't get enough tours, and those reps couldn't hit the floor if they fell out of bed. Getting rid of dead wood will help, but we need more tours in here."

"I know a tour generator in Boston," Farnsworth said. "Maybe he'll talk with Bruce." We all urged him to find out, and he agreed to ask Bruce for an okay.

Kelli couldn't help herself, "What's wrong with your little buddy?"

"You mean Brown?" I asked.

She smiled innocently.

"He's having a bad day," Farnsworth said.

"A really bad day," I added.

Kelli smiled. "Poor boy."

We walked toward the bar, and the pool deck was already jammed with the midmorning crowd. There wasn't an unoccupied lounge chair in sight.

A new bartender greeted us, a thin guy with a long blond ponytail. Danny told us he was from New Jersey, a recently divorced Vietnam vet trying to start over.

A guy in his midfifties sitting across the bar seemed to be watching. "Morning." I called with a wave. "How're you doing?"

He picked up his beer, walked around the bar and sat next to me. "Jim McManus," he said, holding his hand out. "Owner of McManus Ford in Braintree."

I smiled as we shook. "Nice to meet you, Jim. I'm Jake Arril."

Jim smiled. "I watched you work yesterday. You're one hell of a salesman. If you ever tire of this, I have a spot for you on my team."

He'd caught me by surprise. "I appreciate that, Jim. Things are pretty good here, though."

He nodded. "Summer will be good. But I don't think you can even get arrested down here in the winter. No one's around."

Farnsworth piped up. "That's not true. I got arrested here two winters ago." We all laughed.

"You a member at the Castle?" I asked.

He sipped his beer. "Yeah, but I made a mistake."

"A mistake?"

"Bought this week in a studio last year. I should've bought July or August; it's too damn cold. Did you guys catch that lightning storm last night? I thought I was going to die."

"Thought I was gonna die last night too, but not from lightning." We all laughed again. "Why don't I see what's available in a suite? What week would be good?"

Jim smiled again. "Love it. Assume the sale. Wish I had a dozen like you, kid."

"July or August?" I asked.

Jim shook his head. "I'll stick with what I've got. Not moving any cars, with the price of gasoline."

Bruce arrived and took his chair at the other end of the bar.

"Things will pick up," I told Jim as I stood. "Don't let this hiccup keep you from enjoying yourself." I turned to go, but then thought better of it.

"Don't you deserve to enjoy yourself, Jim?" I asked.

He laughed and sipped his beer. "If only I had a dozen like you." I was walking toward Bruce when I heard Jim call my name.

"July."

54

"Superstar's here," Jan said. Robby looked up from a stack of files.

"What do you need, honey?" Jan asked.

Robby frowned.

I leafed through the inventory book. "We've got an owner here looking for a suite in July, Jan."

"What does he own now?"

"This week in a studio."

She reached across the counter and took the book, "What's the name?"

"Maguire, or something like that. First name's Jim."

I leaned over and looked at the list with her. "There," I said. "J. McManus, unit 215. Where is that?"

She laughed. "You sell the crap out of this place, but you don't know what you're selling?"

I did my best to look offended. "I know the unit number is facing the water."

She pointed to the unit number. "Second floor, middle of the building, over the pool."

"Thanks. I can handle it from here."

Jan left the book with me, and I zeroed in on a third-floor suite available during the third week in July. "Can I have paperwork for unit 301, week twenty-eight?"

Robby frowned again. "Sure you can, shooter. Hand in a signed worksheet and we'll be happy to help you."

My superstar status was short-lived with Robby. I went to the pit to get a worksheet, noticing that Kelli wasn't her usual bubbly self, and raised my hands in defense.

"Brown didn't hear anything from me."

She forced a smile. "I know. He found out all by himself. Guess love isn't blind after all."

Way too much to think about.

With a worksheet in hand, I found Jim at the bar, working on a beer. "You waste no time going in for the kill, kid," he said. "What've you got?"

I led him to unit 301, where he asked the question I expected.

"What do I do with the week I already own?"

"SPIF it," I said. He looked puzzled. "Isn't the end of May usually a busy time for car sales? You take the holiday weekend, then give your top rep use of the unit from Tuesday to Saturday."

With that, the deal was done. Ten minutes later, holding the finished paperwork and a check for payment in full, I shook hands with Jim McManus. At the other end of the bar, Bruce grinned.

Man, it's raining money around here.

55

Farnsworth and Camille leaned against the trunk of Jimmy's car in front of the Barracks.

"Bruce will need a Brinks truck to pay you this week," Farnsworth said as he got into the driver's seat. I walked with Camille to the passenger side.

She shrugged when she saw the bucket seats. "I'll sit on your lap."

Fine with me.

We headed for Jimmy's house with the top down, under a sunny blue sky. Camille sat at an angle, moving her little ass around to get comfortable.

"No, no, no!" my big head told the little head, but the little head wouldn't listen.

"Careful of the stick shift," Farnsworth said.

"Is that what I feel?" Camille asked. She put her arm around my shoulder and kissed my cheek as Farnsworth threw his head back and laughed.

"Step on it," I muttered. "This is killing me."

He hit the gas and soon pulled in at a small grocery store. "Need to get a few things. Anyone got cash?"

Still waiting for my first paycheck, I shook my head as Farnsworth pulled his empty pockets inside out.

Camille reached inside her blouse and handed him ten bucks.

"I'll pay you back," I said when he went inside. "Tomorrow's payday."

"Don't you worry about it." She inched her face closer, pressing her open mouth against mine. We were still kissing when Farnsworth opened the car door.

"Well, it's good to see we're all friends," he said.

"Are we almost there?" Camille asked, shifting again.

"Oh, yeah," I said. "We're close."

When we reached Jimmy's place, Camille swung her right leg vertically across the dashboard, then swung the other leg and rolled off my lap.

"Nice move," I said.

"Fifteen years of dance lessons ought to be worth something."

God was she hot.

Inside, Farnsworth unpacked a six-pack of Coke, a loaf of bread, and deli meat from a brown paper bag, then quickly built three rum and Cokes. He handed each of us a glass and raised his.

"To the sun, the sand and the sea."

"And to us," Camille added. I couldn't stop looking at her.

"Aren't you going to raise yours?" Farnsworth asked.

"Might as well," I answered. "I'm raising everything else."

We laughed and drank, then fell silent for a few minutes, until Farnsworth started for the deck.

"C'mon," he said, "I want to show you something."

Drinks in hand, we followed him onto the sand, where a path wound through the scrub pines and chickadees bounced from limb to limb. After a short walk through the seagrass, we were overlooking the ocean from the top of a tall sand dune, nothing in sight but blue water.

"Beautiful," Camille whispered. "Just beautiful."

Farnsworth raised his glass high and jumped from the ledge, zigzagging down the dune like a downhill skier. We watched until he was on the beach. It stretched for miles in both directions, not another soul to be seen. All ours.

"Ladies first," I said.

Camille jumped, yelling, "I ain't no ladyyyy!" I followed, and we laughed all the way down.

Farnsworth tapped his glass when we caught up to him. "Didn't spill a drop."

"God forbid," I said. We sat in the warm sand as Farnsworth rolled a joint. I was looking out at the water when Camille took her blouse off, then her bra. "Let's go in." I couldn't peel my eyes away.

"Don't want to get your shorts wet, do you?" Farnsworth asked her.

"Will you guys come in with me?"

We both nodded as she undid her shorts, one button at a time, until finally she stepped out of them wearing only a smile. "Your turn."

We stripped in a hurry, and the three of us ran to the water and dived in, hollering all the way. One by one we surfaced, yelling, "Cold, cold, cold!"

It was take-your-breath-away cold. Camille laughed and cried at the same time. "I can't walk. My feet are like bricks."

Farnsworth shouted, "Blue balls, blue balls!" I just laughed, so cold that it hurt. We used our clothes to dry off, and I stared as Camille pushed her hair back.

"Yep," Farnsworth said, "she's a beauty."

After two gulps from my drink, I was surprised to see the bottom of the glass.

"Be right back." Naked as a jaybird, Farnsworth scampered up the dune and over the top. Camille sat next to me, shivering.

"Maybe that wasn't my best idea." She rested her head on my shoulder, and I caressed her back as we looked out at the blue sea. "I'm not cold anymore," I said after a few minutes. "Are you?" She shook her head.

"Helloooo!" Farnsworth didn't ski down the dune this time; he just leaned back and took long steps until he was standing next to us. "Did I miss anything?" he asked.

He'd brought a few blankets, sandwiches, Cokes, and the rum.

Camille sat up and brushed sand from her butt. "Very good service, but you'll have to wait until later for your tip."

Farnsworth winked as he mixed the drinks. "I think I got my tip in advance."

Camille took a sip and spread a blanket over the sand. "Life's funny," she said. "We met because there were no paper towels in the women's bathroom."

I nodded. "Less than a week ago, I got fired and hitchhiked here."

Farnsworth laughed. "Can't remember when or why I got here, but I know it's the right place."

I lifted my glass to the sea. "Here's to fate."

We toasted and sat on the blanket until Farnsworth stood and walked toward the water.

"Where you going, honey?" Camille shouted.

"For a walk," he called without turning. "Be back in a while."

I wrapped a blanket around our shoulders. "Farnsworth's one of a kind."

She looked up at me. "He thinks the same of you."

"So what are your plans?" I asked. "I mean, your career, the future?"

She wrinkled her brow. "I've had goals and deadlines my whole life. But no matter how hard I tried, nothing turned out the way I planned." I nodded. "So now I'm going to take it a day at a time, just live for now. I'll deal with tomorrow, tomorrow."

I'd never met such a free spirit. For the next few hours, we talked and laughed about nothing. She was easy, fun, no baggage. Her beauty made it that much better.

I thought about Mandy and Jenn. My feelings for Camille made no sense. Christ, we'd just met. Plus, it was my new best friend, Farnsworth, who found her in the first place.

What did make sense here? Guys were girls, girls were guys, money, booze, drugs ... Maybe there was no making sense. Maybe I just needed to take it for what it was. But I felt the tug on my heart, and deep down I knew it. I was falling for her.

Farnsworth must have walked a marathon. When he finally came back, we were sitting where he left us.

"Nice countryside," he said as he poured a new drink. "Did you know that's the way to Maine?"

I laughed, but Camille didn't. "You okay, Peter?" she asked. "You were gone a long time."

He looked at her, then at me. "I'm fine," he said. "It's all good."

We gathered our stuff and trudged up the dune. "Wonder what time it is," Camille said as we neared the top. "The sun's starting to set."

"Shit," Farnsworth blurted. "I completely forgot Jimmy."

We hurried back to the house, where the kitchen clock read 6:00 p.m. "That's not too bad," Farnsworth said. "I'm an hour late. He only gets mad when it's a couple of days." Camille giggled as we piled into the car and headed for the Castle.

56

Farnsworth hustled to the pool bar looking for Jimmy. Camille and I followed slowly, and she took my hand. "I had a really good time today, Jake."

After a long hug, we walked hand in hand to the bar, where Farnsworth and Jimmy were drinking beer. Danny brought one for me, but Camille declined. She whispered to me, and I gave her the key to my room. After saying her good-byes, she went to the Barracks.

"She wants to stay with me," I told Farnsworth. "You cool with that?"

He raised his glass. "All's fair in love and war."

Jimmy grinned at Farnsworth. "Only an hour late. For you that's almost on time."

Farnsworth apologized. I tried to take the blame, but Jimmy shook his head. "Jake, he's my brother. As long as he gets back safe and sound, no problem."

"When haven't I come back safe and sound?" Farnsworth asked.

Jimmy looked surprised. "What about the time—"

Farnsworth put his hand up. "Okay, okay. A few times, but they weren't my fault."

"Right," Jimmy said. "Somebody forced you to drink a bottle of Crown whiskey."

"That's my story and I'm sticking to it."

We all laughed, even Danny.

Jimmy finished his beer and left, but Farnsworth ran after him. After a few words, Jimmy reached into his pocket and handed over cash. Peter hugged him, lifting him off the ground, and Jimmy left smiling.

He came back to the bar flashing the cash and ordered two shots of tequila.

"Don't worry about it," Danny said. "Bruce left fifty bucks for the sharks. I assume that's you two."

We downed the shots. I reached for a lemon, Farnsworth for a beer.

"Come here," I said to my friend as I stood. "I want to talk with you."

We walked, looking at the sunset over the bay. "What's up, bud?" he said.

"This is going to sound crazy. No, it is crazy. I really like her, but hey, you found her. If you tell me to back off, I will."

He raised his hand to shut me up. "I'm not looking for a relationship, Jake. I'm not built like that. I'm single and I wanna mingle. If you want her, she's yours." Our bottles clinked. "Be careful, buddy," he added. "Women are wolves. Try to put her in a cage, and she'll eat you alive."

57

A few shots later, Farnsworth slapped five dollars on the bar.

"Thanks, guys," Danny yelled as he wiped up. "I appreciate it."

We headed back to the Barracks to invite Camille before going downtown for grub.

"You know what happened this morning?" I asked as we crossed the parking lot.

Farnsworth peered over the rims of his glasses. "What?"

"Tomola made a pass at me when I got out of the shower."

He stopped and planted his hands on his hips. "Now what do you have that I don't."

I shrugged.

Farnsworth winked as we went into our separate rooms. Mine was dark, and when my eyes adjusted, I saw Camille standing next to the bed, wrapped in a towel.

Dinner will have to wait.

She walked toward me, reached up to stroke my face, and let the towel fall to the floor. Our mouths found each other as we fell onto the bed.

After a while, as we were lying in each other's arms, Camille leaned up, kissed my neck and whispered, "Cammy's hungry. Want me to go get us something? Or do you want to go together?"

I swung my legs over the side of the bed. "Give me five minutes to shower."

We went out just as Farnsworth crossed the tennis courts, Cape Codder in hand, dark glasses where you'd expect. "Good morning," he said. "Or night. Or whatever."

After a quick bus ride downtown, Farnsworth said, "Let's go check out the bug and see if he's in a better mood."

205

He wasn't. Oscar pointed his antennae at me and retreated. "Rejected by a sea bug," I said.

Farnsworth patted my back. "Mojo's or someplace else?"

I looked at Camille, and she shrugged. "Anything's fine."

"Forward, but never straight," Farnsworth said as he crossed the street ahead of us.

Holding hands, we ran to catch up with him. "Oh man," Camille sighed when we reached the line at the window. "Everything smells so good. I want one of everything."

"Wouldn't recommend it," I said. She looked curious. "Long story."

She settled on a chicken Caesar wrap and a bottle of water. Farnsworth and I got burgers with fries. We were eating happily at a picnic table when he stood and yelled, "Hey, Andy! Andy, wait up!"

He grabbed his half-eaten burger. "Excuse me. Gotta go." With that, he trotted down the road.

"There is no Andy, right?" Camille said.

"Farnsworth is a bird who likes to fly solo. Don't worry. He'll be around."

She reached over to hug me. "I'm not worried. I have what I want."

"A chicken Caesar wrap?" She punched my shoulder. "Why don't we finish and head back?" I said. "I don't know about you, but I'm exhausted."

She nodded. We got up, walked back to the center of town, and caught the last bus back to the Barracks.

In bed, nestled in the curl of my arm, she gently kissed my cheek and said, "Thank you."

She's thanking me?

58

After a quick shower the next morning, I leaned over the bed and kissed Camille. "Gotta go. No need to get up."

She reached out to hug me. "Have a great day, honey. Don't worry about me."

I couldn't have been happier. It was a beautiful day—payday to boot—and she'd called me *honey*.

I said good morning to Kelli and went into the pit to find my name had been boarded for yesterday's deal.

"Attention!" Akers called out. "We have greatness among us. This guy can make money out of thin air."

I took the chair next to Peter, who wore his dark glasses.

"Roses," he muttered.

I laughed. "That vodka's gonna get you."

"Actually, it's the cranberry."

"You can see we're a smaller group today," Bruce said. "I wish them well, but keeping the weak around would only hurt you guys."

He was holding a cardboard box. "I just received a sales tool, a film from RCI. Anyone seen it?"

I raised my hand. "It's a joke. Insulting. If I were you, I'd chuck it."

He produced an envelope. "Well, based on the size of this paycheck, I'll take your recommendation." He handed me the check. "For you, my great white." He then tossed the "sales tool" into the trash barrel, where it belonged. That was it. Another classic Bruce meeting.

The check was silver, with a black stripe across the back. Printed next to my name was the amount: $2,660.

Peter lowered his glasses to get a better look and whistled. "Drinks are on you."

"Hold on," I said, laughing. "I'm a family man now."

"Oh, God," he muttered, "you're done for."

59

During the next month, I made trips to the Holiday Inn almost daily to cash my big checks. Counting Bill and Edna Thomas's referrals, my first week at the Castle netted me more than $16,000. I kept the cash under my mattress, stuffed into a slit I'd made with Niles's knife.

With my first paycheck, I bought a new wardrobe: khakis, linen shirts, polos, topsiders, bathing suits—money was no object. I had plenty to take care of Camille, too. *Gotta have my gal looking good.* With or without me, she did.

We ate at fine restaurants every night, drank top-shelf, and basically acted as if we had an endless supply of cash. With the July start to the season still ahead, I always had a couple grand in my pocket.

The sales community soon heard that there was money to be made at the Castle, and the characters began showing up. Leon Boule was one. A commodities broker from Los Angeles, he'd worked for Michael Milken, the junk bond trader who got busted for insider trading, fined a few hundred million dollars, and sent to jail. Boule was at the office on the day of the raid.

"What did you do when the doors got kicked in?" I asked.

"Threw my sport jacket in the trash"—his tone reflected that of a conversation on the day's weather forecast—"and hid in a closet for three days."

I laughed and asked what he ate and drank.

"Cheezies and a cola," he said. Boule was okay with me. Some of the others weren't. Carl Crabtree, a good-looking guy dripping with gold and diamonds who drove a Lincoln and had a pocket full of cash, had sold "swampland" in Florida before being run out of town. Like most of the flashy guys, he owned nothing more than his car, clothes, and jewelry.

The Castle was building a powerful sales team, and it didn't take long for old faces to join the new. Camille and I were returning from lunch one day when I spotted *it* parked at the Barracks—the green Cadillac. *The Bull.* I gave Sweets and Becky big hugs.

Peter hooked Bruce up with the lead generator from Boston, and Bruce, without worrying about approval from the developers, upped the tour invitations from five thousand to twenty thousand per week. That would bring in thirty tours a day—three each for a sales staff of ten.

Former waiter Doug Webber had made close to $1,000 his first week. He was ecstatic. Everyone was. The buzz was contagious. Tours were slow in June, but between OPC and in-house sales, Peter and I still made money. We were all waiting for July.

I was in the pit one morning when a tan, two-seat, English-made 1974 Jensen Healy pulled up to Reception. A tall, slim guy got out and stretched, checking the place out. Doing a crossword puzzle with Warren Lynch, Akers moaned, "Oh, great. Another hotshot."

The guy found Kelli, and we could hear him from the pit. "I'm Matthew Marroni," he said. "Most people call me Matt. If you're lucky, maybe someday you can too." He winked. "Saw an ad in the paper: 'Only apply if white shark.' What does that mean?"

Kelli answered, but all I could hear was Marroni's thunderous laugh. I went out to meet the guy. It was apparent that from the look in her eyes, Kelli liked what she saw. The man had thick brown hair, neatly cut, and was clean-shaven. Clad in a sport coat, he flashed a quick smile as he introduced himself. Another commodities broker, this one from Boston, he claimed he was tired of losing people's money and wanted a career change.

At the bar, after a quick interview, Bruce looked at me. I nodded. Marroni was hired. I walked him to his car, eager to take the short drive in the Jensen. The Lotus engine purred like a sewing machine. Before stepping out, Marroni reached across with his hand open. "That'll be ten quid for the lift." His face showed no signs of humor.

"Consider yourself stiffed." I got out. "Welcome home."

At the Barracks, Marroni tossed a copy of the *Framingham News* on his new bureau.

"Can I take a look at the sports page?" I asked.

"Help yourself."

"I wanna check out some scores."

He lifted neatly folded clothes from his suitcase. "Got money on some games?"

I shook my head. "My dad coaches Natick."

"Just spent a year living in Framingham."

Paper tucked under my arm, I headed out the door. Marroni whined, "Hey, that'll be fifty cents."

"Consider yourself stiffed."

"Again?"

"Welcome to the Sandcastle," I said as I left.

I kind of liked the cocky bastard.

60

Sitting next to Bruce at the bar, I found the headline in the sports section: "Natick Wins Championship." Coach did it again.

The quotes from my father were the same as always, giving all the credit to his team, complimenting them as young men, not just baseball players.

"A whole family of great whites," Bruce said when I showed him the article. "I'm not surprised."

"Okay if I call home later?"

He nodded.

A bunch of the other guys joined us, and I introduced Marroni as the new shooter from Boston. He grinned as he sized up each rep. *What a cocky prick.*

That afternoon, Farnsworth and I went to the Holiday Inn to cash our checks. One of the developers, Freddy, came out of his office and was followed by a big guy—six feet two inches, 250 pounds, big nose, big lips.

"Okay, Barry," Freddy said, "lie low for a couple of days, then we'll make the move."

Only when he turned to go back to his office did he notice us. "Hey, Peter," he said, and he gave a quick nod in my direction.

"Have you met Jake?"

The developer took off his glasses and smiled.

"Meet Freddy," Peter said, "the guy who signs the checks."

I shook his hand. "Hope you've got lots of checks, and a pen that works."

"Call me Freddy. Don't worry about that, kid. You write 'em, I'll buy 'em."

My pockets filled with cash, we went back to the Barracks, found

212

Tomola leaving my unit holding an armload of towels, and headed for the pool. As we passed Reception, Kelli waved us inside.

"Who's the new guy?" she gushed.

Peter shrugged. "He's gay. How's that work for you?"

Kelli frowned. "It doesn't. Freakin' fags."

Peter looked at me. "Confusing, don't you think?"

The big guy from the Holiday Inn was sitting with Bruce at the bar, smoking a thin brown cigar, doing most of the talking. Bruce looked straight ahead, almost ignoring him. Who ever knew what Bruce was thinking?

"Barry, these are two of my sharks," he said as we sat down. Barry rested his cigar in an ashtray and reached out to shake hands.

"Just saw you at the Holiday Inn with Freddy," I said. "How's it going?"

Barry looked like a deer caught in headlights. His eyes moved from Bruce to me and back to Bruce, who grinned and stood. "Do me a favor, Peter; have your marketing friend from Boston give me a call."

Barry excused himself and wandered toward Reception after Bruce left.

"Be careful of him," Peter said. "There's no loyalty in this business. I bet they're gonna blow Bruce out, but there's nothing we can do about it. We're just the foot soldiers."

He was right, but I didn't care. "Bruce has been good to me. He deserves a heads-up if they're going to replace him with that slob."

Becky and Sweets walked in and met Peter, then Sweets turned to me. "I hear you're the top dog here, buddy. Is it true? About the money you made last month?" I nodded, still thinking about Bruce.

Becky smiled. "Congrats, sweetie. After Jiminy Peak, you deserve it."

"Morning," Marroni and his cocky grin interrupted, "or maybe afternoon! Slow day, but it's a nice day in paradise." I stood and started toward Reception.

"Where you going, bud?" Farnsworth called.

Without turning, I raised my hands, palms up.

Farnsworth and Marroni caught up with me as I reached the contract office, where Barry was holding court with Jan and Robby. "Look at that," I said. "I've sold more than a hundred thousand dollars of business and I can't get behind the counter. This guy's here ten minutes, and he's in the back."

"C'mon," Farnsworth said, "bet I know where Bruce is."

"Trouble in paradise?" Marroni didn't have a clue. "Christ, I've only been here two hours. Usually takes a day before things get screwed up."

Peter managed a chuckle. Outside, the bus was just pulling into the Castle. The three of us ran and boarded. We found Bruce at Rose's, a beer and a lit cigarette on the bar in front of him. Without asking, Aaron opened three more beers.

"What do you want us to do, Bruce?"

He smiled. "My great white, you've already done it. Thanks."

Peter seemed to understand. I was confused.

"Get your buddy on the phone quick," Bruce said to Peter. "I can't stop them from blowing me out, but I still gotta take care of my men."

He stood, dropped a fifty-dollar bill on the bar, and for the first time took off his sunglasses. "You really are a rare species, little brother," he said to me. "Almost extinct. A loyal killer."

61

"Will someone tell me what the fuck is going on?" Marroni was almost frantic. "Should I start packing? Christ, I just unpacked."

Peter slapped him on the back. "Let's go out on the deck. We'll fill you in."

We sat in the sunshine and brought Marroni up to speed on the politics.

"It's nothing I haven't seen before," he said. "A manager babysits a project while it's slow, barely getting by, and as soon as it picks up, bang! He's replaced."

Aaron came to the table with seven shots, put six on the table, and raised the seventh. "To Bruce," he said, "a good guy."

We downed the tequila. Marroni choked and took a slug of beer. "Do you guys always do shots at this hour?"

Peter threw his head back and laughed. "No. Sometimes we start earlier."

Marroni looked serious. "I understand how you feel about Bruce, but we need tours. Are we gonna get 'em or what?"

"We'll start seeing them tomorrow," Peter said. "Monday's the Fourth of July. I know the guy Bruce hired to supply the UPs. What I don't understand is why he wants to talk to him again."

"Bruce won't do anything to hurt us," I said. "I'll bet the house on that."

Peter reached for another shot. I grabbed mine, and Marroni reluctantly took his.

This time we toasted silently.

"Thought I'd find you here." Camille kissed my cheek and sat in the empty chair. I introduced her to Marroni, who was clearly impressed. We chatted about nothing for a while, then Peter stood.

"Gotta head back to the Castle, make a phone call for Bruce."

"I'll go with you," Marroni said.

"Hope I didn't interrupt anything, honey." Camille looked beautiful in a loose cream-colored shirt over a brown sarong. She moved her chair closer to mine and leaned back in the warm sun. I stroked her naked leg, my hand resting on her upper thigh.

"Hungry?" I asked.

She opened one eye. "No. I'm starving."

Aaron came to the table. "Need something, Jake?"

Camille sat up. "Plain omelet, bacon, two small pancakes, and an orange juice, large, please."

Aaron laughed. "Little lady knows what she wants. Anything for you, Jake?"

I shook my head, and he left. Camille and I leaned back in the sun again, eyes closed.

"What do you have planned today?" I asked.

"Walk downtown," she said. "See what's happening. Think about you 'til I see you later."

She knew all the right things to say. Cute as she was, she was tough, independent—not someone I needed to worry about. That was one of the main reasons I loved her.

After breakfast, as we stood on Commercial Street, I reached around her waist and pulled her close, kissing her lips.

"Let's go someplace nice for dinner," I whispered.

"Love you, Jake," she said, then she turned and walked toward town.

It was the first time she'd used the L-word. I stood watching her, feeling good, until I remembered the drama unfolding at the Castle.

Barry was talking to Kelli at her desk when I reached Reception. The conversation stopped when I arrived.

"What can I help you with, honey?" she asked.

I looked from Barry to her. "Bruce said I could make a call. What phone can I use?" She pointed to the contract office. "Thanks."

Jan and Robby seemed to be having a spat, and Jan was on the verge of crying.

"What do you need, Jake?"

"Sorry to bug you, Jan, but Bruce said I could make a call."

"Her name is Janice now!" Robby snapped. She looked as if she might kill someone.

62

"Coach here. How can I help you?"

I almost laughed. "Hey, Coach. How're you doing?"

There was a pause, then, "Jake, is that you?"

"Wanted to say congrats on another great year, Dad."

"Good bunch of boys," he said, true to form. "They work hard. They did things right. But how's everything with you, Jake? Must be pretty in the mountains."

It was my turn to pause. "Actually, Dad, I'm in Provincetown, working at a new resort. And things are great."

There was silence, then, "Okay, Jake. Got to get going. Mowing the lawn. Take care of yourself."

"Hi to Mom and the kids," I added quickly. "And congrats again, Dad." Click.

I wasn't sure he heard the end of the conversation.

The silence in the room was thick. Janice sat at her desk while Robby stared out at the parking lot. *Man. A lot of drama around here.*

Kelli waved me over. "What's going on?" she whispered, nodding toward the sales pit. "Who's Barry? And what's with the third degree?" Her posture told me Barry was in the next room. "That guy makes me nervous," she said. "Christ, he's even drilling in on Bruce."

"Big changes are coming," I said. "And fast. Better to mind your own business." She ran an index finger across her closed lips.

In the pit, Sweets and Akers were talking to Barry, and again the conversation stopped when I arrived. Akers offered a fake smile. "We're talking about what's needed around here."

I was quiet.

"What do you think is needed, Jake?" Barry asked.

I hesitated, but not for long. "I think people should do their jobs, stop blaming everyone else for their own failures. Everything here is great. For God's sake, I made more money in two hours than in six months at the last place."

No one responded, so I turned and walked out.

I was still shaking my head when I found Marroni, Farnsworth, Boule, and Doug at the bar. "Drama," I said.

"It gets worse," Peter replied. "You just missed Bruce. He's gone."

"Gone?"

"He called Boston, bumped the contract to fifty thousand letter drops a week for the summer, then went to the Holiday Inn and had it out with Freddy. Called him a back-biting bitch, then quit."

"That was quick."

"Said to say good-bye to you, Jake, and to thank you again." I just stood there.

"What does that mean for us?" Doug asked. "Do the developers know what he did with the letter drops?"

Peter shook his head. "No one knows but us." Doug looked confused.

"In the next few days," Farnsworth said, "this place is going to be flooded with tours. Put on your skates, my good man, 'cause you're gonna need them."

Marroni chuckled. "Fucking Bruce kept his promise, took care of his troops. And there's not a damn thing the developers can do about it."

Boule piped up. "Spin 'til you win, baby."

This was way too much information for Doug. "What does that mean?"

"Step up the pitch," Peter told him. "With that many tours, you need to get tougher about breaking the pact. If they even blink, you spin 'em. Get another, and another, until you've got a firm commitment on business today."

"I've seen this before," Boule said. "Some guys won't even throw down a pitch until they know how much is in the checkbook."

Marroni roared with laughter, "That's great, just great."

I had to agree. "Bruce really stuck it to them."

"And gave it to us," Marroni added.

"No more barbecues," Peter said. "Now the gift's a ceiling fan."

"As long as it's not a faux-leather bathing suit," I muttered.

Heading back to the Barracks, Farnsworth, Marroni, and I spotted Janice on a cottage porch, kissing a guy who was about six foot seven, 250 pounds, and black.

"Uh-oh," Peter said. "Trouble in the contract office. Looks like Jan's converted." Marroni looked confused.

"Until this morning, she was hooked up with Robby," I explained, "the office manager."

Marroni shrugged. "Sometimes couples break up."

"Robby's a woman," I added.

"This place should be called Dramatown," Marroni said.

We were smoking a joint in Peter's room when Akers knocked. "Barry wants to see you, Jake," he said, then he sniffed the air. "That is, if you're not too busy."

Barry was alone in the pit. "Got a few questions for you, Jake."

"Shoot."

He took his bifocals off. "I know what Bruce did with the tour production. Frankly, I agree with the move, but we have a problem. No, two problems."

I waited.

"I'm sure Bruce is a great guy," he continued, "but it's dog-eat-dog in the sales world. If I hadn't taken this job, someone else would have."

I didn't say anything.

"You've really done a job here, and the other guys look up to you. I could use your support."

I didn't respond.

"We need more staff," he said, "and a guy sitting at the bar wants to work here. Frankly, I think he's off his rocker, but he says he knows you, says you'll vouch for him. And it seems like he really needs the job."

We were sparring. If I'd support Barry, he'd hire the guy.

"Who is he?" I asked matter-of-factly.

Barry grinned. We were speaking the same language.

"John Niles," he said.

63

Holding court with a lit cigarette in one hand and a beer in the other, Niles spotted me as he took a swig. He then set his can down and walked toward me. "Nice foxhole you found, little brother. Any room for your sarge?"

"If there's room for me, Niles, there's room for you."

"Semper Fi."

"Grab your gear," I said. "I'll take you to the Barracks."

"Barracks," he repeated. "That's funny."

We were passing the tennis courts, crowded with kids, when he spotted the green Caddy. "Sweets is here. Right on. Anyone else from the Peak?"

"Just Charlie and Herbie."

He dropped his duffel bag, looking pained. "You gotta be shittin' me."

"Yeah. Just kidding."

I led him to his room and handed him the key.

"Welcome home, Niles. Let me find out what's happening, and I'll catch you in a few. We'll go grab some dinner."

Billy Joel's "It's Still Rock and Roll to Me" blared from the radio in Farnsworth's room. He was dancing with Becky while Sweets, Doug, Donna, Marroni, and Camille stood around talking, drinks in hand, the air heavy with the smell of pot. I kissed Camille's forehead.

Farnsworth turned down the volume. "Everything okay with the new boss?"

"We've got another player," I said, looking at Sweets. "Niles."

Becky squealed and Sweets beamed. I tugged gently at Camille's waist, leading her from the crowd.

"Is Niles the guy you told me about?" she asked. "The deer story? The bar fight that landed you in jail?" When I told her he was, she frowned.

"Don't worry, honey. He's got issues, but he's a good guy."

221

As if on cue, Niles showed up. When I introduced him, he snapped to attention, bent forward, and kissed her outstretched hand. "Sergeant John Niles, USMC, at your service, ma'am."

Camille laughed. "Your reputation precedes you, Niles."

Marroni showed up next, with the gang behind him. "Let's get something to eat. I'm starving."

I looked at Camille. "So much for a quiet dinner."

"Whatever, honey. Let's go."

Everything was easy. She rolled with the punches.

"We can jam seven into my car," Sweets said.

"And I'm good for two," Marroni added.

I did a head count. "Nine. Perfect."

"Make that ten," Akers said as he joined us. Marroni and Farnsworth looked at me.

I shrugged. "Guess it's the bus."

As we walked to the road, Warren Lynch called out from the Barracks. "Hey, wait up. Where's everyone going?"

Marroni groaned. "Anyone we forgot?"

"Just Barry," Peter said.

"Let's go before he shows up," I said, but then I remembered our deal. "Do you think we should look for him?"

"Troops only," Peter answered. "No management."

At Rose's, Aaron pushed four tables together. I sat at the head of the table, my back to the wall, Camille to my right and Farnsworth on my left, as the other chairs filled.

"What'll it be, Jake?" Aaron asked.

Peter answered before I could. "As long as there's a lot of it, who cares?"

Marroni shook his head while Doug, with Donna next to him, stared out at the sunset. "Man, is that beautiful."

I leaned closer to Camille. "Champagne?"

She smiled. "What's the special occasion, honey?"

"I have you, don't I?"

"You're so sweet, Jake."

Niles tapped his fork against a water glass as we kissed, and the others followed suit.

"For God's sake, get a room!" Marroni yelled.

I ignored them and turned to Aaron. "Three bottles of your best champagne, my good man."

He bent down and whispered. "Jake, that's Dom, a hundred twenty-five a bottle."

I'd never ordered a bottle of champagne in my life, let alone paid for one. The price floored me. "You're right, Aaron. Thanks. Better make it four bottles."

I sat back and took in the room. Three couples sat at separate tables, enjoying quiet dinners.

Aaron and an attractive waitress strategically placed the Dom in silver buckets around our long table. Another waitress arrived with a tray of ten glasses as Aaron pulled one bottle from its bucket and showed the label to me.

"So that's what it looks like," I said. "Let's see if it's any good."

He teased the cork from the linen- wrapped bottle, then poured a thimbleful into my glass.

"That's all I get?"

The group laughed, and he started to pour more, but I stopped him. "Just kidding," I said, then I held the glass to Camille's lips. She sipped, then took the glass and held it to mine. "A fine vintage," I said. "Drink, my friends."

They cheered, and three of them grabbed the closest bottles.

Across the room, a portly man sat alone, wearing a three-piece suit with a white cloth napkin tucked under his chin, about to dip into a bowl of clam chowder. Just as the silver spoon reached his mouth, Doug opened a bottle, pushing at the cork with both thumbs. A loud pop erupted, and the cork took flight.

The rest happened in slow motion.

The whole table watched as the cork ricocheted off the ceiling and headed for the other side of the restaurant. It landed smack-dab in the portly man's bowl, covering him with chowder. Marroni burst into laughter, slapping his leg. Farnsworth covered his mouth with his hand.

The guy grabbed for napkins as Doug jumped up and ran to him, still holding the bottle. "Sir, I'm so sorry ... I mean ... I guess ..." The guy didn't even look up, which made the whole thing funnier. Camille laughed so hard I thought she'd fall off her chair.

Doug ran back to the table and began to fill a champagne flute, but the guy held up his hand. He slowly emptied his water onto the floor, then set the glass on the table and pointed to it. Doug laughed and filled the glass to the brim. The gang erupted in applause, as did the other tables.

Doug started back to his seat but stopped and turned, hearing the guy clear his throat. Grinning, he tapped an open spot on the table. Doug looked at the half-empty bottle, set it down, and patted him on the back. There wasn't a dry eye in the place.

The guy never blinked. He tucked in a fresh napkin, sipped the champagne, and went back to his chowder.

Aaron appeared with a new bottle. "On the house, Jake."

"Priceless," said Niles, raising his glass. "To old friends and new, especially my little brother."

Menu in hand, I canvassed the group and ordered an assortment of appetizers: escargot, calamari, stuffed clams, shrimp cocktail, mussels ...

After that, we ordered steaks, lobsters, and locally landed fish with gallons of beer, wine, and cocktails. We talked about what brought each of us to Provincetown to sell time-share. That was one crazy bunch of storytellers.

At one point, Marroni looked down the length of the table and bellowed, "What did Barry want, Jake?"

The group quieted, all eyes on me.

"He told me his side of the story," I said, "about Bruce getting sacked. It wasn't his fault, so no hard feelings. He's here to make a buck like the rest of us."

"Are we gonna see more tours?" Akers asked.

I wondered whether he'd complained to the "powers that be" about Bruce. "Yeah, Akers, we're gonna have more tours than you can count, but not because of Barry. Bruce took care of that."

Farnsworth nodded, and Marroni clapped. "That's what I need. Gotta make some cash." Everyone raised whatever drink he or she had—some had three or four to choose from—and we toasted. "To the season," I said.

The portly guy finished his meal, drank the last drop of champagne, and pulled the napkin from his shirt to dab the corners of his mouth. As he stood and dropped money on the table, he caught my eye and winked.

"Bet he's a hell of a poker player," I said. Aaron handed the bill to me: $1,200!

A few guys reached into their pockets for cash, but I stopped them. "Next time," I said. "Tonight's my treat." Then I peeled off fifteen hundred-dollar bills, handed them to Aaron, and thanked him for a great night.

Outside, the group split up. Some headed downtown, others to the Barracks. It was close to midnight, and Camille looked tired. "Want to go home, honey?" I asked.

It was the first time I'd referred to the Barracks as *home*. She fought off a yawn.

"Whatever you want, Jake." I put my arm around her, and we walked home.

64

Camille pushed gently on my shoulder. "Honey," she said, "someone's knocking." I got out of bed and wrapped a towel around my waist.

"Mornin' Jake," Barry said when I opened the door. He was wearing a bright red shirt, smoking his brown cigarette.

"What time is it?" I asked.

"Eight o'clock. Truck just arrived with a shitload of ceiling fans. We've got to unload them and get ready for the UPs. Fifty on the schedule."

Christ. That's a week's worth of tours.

"Let me take a shower," I said. "I'll be right over." I turned to find Camille fast asleep, hair tumbling across her face. Beautiful. She didn't stir until I opened the door to leave.

"Good luck, honey," she said softly.

"Luck's got nothin' to do with it. I'm Jake Arril."

She sighed and smiled.

The troops were unloading cardboard boxes from the truck, some three feet long and four inches thick but light; the other little buggers only five inches square but weighed about ten pounds. An hour later, the truck almost empty, everyone was sweaty and grumbling. Sales was supposed to be white-collar work, not manual labor.

"Take pity, Massa," Niles yelled, "I's just a poor field nigga!"

We laughed as he broke into a soulful rendition of "Amazing Grace." He knew the whole song and knew it well. When he finished—"was blind, but now I see"—everyone was quiet. Then Sweets started clapping, and the others joined in.

I didn't. Niles gave me a sad smile.

Where has he sung that song before? How many times?

We finished unloading and went to the pit, where Barry introduced his new assistant, Jim Dewey. Dressed in blue jeans and a plaid shirt, Dewey was short. He needed to get a haircut and shed thirty pounds. "I'm here to give you guys every opportunity to fill your pockets with cash," Barry said.

He glanced at me, and I started a weak round of applause. When he announced the expected tour count, the room erupted.

"Thanks for unloading the truck," he said as he wrapped up. "The new gift comes in two parts: the fan and the motor. Remember to give your tours both. Any questions?"

Boule, who had somehow managed to miss the previous night's party, piped up. "Do you guys use a standard power line?"

Barry nodded. "Bruce set it up right. I see no reason to change it." He turned to Dewey. "Start with Jake and Peter. The others draw straws."

Kelli poked her head inside. "The first five are ready to go." She nodded toward the parking lot. "And more cars are pulling in."

We all scrambled. I grabbed a directory, yellow pad, Bic pen, and worksheet.

Larry and Hazel Phluck from New Haven, Connecticut, get ready to meet Jake Arril.

The pitch was going well. Too well. The Phlucks had all the right answers, as though they were reading from a script. They looked at each other after every question, as if to see whose turn it was. When Larry answered, Hazel giggled.

Something wasn't right.

A few hours later, after touring the entire property, we walked into the studio. Their animated enthusiasm convinced me they were putting on an act.

"This is absolutely beautiful," Larry gushed.

"I'll bet the suite is unbelievable," Hazel giggled.

I hadn't mentioned the suites.

We went back to the pitch room and sat at the round table.

"How does the property look today," I asked, "compared to the last time you saw it?" They looked at each other, confused.

"When were you here?" I asked.

"Last year," Larry said.

"Did you join?"

"Naw." He was smug. "We're not interested."

I'd been taken for a ride. "Do you realize this is how I make my living?"

"You guys invited us!" Hazel protested.

"We only came in for the ceiling fan," Larry added.

I stood. "Come on, then, let's go get your gift."

I stormed past Kelli and grabbed a three-foot package.

"Jake, that's just the blades. The fan won't work without the motor."

"I know, Kelli."

She got it. "Good tour?"

I didn't answer. The room was packed with UPs waiting to go. Outside, I handed the box to Hazel. Larry held out his hand. I turned without taking it.

"Enjoy the gift," I said. "You two deserve it."

Back in the pit, a few names were already on the board. Niles had a big sale, Marroni a small one. *At least we're writing business. Too bad I got Phlucked.* But I did enjoy the thought of the two of them trying like hell to turn on their new ceiling fan.

Maybe they'd reach up and spin it from time to time.

Back to Kelli. New survey sheet, new tour, new chance. "Alexander!" I yelled in the crowded reception area. A couple in their thirties waved, and I ushered them into the pitch room. "Ever been here before?" I asked.

Billy and Sara Alexander shook their heads, obviously surprised by the question. I decided to break the pact right away.

"Don't want to waste your time or mine," I said. "If I show you something you want and can afford, is there any reason on earth you wouldn't buy today?" They shook their heads again, but that wasn't good enough. "If you like it and it's affordable, you'll buy today, correct?"

"Sounds fair," Billy said.

Still not good enough. To hell with breaking the pact; I wanted to smash it.

After my third attempt, they both agreed verbally. If they liked what they saw and could afford it, they'd buy today. I relaxed a little and got into the pitch. They'd been married five years; Billy was a mechanic, Sara a stay-at-home mom with a three-year-old. We toured the property, passing the other troops at work, some headed to the indoor pool, some to the units, others in the pitch room, warming up or closing. This was action for the reps and the UPs. Excitement filled the air.

Returning to the pitch room, I was sure they were going to buy. But when I started talking about money, Billy took a left turn. It wasn't affordable, he said.

Sara told her husband she'd get a job, tighten the budget. She could just about taste the vacations.

But Billy was adamant. They couldn't afford it. I looked only at him. "Do you remember your wedding day?"

He nodded.

"Sara was beautiful walking down the aisle, wasn't she?"

He looked at her. "The most beautiful bride in the world."

I knew then I had the sale.

"Before you took your vows, if Sara had said, 'Honey, I'll raise your kids, keep house, and cook for you. All I want in return is a week of time-share on Cape Cod,' what would you have said?"

He was, as they say, in a box. Sara and I, now allies, waited for his answer.

She raised an eyebrow. "Well, what would you have said?"

He squirmed. "I guess it would've been okay."

He looked at me for mercy but didn't get any. It was time to move in for the kill.

"After five years," I said, "has she kept her side of the bargain?"

He knew the game was over. "Show me how I can afford it, and I'll join."

I wrote up financing from the Sandcastle. Even with 16 percent interest, the payments came to only $135 per month.

"Imagine that," I said. "For thirty-five dollars a week, you guys have a vacation every year. That's five dollars a day—a Big Mac and fries." He took my pen and signed.

Sara mouthed "Thank you."

I wasn't done. "You see it all in this business," I said as she signed. "You wouldn't believe how many men who've been married for thirty-five years won't spend the cost of a burger and fries on their wives. I feel good helping couples like you realize how much you love each other."

Sara kissed Billy's cheek. He reached across the table and shook my hand.

Carrying the paperwork to the contract office, I realized the Phlucks were going to make me a lot of money. This was war. Reps against UPs. Take no prisoners. Winner take all.

I had myself a new motto: "Get the deal or cause a divorce."

65

"Moving up in the world," Kelli said as I passed her desk. "Got an assistant."

Becky rolled her eyes. "Just helping out today. Wouldn't want to do this all the time. Some of these UPs are crazy."

"Try spending an afternoon with them," I suggested.

In the pit, I boarded the deal, the seventh of the day. Farnsworth was on the board, and so were Doug and Boule. Akers, Lynch, and Sweets were still on tour. Crabtree had gotten into a fight with Barry, Kelli said, and quit.

Farnsworth and Marroni came in laughing.

"Come here," Marroni said. "You're not gonna believe this."

The pool deck was packed, the Saturday crowd already checked in for the Fourth of July weekend. Farnsworth grinned. "Notice anything?"

"Just a mob scene."

Marroni nodded toward the lounge chairs, where a bright yellow head of hair sat in a matching yellow Speedo, basking in oil.

"So the canary's here," I said. "What's so funny?"

Farnsworth choked back a laugh. "Look at the chair next to him."

In the chair sat an attractive woman with two little kids playing in front of her.

"What's the big deal?" I asked.

Marroni could barely contain himself. "That's Warren Lynch's wife," he said. "She brought the kids down from Boston."

"You gotta be kiddin' me. Does Lynch know?"

"Doesn't have a clue. She just got here, and Lynch is on tour."

As if on cue, Lynch appeared at the far end of the pool, walking toward us with his tour.

"Christ," Peter said, "he's headed for room one, right next to them." Marroni looked as if he were having a heart attack.

"We've gotta warn him," I said. "This is gonna be a disaster. I mean, think of the kids."

Marroni stopped laughing.

"C'mon," I said. "Let's run interference." The three of us walked toward Lynch.

"Got a second, Warren?" Peter called.

Lynch kept walking toward Pitch Room 1.

"Shit," I said. "Either he didn't hear you or he's ignoring you. Lynch! Hey Lynch!"

He stopped. "For cryin' out loud, guys, can't you see I'm busy? This is the best shot I've had in a month."

I positioned myself so Lynch's back was to the lounge chairs. "Listen, man, this is none of our business, but if I were you, I'd turn—slowly, don't be obvious—and look who's sitting in front of your pitch room."

Farnsworth and Marroni gathered in close as Lynch slowly turned. Both the canary and the wife waved. Because of the crowd, neither knew who the other was waving to.

Warren the Bible thumper pretended not to see them, turning back to us. "Sweet Mother of God. I'm screwed. What should I do?"

"Be a man," Marroni said. "Get the hell outta here."

"Wave at them," I said.

Farnsworth and Marroni looked at each other, then waved wildly as Lynch exited down a side corridor. "Take my tour," he called back. "See you in another life."

As we headed back to Reception, the canary and the wife beelined toward us.

"Split up," I said. "Separate them."

Marroni took the canary, Farnsworth the wife, so I went for the tour. We all took care of business. Twenty minutes later, I had a worksheet signed. And the only person who saw Lynch sprint across the parking lot was Kelli. No one in the history of man ever packed a car so fast, she said. He didn't even put his stuff in a suitcase, just stuffed the backseat and split.

"I think it's safe to take his name off the line," Farnsworth told her.

Marroni and I agreed.

A few more tours came in that afternoon. The final tally was thirty-eight tours, nine sales, $69,000 in business. When the dealing was done, Barry looked at the board and said, "Not a bad first day."

"This doesn't seem too hard," Dewey added.

"Dicks," I said as I left the room with Farnsworth and Marroni. "They're dicks."

66

◆

Niles was holding court again, a beer and a shot of whiskey in front of him. "Semper Fi!" he shouted to us, and the guys who'd been listening took the opportunity to leave. Farnsworth and Marroni went to the other end of the bar.

Niles was already drunk. "Little brother," he yelled, and almost fell off the stool.

He hugged me and kissed my cheek, reeking of booze. I practically had to push him off.

"Niles, why don't we go back to your room? Call it a day."

He frowned. "Can't. Got no money for the tab. Gotta wait here 'til payday."

I looked at Danny, who ran a hand across his throat. Niles was cut off. I asked for his bill: one hundred dollars! "Sorry, Jake," Danny said. "He's been buying drinks for everyone all afternoon."

I paid the tab, helped Niles from the stool, and steadied him as we walked to the Barracks.

"That was some firefight," he said when we reached his unit. "Secure the perimeter. Double the watch. They'll probably hit us at first light."

He fell face-first on the bed, and I took off his shoes. After shutting the door gently, I went back to the pool bar. Marroni and Farnsworth were drinking beer, and Danny put one in front of me.

"Sorry you got stuck with that tab. This one's on the house."

Marroni slapped me on the back. "Your first tour was a marathon. Thought for sure you had them."

"Got Phlucked." He looked confused. "That was their name. The Phlucks."

Farnsworth grinned. "Do they have any kids?"

I didn't get it until Marroni said, "That would make her a true mother Phluck." We all laughed.

"It was a real Phluck-up," I added.

"Nice touch giving them just the blades," Farnsworth said. "Kelli told me."

"That's the last time I get stroked. If an UP even hesitates when I'm breaking the pact, see ya later. I was pissed but ended up with a couple of deals anyway."

"Where do you think Lynch is now?" Farnsworth asked.

"Screaming into the night with his hair on fire," Marroni answered.

I nodded. "The devil was almost paid his due."

"Sounds like a country western number," Marroni said.

Barry and Sweets walked out on the pool deck, looked around, and then left.

"Looks like Sweets is sidling up to new management," Marroni said.

I shrugged. "Never did at Jiminy. Wonder what that's all about."

As the bar quieted down, Danny asked, "What do you want me to do if your friend runs a tab again?"

"Cap him at twenty bucks. I'll cover that much."

"I was in 'Nam," Danny said. "I understand why he has issues. Poor guy."

"That's not the half of it," I told him. "But you're right. Poor guy."

Peter got off his chair. "Anyone up for dinner?"

Marroni slapped his hands together. "Must've read my mind. Tonight's on me."

At the Barracks, Akers was complaining about the quality of the tours. "These UPs don't travel, and they've got no money. Even if they wanted to buy, they couldn't."

Doug walked over to us. "That freakin' guy complains about everything. He's the only one who didn't get a deal. Maybe he should look in the mirror."

"Want to get something to eat?" I asked.

He nodded. "Donna's working tonight, so I'm solo. Where're you guys going?"

I shrugged as the four of us headed for the bus.

"Saw you at the close with your first sale," Doug said on the way downtown. "Guy had his arms folded across his chest, shaking his head. How'd you turn him around?"

"Marriage close."

Marroni leaned forward. "What the hell is that?"

My explanation caused an eruption of laughter. "He fell for it?" Marroni just about choked on the words.

"After the first tour, I figured it's us or them. Deal or divorce."

"That's great," Marroni said. "Just great."

"Come here," I said when we reached the center of town. "Check this out." I took them to the tank, standing to the side so Oscar couldn't see me. "Go ahead. Lean close."

Marroni and Doug stared in at the goliath. Oscar aimed his antennae and inched toward them. "Big bug!" Marroni hollered.

"Watch this. My turn." When I leaned toward the tank, Oscar retreated. Peter laughed.

"Bad blood between those two."

"How long has this been going on?" Doug asked.

"Since the first time we met," I said.

"Careful, buddy," Marroni told Oscar. "You don't know who you're screwing with. He'll either sell you or eat you."

We walked to Mojo's, and as we looked up at the menu, I heard a familiar laugh.

Camille was seated with another couple. I walked over, excited to see her.

I didn't get a warm reception. After an uncomfortable silence, she excused herself and took me aside. "Listen, Jake," she said, "don't get me wrong. I really enjoy being with you, but I also need my space. Can you handle that?"

I glanced over at the couple, who were watching. Midthirties and good-looking, the guy smiled. It wasn't friendly. His wife's smile was. She gave me a once-over.

I held up my hands. "You want space, Camille, you've got it."

She moved close to kiss me, but I stepped away. She walked back to her table, and I could feel them all watching as I rejoined my friends.

"Everything okay?" Marroni asked. "We don't have to eat here." Peter and Doug agreed.

I perked up. "Actually, I'm tired of Mojo's. C'mon, change of plans." We went back to the Lobster Pot. "Payback's a bitch," I said as we went in.

A handsome waiter seated us. Peter whistled and the other two laughed as I ordered four shots of tequila and four beers before Stephan had a chance to give us menus.

"Are we celebrating?" he asked excitedly.

"Yup," I said. "Independence Day."

My buddies looked nervous. "Don't worry," I told them. "She needs space."

Farnsworth started to speak, but I cut him off. "I know, I know. You warned me."

"Takeaway, Jake; she'll be back." Doug laughed. "You believe in b-backs?" When no one else laughed, he raised his glass. "Down the hatch!"

"And the hell with snatch," Marroni added.

Stephan was quick to agree.

Two shots turned to three, then four, and then more. As the liquor took hold, the light mood turned joyous. The jokes were even funnier when the nearby tables got annoyed. Three pretty girls took the next table, and a few minutes later, we were a party of seven. Stephan was delighted to see the beverages shift to champagne, meaning a sizeable bill and a bigger tip. He came to the table with seven menus.

"We don't need those," I said. "Everyone okay with me treating to a lobster-fest?"

They were. Feeling my drinks, I motioned for Stephan to lean over and whispered in his ear. He bolted upright in horror.

"Oh no, you can't do that! He's like family!"

Marroni clapped. "He's going for the big bug!"

I didn't give in, and soon Stephan huffed away in search of a manager. A handshake later, with a fifty-dollar bill tucked into his palm, the manager instructed a distraught Stephan to bring the guests their dinner.

The girls didn't realize what had transpired until a sniffling Stephan returned, assisted by another waiter, carrying a tray normally used to bus tables. In the center was Oscar, surrounded by steamed clams, mussels, corn on the cob, and boiled potatoes—a New England clambake.

Oscar looked big in the tank, but now, steamed a crimson red, he looked enormous. A few of the annoyed from nearby tables asked whether they could have their pictures taken with the bug.

Marroni filled our glasses and stood. "To a man who won't take *no* for an answer!" The girls didn't understand, but the salesmen did. "Here, here!" they chorused.

The bug was good, the company great, and in the wee hours of the morning, four salesmen and three secretaries made their way back to the Barracks.

Donna was waiting at the door for Doug. He tried to kiss her, but she pulled away.

"My God, you stink! What the heck did you guys get into?"

The rest of us headed to our rooms, each with a secretary in tow. But when I opened my door and flipped on the light, I stopped dead in my tracks. Camille was in bed … with the lady from Mojo's. They were sitting up, naked as far as I could tell. Camille smiled.

I turned to the secretary. "Sorry, looks like we're sold out."

She frowned. "What am I supposed to do?"

Peter opened his door. "There's an opening in this suite. Even has a view of the water." She looked at me and shrugged, then went into Peter's room, closing the door behind her.

Without a word, I turned out the light, undressed, and crawled into bed between them. Camille snuggled up and whispered, "Say hi to Vanessa."

"Nice to meet you," Vanessa said.

I slid my arm under her shoulders and pulled her close.

67

Nobody could remember exactly how one of Oscar's claws ended up on the Barracks roof, but it stayed there all summer.

The morning after the lobster-fest, as kids squealed on the tennis courts, I showered, dressed, and then paused, remembering the cash. I reached under the mattress, careful not to wake the sleeping girls, and even more careful not to cut myself on the knife, and tucked nearly $25,000 into my pockets.

Niles had joined the dodgeball game. He was the main target, to the delight of the kids attacking him. He saluted. I waved, then headed to the restaurant.

"What did you guys do to my boyfriend?" Donna asked as she poured my coffee. "I've never seen him so drunk. And his clothes smelled like fish."

"I don't know why he smelled like fish," I said.

Niles joined me, sweaty from all the running around, and thanked me for covering his tab. He looked rough. When Peter, Marroni, and finally Doug showed up, we headed to the pit. Donna seemed pleased that Doug was suffering from the night before.

Barry's meetings were more formal than Bruce's. He reviewed the prior day's activity and talked about the tactics that resulted in sales. He wrapped up by passing out checks to a round of applause.

The next month flew by. Camille would show up, stick around for a few days, and then disappear again. If I had company, sometimes she'd stay, sometimes not. It was all okay with me.

Janice and Robby were still on the outs, and the office was tense. Barry handled their meltdowns, usually consoling Janice. More and more often, we spotted her at the cottage next door with "that really big black dude."

239

Brown returned towing his sailboat, making Peter happy. Niles continued to sell, and to drink at the bar until he was cut off. Marroni, Peter, and I kept cashing checks and hitting the town at night. My pile of cash had gotten so big that I hid it in different places. I worried about getting ripped off but never considered a bank account. Who pays taxes, after all?

One August day while Camille was around, I took the afternoon off. The tide was out, and we hiked to the water's edge with a bucket of frozen margaritas. We stripped, jumped into the water, then laid on a blanket under a blue sky, enjoying the soft breeze.

"Excuse me, do you have a light?" A middle-aged man stood over us, naked, with a joint in his mouth. Camille giggled as I searched through the pockets of my shorts and finally came up with a lighter.

"Feel like smoking pot?" the guy asked. Camille nodded.

Lighting the joint, Tim sat down, a lawyer from Boston. He asked whether we were vacationing. When I told him what I did for a living, he seemed genuinely interested.

Soon I was putting on a full presentation, using my finger to write in the sand.

"Where is the property?" he asked.

I pointed to the Castle.

"Will you meet me in a half hour? I'll go back to my hotel and get a check." I shook his hand.

Tim left, and Camille smiled. "So that's what you do for a living?"

"Yeah, but I don't usually do it naked."

We laughed and got dressed, met Tim, and did the paperwork. That sale was the topic of conversation at the Castle for quite a while: "Jake Arrill can make a deal out of thin air."

It was all catching up with me now. The fast-paced, self-indulgent lifestyle became the norm, and it didn't take me long to realize that if you have pockets full of cash, there will always be people around to help you spend it.

Living life at one hundred miles an hour no longer excited me. There was a change coming, and it wasn't just the season. Summer was ending, and I found myself sneaking away from the crowd to find a quiet space to be alone. I was sitting on the deck at Rose's, enjoying the warm sun on my face, listening to the soft cry of the seagulls. I was content. The rustling of a nearby chair interrupted the moment. I opened my eyes to see Marroni sitting next to me.

"Found ya," he said with a grin.

Though I was enjoying the quiet, I was glad to see him. "Great." I frowned. "What do you need?"

"Nothin'. Just looking for my friend."

We both leaned back in our chairs, appreciating the sun's final moments. After a while, Marroni broke the silence. "What a beautiful day."

"Yup."

He sat up. "You okay?"

"Just tired." Exhausted is more like it.

"Have you ever left P-town? I mean, have you seen the rest of the cape?"

I shook my head. Aside from our occasional trips to Jimmy's place in Truro, I hadn't ventured out of Provincetown.

"Tomorrow morning we'll take a drive," he said, "to the prettiest part of the cape."

I was up for a day away from the madness.

68

Top down on the Jensen, Marroni and I sped toward the elbow of Cape Cod, following Shore Road along Pleasant Bay. My eyes were wide open, taking in the waterfront estates, boats on their mooring lines, pink beach roses, soft scrub pines, and manicured lawns.

"Beautiful," I said. "Just beautiful." Marroni kept grinning.

He stopped in front of a lighthouse overlooking an expanse of white sand and a small harbor that opened to the deep blue ocean.

"Welcome to Lighthouse Beach," he said, "one of the prettiest spots on earth."

He wasn't kidding. I got out of the car and just stood there. It was truly breathtaking. I looked down three levels of wooden stairs that led to the beach and out to the glistening bay. The soft green sea grass that dotted the sand dunes swayed silently in the breeze. Families basked in the late morning sun, lying atop their beach blankets. It was like a postcard. I took a deep breath, allowing the warm, salty air to fill my lungs.

"C'mon," he said, "let me show you the town."

A few minutes later, we parked on Main Street in the center of Chatham. Small shops and restaurants—the Candy Manor, the Squire, the Improper Oyster—were peppered among high-end art galleries, clothing stores, and a quaint movie theater. This town had money, and lots of it.

The Squire's door opened to an old wooden bar and floors, friendly people, and fabulous aromas. The bartender poured two cold ones and told us about the specials. Marroni decided on fried clams and a bowl of chowder. I got a fish sandwich. We ate in silence, feeling the good vibes around us.

"You know," I said when we finished, "we've spent thousands on steak, lobster, and champagne, but that was the best meal I've had on Cape Cod." Marroni nodded.

We were quiet on the drive back to Provincetown, taking in the beauty along the winding road. With Marroni, the silence was nice; at times, the guy wouldn't shut up. We spent more than enough time calculating words when we were at work.

"Someday I'm going to build a beautiful home in Chatham," I said.

With one hand on the steering wheel, Marroni glanced over. "I'll visit every chance I get."

"You like to fish?" I smiled.

We'd been quiet for a while again when he asked, "What plans do you have after Labor Day?"

I didn't answer right away. I knew the tour count would slow after the season, but I hadn't given it any real thought. I lived day-to-day.

He looked over at me again, waiting.

"Maybe follow the birds," I said.

He nodded. "Florida. Judging from the photos in the directory, some of those properties are beautiful."

That was all we said. But for the first time, I was thinking about the next move.

It was coming.

69

The sun was beginning to set as Marroni and I pulled in to the Barracks. The kids were playing on the tennis courts as usual, making the most of every last minute of summer. Their parents had the same idea. The bar was packed.

Seeming nervous, Danny nodded toward a lounge chair, where Niles was sound asleep. "He's lost it," he said. "The horse has left the barn."

"What'd he do?" I asked.

Danny answered in a hushed voice. "After he drank your twenty dollars, I cut him off. He just stayed at the bar with this grin on his face, but his eyes … Jake, he never took his eyes off me. He looked right through me."

"Did he say anything?"

Danny leaned closer. "Yeah. Just before he got off the stool, he said, 'I'm gonna send someone over to give you a shoeshine.'"

A chill ran through me, remembering his story.

"I don't know what that means," Danny said, "but it sure ain't anything good."

"How long has he been asleep?"

Danny checked his watch. "Couple of hours."

I walked over and shook Niles's shoulder. Instantly, he grabbed my wrist and twisted, almost breaking it. When he looked up, I knew what Danny meant. His eyes looked right through me. Slowly, as he focused, he loosened his grip.

"C'mon, Sarge," I said, "let's head to the Barracks and get some shuteye."

He struggled to get up, and I tried to help, but he shook me off. Unsteady on his feet, he left the pool area, walking toward the Barracks.

Marroni and I followed as far as the parking lot. When I called out his name, he raised his hand but didn't turn around.

"I don't know about you," Marroni said, "but I'm locking my door tonight. He's gone, man. Gone."

If Marroni had seen what Niles could do, locking the door would've seemed less reassuring. Back at the bar, Danny opened a couple of beers for us. We exchanged glances but didn't say a word. We were on the same page.

"Let's catch what's left of the sunset," Marroni said. "We've had a great day. His problems aren't ours."

I followed him to the beach, thinking that Niles's problems could very easily become ours. The sun was dropping into the bay, sending sprays of brilliant orange, yellow, and purple across the sky. Fall was just around the corner.

Marroni and I kicked off our shoes and walked to the edge of the water. The tide was high, the water warm. We stood in silence as the last of the sun disappeared.

"Did you see that?" I asked.

He nodded. "Farnsworth told me about the green flash. I thought he was full of shit. What does it mean?"

"Something about good luck."

Marroni looked over my shoulder. "Is that who I think it is?"

On the dimly lit balcony of a second-floor studio at the Castle, a couple hugged and kissed. It was Janice and—rather than the big black dude—Barry. "He's either really brave or really stupid," Marroni said.

I groaned. "I don't even want to see this. You hungry?"

"Haven't you noticed? I can always eat. I'm Italian."

It was true. Slim as he was, he could sure pack it away.

As we walked to the bus stop, I noticed the light on in my room but kept walking.

"Lately it seems she shows up only to be fed. Kind of like having a dog."

Marroni laughed. "Hope she doesn't have fleas."

From the bus, I glanced back to make sure Niles's lights were still off. I was afraid for my friend, but I was even more scared of the damage he could do to someone else.

Downtown, the festive mood was missing. The end-of-summer blues had set in. We grabbed a few slices of pepperoni to go for each of us and one to take back to Camille.

Noticing the extra slice, Marroni gave me a look. "It's none of my business, but if you headed south, would you bring Camille?"

I couldn't answer right away. I'd bitten into a slice and needed to shift the molten cheese from side to side in my mouth. "Haven't given it much thought," I said when I could. "What do you think?"

He shrugged. "That's your call, buddy. How do you feel about her?"

I took another bite. "It was great for a while, but she's not exactly a 'bring home to meet Mom' type. To tell you the truth, she takes the term 'free spirit' to a whole other level." Marroni just nodded. He never offered unsolicited advice.

Hearing our names, we turned to find Farnsworth and Brown behind us, each with a girl. Peter was wearing shades and a smile; Brown, his mousy grin.

"What're you doing?" Peter asked.

Marroni checked out the girls. "Looking for a couple of beautiful women, but you guys beat us to it."

Brown frowned. Farnsworth laughed and asked if we wanted to go to a club. Marroni liked the idea, but I was tired. My mind was elsewhere—thinking of Camille. And Niles.

They headed off, and I jumped on the bus back to the Barracks. All was quiet, and as I closed my door, I remembered what Marroni had said about locking it. I reached for the handle but then stopped. No way Niles would hurt me or Camille. No way.

She was asleep, so I put the slice on the nightstand and got into bed. I didn't feel like hugging and kissing her as I normally would. I lay still, sensing she was awake. I didn't care.

Niles. For some reason, I felt responsible for him. I felt his pain.

70

◈

Bang! The door flew open. A silhouette stood in the doorway.

"I am Jesus Christ," it said. Camille screamed.

Wearing only BVDs, I jumped up and flipped on the light. "Jesus Christ, Niles, you scared the shit out of me. What do you want?"

He was dripping wet, wearing cut-off blue jeans and no shirt, a mask and snorkel perched on his forehead. His face, chest, and arms were coated with black goop, his eyes so bloodshot they looked like they were bleeding.

Camille pulled the sheet over her head.

"One less rapist homosexual is alive tonight," Niles said.

Whatever he was planning couldn't happen here, in front of Camille. "C'mon, Sarge," I said, "let's head to your room and talk about it." He looked as if he might cry.

As I led him out, Farnsworth and Marroni opened their doors.

"What the hell?" Farnsworth said as he walked into the hallway. "Jake, you okay?"

I signaled for him to go back inside. From behind me, Marroni said, "Christ, what the fuck is this?"

Niles's head snapped to look at him.

"Sarge," I said, "it's just the two of us. You're safe with me."

I turned on the light in his room as he sat on the unmade bed. The place reeked from overflowing ashtrays, crushed beer cans, and empty whiskey bottles. I settled on a wooden chair, careful not to sit on anything foul.

"What's all over your face?" I asked.

Slowly, he rubbed his cheek. "Camouflage. Couldn't let the gook fag catch on to me, but I had to swim underwater to his hut before I took him out."

"Did you use the mask and snorkel?"

He dropped the mask on the floor, pulled a Bic lighter from his pocket, put one end of it in his mouth and pushed the butane lever, inhaling deeply.

"Underwater breathing apparatus," he said. "A brother in the force taught me this."

He mumbled about keeping the troops safe and securing the perimeter, but his eyes were closing. Eventually, he fell back and went to sleep. I lifted his legs onto the bed and took another glance around the room. On one night table sat the knife—his knife. On another were a dozen commission checks from the Castle, totaling more than $10,000, all uncashed. No wonder he was always broke.

Marroni was waiting in the hallway, shaking his head. Farnsworth was with him.

"Man," Marroni said, "I get fucked up, but never like that. The guy's a mess."

I said good night and went into my room, locking the door behind me. Camille was eating her slice of pizza. When I turned out the light and lay on the bed, she asked, "Is he gonna be okay?"

"Don't know," I said. "Right now, he's lost in a place that's pretty dark."

She laid her head on my shoulder. "I'm sorry. He's lucky you're his friend."

After a restless night, I'd finally fallen into a deep sleep when someone banged on the door again, calling my name. This time it was daylight. I flung it open to find Marroni screaming.

"It's Niles. He's in a room on the second floor. And Jake, he's got kids locked in there with him."

"Shit!" I yelled as I pulled on my clothes.

"A ton of cops," Marroni continued, "and more coming." Camille held a pillow over her face.

Outside, the tennis courts were empty. No kids.

Farnsworth, Marroni, and I ran toward the scene, but I stopped and ran back to Niles's room. Pushing his door open, I saw what I was afraid I'd see.

The knife was gone.

71

Pistols drawn, the cops blocked all doors to the building. Off to the side, Barry, Janice, Sweets, and Danny stood with a cop who held a walkie-talkie to his mouth. More sirens approached. Janice had been crying, but that was nothing new. Barry looked sick.

Danny was the first to speak. "I told you, he's gone, and I mean gone. When I was setting up this morning, he went straight to the charcoal grill and smeared ash all over his face and arms. All he said was, 'Hold the position to the last man.'"

"He thinks he's in 'Nam," I said. "But how did he end up with the kids? How many are with him?"

The gold shield on the cop's chest told me he was the chief. "Secure the back perimeter," he ordered into his walkie-talkie. "Snipers on the roof of the single-story by the tennis courts."

We watched as a few guys scrambled up ladders to the roof of the Barracks, then Barry turned to the chief.

"This is Jake," he said, "Niles's friend."

The chief checked me out. "When did you last talk to your friend?"

"Last night."

"Did he seem off? Did he threaten you? Anything about him seem unusual?"

Usual was a distant past. More sirens roared in, and parents who'd tried to break through the barricade were being restrained by the force.

"He was out of it," I said. "He's a Vietnam vet, and he has some serious issues, but he usually calms down by morning."

"Does he get physically violent?"

I thought about the three guys Niles had dismantled at the Peak.

"He'd never hurt an innocent child," I said.

A cop had been calling to Niles through a bullhorn, and at that moment, he bellowed back. "You might get us, you fuckin' commie gooks, but a lot of you are gonna meet your creator today. Semper fi, motherfuckers!"

And then there came a little voice. "Mommy!"

The chief went back to the walkie-talkie. "Sniper one, do you have a clear shot?"

There was a crackle, then, "Negative. Glass doors open, but curtains closed." The chief looked at me.

"Jake—that's your name, right?" I nodded. He leaned close. "Does he have a weapon?"

I froze, and I thought about the kids. "Yes," I said reluctantly. "He has a knife. A big one."

The chief lifted the walkie-talkie again. "Snipers one, two, and three, the suspect is armed and dangerous. If you get the shot, it's a go."

My heart sank. Did I just kill Niles?

72

"You can't do this. He's not in his right mind. He's fighting in 'Nam, and those kids are his buddies, his marines. He'd never hurt them. He'd die for them. Let me go up there. He'll listen to me."

The chief shook his head. "Don't need another hostage."

Janice was crying again. Danny slowly shook his head, turned around, and walked away. He'd seen enough.

"Thanks for the help, Jake," Barry said. "It's about the kids now." I wanted to punch him in the face.

With a tilt of his head, Farnsworth directed Marroni and me to the other side of the indoor pool building, out of earshot of everyone else.

"They don't know about the secret staircase from the basement under the restaurant, where they store the liquor."

"We can cause a scene at the side door," Marroni said, "so you can get up to the second floor. But there's probably a cop there, too."

I had to try.

They went back to the action, and I went inside, careful to steer clear of the windows. Through the doorway, I saw a cop standing in front of the stairs to the basement.

"Hey, you two," he shouted, "can't you see we have a situation here?"

"You mean the restaurant is closed, too?" Farnsworth whined.

"Where in hell are we supposed to get breakfast?" Marroni yelled.

The cop walked toward them, and I hustled down to the basement. I could make out the boxes of liquor but not much else, so I felt my way around as my eyes adjusted to the dark. When I found the stairs, I crept up, sure my pounding heart would give me away. At the second floor, I opened the door.

A cop, crouching in the hallway, whipped around and pointed his gun at my chest. "Who the fuck are you?" His voice was shaking.

I froze with my hands up. *See you later, Mom.*

"I'm here to help," I managed, "to make sure no one gets hurt. Or killed."

He reached for his walkie-talkie.

"No," I pleaded. "Don't call. That guy in there is my friend. He's a vet, and right now he's back in 'Nam. Those kids are the buddies he held when they cried out with their last breaths."

The cop paused, the walkie-talkie still raised.

"They're gonna kill him. And he thinks he's still fighting the war he didn't want any part of. He'll never surrender to you, but he'll listen to me."

The gun was still trained on my chest.

"For the love of God, let me give him new orders. If you make that call, another marine will die in that war."

The cop lowered both hands. "I was a marine," he said. "I did 'Nam."

He put his finger to his lips and together we crept down the hall until we heard the kids on the other side of a door.

"Don't worry, buddies," Niles was telling them, "I'll get you home. Just hang in there. Semper fi!"

The cop nodded at the door then took two steps backward and stood against the wall with both arms outstretched, clutching the pistol. I knocked.

"Sergeant Niles?" The room went quiet. I knocked again.

"What's the password?" he called out. The cop looked really nervous. Slowly, I raised and lowered my hand, telling him it would be all right, remembering the nickname Niles had given me at the Peak.

"Blue Dolphin," I answered.

"Kinda busy here," he said. "Surrounded on all perimeters."

"I'm here to relieve you and your men. The men outside are friendly. Repeat, friendly. The war's over, Niles. You and your men are going home."

He unlocked the door. It opened slowly, and there he stood, tears streaming down his charcoaled face. My mouth opened, but no words came out.

He stepped into the hall and reached out to me with one arm behind his back. Standing between Niles and the cop, I hugged him. I heard a thud on the carpet. Niles had dropped the knife.

I hugged my friend as the cop cuffed him and called for help. I leaned against the wall and slid down until I was sitting. It was over.

The hallway filled with cops. Two frisked Niles, and one kicked his legs apart.

"Go easy!" I yelled. "He's a vet."

The cop who'd helped offered his hand. "Daniel."

I stood up and shook. "Thanks for not shooting us, Daniel."

"Balls, man. You've got balls." He turned and took Niles by the arm.

Niles looked at me, then down at the floor, then at me again. "Is it true?" he asked. "Is it over?"

"I hope so, Niles. I really hope it's over."

"We'll take care of him," Daniel said. "Semper fi, brother."

He led Niles down the hall as the other cops ushered the kids to their waiting families. A cheer went up from the crowd outside.

Marroni and Farnsworth emerged from the stairway and walked on either side of me, their arms around my shoulders.

"Hungry?" Marroni asked, and we all laughed. Inside, though, I was crying.

73

Kelli's sad eyes met mine when Marroni, Farnsworth, and I walked into Reception.

She got it.

In the sales pit, Barry stopped talking as the three of us took our seats, then said, "Jake, everyone knows what happened. Anything you want to say?"

The faces all around me reflected sincere sorrow.

"It's Labor Day weekend," I said, "the last big hurrah. The show must go on. What's the SPIF?"

After a brief silence, the room filled with applause. Barry looked at me, his expression serious, and then put out a good SPIF. Niles would want nothing more. And wherever he ended up, he'd put on a show of his own.

The meeting broke, and some reps murmured "congratulations" as others patted my shoulder. Soon it was just Marroni, Farnsworth, and me sitting in front of Barry.

"Saw the knife," he said. "Big knife. Nothing scares me more. That took guts."

"Thanks," I said, "but I knew Niles would never hurt me."

Kelli stuck her head into the room. "Jake, some people are here to see you."

A bunch of kids were in Reception, their parents gathered behind them. One little girl stood in front of the rest.

"Mr. Jake," she said, "we want to thank you for saving us from that man."

I crouched so we were at eye level. "You were all very brave. That man was confused. He didn't know what he was doing, but he never would have hurt you."

She reached out to me, and the other kids circled in a group hug. When I stood, the parents hugged me too, one by one. Tears streamed down Kelli's face. Even Marroni and Farnsworth looked choked up.

The room was filling with new UPs, and after a bit we all got back to business. Once the sales machine was in motion, it didn't stop. Labor Day weekend was busy, and soon I was on tour with Al and Hazel. As we walked by the pool, Danny gave me a thumbs-up from the bar. People on the crowded lounge chairs stared at me, even pointed. Some tilted their heads and recounted the day's events to one another.

As we toured the Castle, a guy came over and stuck out his hand.

"Good job this morning," he said, and then he looked to Al and Hazel. "This guy's a hero—a real hero."

When he walked away, my clients asked what he'd meant.

"Some kids were in trouble," I told them, "and I helped."

Al and Hazel grew more skeptical as others interrupted the tour with accolades. When we finally sat at the round table, they pried the full story out of me. Al reached across the table, took the pen from my hand, and filled out the worksheet himself.

"Sign us up. We want to be part of something that includes people like you."

I had thought the morning's events would be best left alone, but I was wrong. When I brought the worksheet and check to the office, Janice smiled.

"We're proud of you, Jake. And we hope Niles will be okay." Even Robby gave me a thumbs-up.

After I finished the paperwork, Marroni stopped me as I walked across the pool deck. "Nice work this morning, pal. Everyone appreciates what you did."

He introduced me to the guy he was pitching, who held out his hand. "Brave thing you did for your friend, and for those kids. I'm proud to meet you." Soon Marroni was on his way to the contract office.

Sales continued all day; the Castle buzzed. Something had happened, and everyone wanted to be part of it. A lot of money was generated. I sure made my share.

When the day finally drew to a close, Marroni, Farnsworth, and I headed back to the Barracks. On the tennis courts, the kids had resumed their game.

74

My room seemed different. Empty. And it was. Camille's note was on the nightstand.

> Dearest Jake, Thanks for a great summer. Had so much fun being with you, but it's time to move on. I'll always love you. And I was so proud of you this morning.

I sat on the bed and felt … nothing. Not happy, not sad. Just empty.

But after a few minutes, my thoughts returned to the day's sales and I went to find the guys.

Doug and Akers were in the hallway. "What you did this morning was crazy," Doug said as he shook my hand. "You probably saved Niles's life."

Akers smiled sheepishly. "Good tours today. I got a big sale." Akers was an idiot.

Farnsworth and Marroni joined us. "Let's go to Rose's for a bite," Marroni said, "on me."

Doug shook his head. "No, tonight's on me."

Marroni laughed. "Even better."

On the way to the bus, I stopped. "You guys go ahead. I'll meet you there."

"You okay?" Marroni asked. "Need help with anything?"

I shook my head. "I've got to do this by myself."

75

When they left, I headed to Niles's room. I packed his clothes, gathered his paychecks, and looked around to make sure I hadn't missed anything. Holding his green duffel bag, I looked around at the empty room. "See you around, brother. I hope it's really over for you."

With his stuff safely stashed in my room, I walked to Rose's. The cool bite in the air felt good, and the sky was awash with fall colors as the sun ducked behind clouds on the horizon. Camille was gone, Niles and the kids were safe, but all I focused on was sales. The day could have been a disaster on so many fronts, but it hadn't been. *Why?*

Somewhere along the open stretch to Rose's, I got the answer. A situation could be interpreted in a variety of ways. It's the salesman's job to paint the picture that works to his advantage. Is it a cloud or a silver lining? A glass half-full or half-empty? Sales is about seizing the moment, taking control.

The guys were at a table, and Brown was with them.

"Way to go, Jake," Aaron called. "That was really something."

I waved. Small town. Word travels fast.

"Just got back," Brown said when I joined the table. "Heard you saved the day."

I expected something stupid to follow but was pleasantly surprised. He left it at that.

"Camille coming?" Marroni whispered.

I shook my head.

"She's packed and gone."

He looked blank.

"It's all good," I told him. "It was time."

Aaron came to the table with another round. "What'll it be tonight, champ?"

I ordered a Cape Codder as Farnsworth sipped his. The table was oddly silent. Everyone was drained.

After a gulp of my drink, I broke the quiet. "Today's sales didn't just happen. It wasn't dumb luck. We did something different. Anybody know what it was?"

Brown didn't disappoint. "Better UPs?"

No one else took a shot, so I continued. "We have tools—the directory, the story, the beach—but today I discovered another tool: the in-house members at the resort. They were proud to know us. The UPs trusted them. That's why we did so well."

I raised my glass. "To the living, breathing pitch book."

Marroni grinned, but Doug looked confused. "What happened today doesn't happen every day."

Farnsworth cleared his throat. "But I see it. Get to know the in-house crowd, buy them beers at the bar, and then use them during the tours. Even if they don't interact directly, point them out, tell their stories."

Brown didn't get it, so Marroni spelled it out. "John and Mary, you're both in the medical field. See that guy reading over there? He's a doctor from Chelmsford."

"What if John and Mary are truckers?" Brown asked, true to form.

"For fuck's sake," Marroni said, "then make the guy a trucker. Mold the pitch."

"But what if they end up talking?" Doug asked.

"It's all about control, Douggie," I said. "We have to use all the tools. Pictures and words are fine, but living, breathing proof? It doesn't get any better than that." My head was spinning. I was done for the day.

"What's everyone doing when the Castle shuts down?" Farnsworth asked after we ordered dinner. "Weekends will be okay through September, but October will be slow except for Halloween weekend."

"What happens on Halloween weekend?" I asked.

Farnsworth smiled. "You haven't heard? The owners come for free, and they're encouraged to bring friends."

"So the resort's filled with members and guests," Doug said. "So what?"

"So it's reload time," I told him. "Sell the members more time, and pitching their guests is like shooting fish in a barrel."

Farnsworth nodded, sipping his drink. "The whole town turns into one huge party. Big parade. The king's a girl—"

Marroni cut him off, slapping his leg. "Let me guess. The queen's a guy."

76

The tab was modest for our group—no expensive wine or champagne. Doug paid it happily and then went into town with Brown and Farnsworth. Marroni and I walked back to the Barracks. He was unusually quiet, and that was fine with me. My mind was numb.

He followed me into my room and sat in the only chair while I rolled a joint.

"She didn't have much stuff," I said, "but the place sure seems empty."

"What happened?"

I shrugged. "She left a note. Said 'See you. Thanks for everything.'"

"Probably for the best."

I must have looked confused, because he continued. "We've had a good run here, buddy, especially you. But it's time to figure out the next move. In another month, we're homeless and unemployed. Better to be on your own. Travel light."

"I'm good with it. We had fun while it lasted. Guess I shouldn't have fallen so hard for a girl Farnsworth met in the bathroom." Marroni left the room laughing.

Noticing a light on in the room across the hall, I opened the door. Tomola had been there. The only reminder of Niles was the stale smell of cigarettes.

All sorts of people were vanishing. Like a light switch flipped off, the town went quiet after Labor Day. Even the sky was different, with wispy clouds hung high. Breezes were chilly and nights were cool. The people looked different, too—more serious, focused on the task at hand. Close it up.

Weekdays at the Castle were slow, but weekends were busy. Sales were good on sunny days, terrible when it was rainy and cold. For people with money, the place was great. Restaurants weren't crowded, streets were empty, and the sunsets were surely painted by God's hand.

More and more, I felt lonely. Camille was part of it, but I missed the action, too, the excitement. I was a hunter on grounds with no game, a fisherman on waters with no fish. Gradually the sales crew took off, most without so much as a good-bye. The cream of the crop stayed, picking off a deal here or there, making a living, but nothing more.

The in-house guests at the Castle were an older group of retirees, adding to the quiet. Bill and Edna Thomas showed up with their friends and invited me to dinner a few times, but I always found an excuse. Marroni made frequent trips to Framingham, searching for employment, working only weekends at the Castle. Sweets and Becky moved into an oceanfront suite. Barry did, too, and more and more often I saw Janice heading to or from his place. Farnsworth and Brown made plans to tow the sailboat to the Florida Keys to work at Matecumbe Resort on Islamorada. The days were quiet—most were dead—and the sun was setting earlier and earlier each day.

One morning after Donna poured my coffee, I picked up a directory and paged through the resorts, pausing when I got to Las Vegas. At the end of that day, I went to my room and pulled the knife from under the mattress. Concealing it inside the sleeve of my jacket, I walked downtown and to the end of the wharf. I looked at it one last time before throwing it into the ocean. Camille was right. It had been quite a ride, but it was time to move on.

SECTION IV |
| Las Vegas

The Hacienda / Roll of the dice

77

"You can always come back if it doesn't work out," Marroni said as we drove over the Cape Cod Canal. The last time I crossed the Sagamore Bridge, I was arriving, a lifetime ago. Now I was leaving, excited, scared, but, most of all, sad. I loved Cape Cod.

At Logan Airport, I pulled the backpack from the trunk and Marroni opened his arms.

"Thanks for the lift," I said, hugging him. "Remember, I'll be at the Hacienda Resort and Casino."

"You bet," he said, and then he frowned. "Be careful. Those hotels weren't built because people won big money."

I wasn't concerned. Gambling wasn't an issue.

Backpack checked and cash stashed in my pockets, I settled into my seat on the plane. Just a few days earlier, I'd told Barry I was leaving the Castle. He was good enough about it, thanked me for my support and for a job well done. He recommended a resort, and I took the phone to make some calls. In no time, I'd reached Mr. Roy Corkem, vice president of Sales at the Hacienda, through his toll-free number.

Roy told me the resort had just added three hundred rooms and was pushing time-share sales. I'd have to get myself there, and the hotel would put me up for a week; then it was up to me to find housing. Just like that, I had a job in Las Vegas.

As the plane made its way cross-country, I noticed a newspaper tucked into the seatback in front of me. *Oh, shit. September 20. Mom's birthday.*

When we landed, I knew I was in the right city. Slot machines were everywhere—even the bathroom. Leaving the terminal and the *ching-ching* behind, I caught a cab to the Hacienda. Vegas was everything I'd imagined. Even in daylight, the place was electric.

"First time to Vegas?" the cabbie asked.

"Yep. Gonna sell at the Hacienda."

"You with the time-share group?"

I nodded.

"I think it's a great concept. But I sure don't understand how they can afford to give all that stuff away. And to pay me just for sending people to their show." He held a brochure up to the rearview mirror. "They pay me twenty dollars to send people to their sales center. They give away show tickets, and other stuff, just for attending a presentation. Sounds a little fishy, if you ask me."

As I took the brochure, the Hacienda's version of the OPC, thinking of Bruce barking and slurping up the puddle made me smile.

Corvettes, Porsches, Ferraris, and limos were everywhere. I could smell money. Only later did I realize the cabbie turned a ten-minute ride into a half-hour trip. Welcome to the money grab.

Donna Summer's hit "Dim All the Lights" blared through the speakers as we drove past world-famous casinos—The Stardust, Golden Nugget, Aladdin's, Caesars—each bigger and fancier than the last. The Dunes Hotel's massive sign boasted headliners Lou Rawls and Natalie Cole. I'd quickly gone from a white shark to a minnow.

The cabbie shouted over his shoulder and pointed. "MGM Grand, crown jewel of the Strip, twenty-three stories with two thousand rooms!"

Twenty-five dollars later, we'd arrived. Peering out the window, I looked up at an enormous neon sign of a horse and rider that towered over the hotel. Below it, old letters advertised that Redd Foxx, star of the hit TV show Sanford and Sons, was performing his stand-up at the hotel.

A young guy wearing a red suit opened my door, welcomed me, and offered to help with my pack as I slung it over my shoulder. He held out his hand, and I gave him a three-dollar tip. He wasn't impressed, but what the hell? He opened a door.

Inside the grand entrance, slot machines chimed and scantily clad waitresses carried trays loaded with cocktails to packed gaming tables. I expected a glitzy, high-rolling, well-dressed crowd, but I was wrong. Elderly people sat at the blackjack and roulette tables. Their parents played the slots.

A pleasant girl at a reception desk greeted me at the back of the casino. She didn't recognize Roy Corkem's name. When I said I was a new rep, she pointed to a door posted "Sales Center."

Inside, the action was on. The sound system blasted Supertramp's new hit "Take the Long Way Home." Presentations were in progress at about fifty round tables, and the reps were practically yelling to be heard above the music. A few guys in well-tailored suits strolled around, standing behind UPs, making hand gestures. Each rep answered with a slight nod, all the while continuing the pitch. The room buzzed.

The suits occasionally sauntered over to a big guy in a white suit to exchange a few words. Must be the boss.

I headed toward him but was intercepted on the way. "Can I help you?" asked a suit.

I introduced myself and explained that I was looking for Roy Corkem. As I spoke, the music died down and an announcement blared: "Ladies and gentlemen, fasten your seatbelts. The Hacienda of world-famous Las Vegas is about to launch you into the future, on a journey that will guarantee incredible vacation experiences for you and your family. You will now be able to provide champagne holidays on a beer budget!"

The reps and UPs all stood and headed for the casino. The room fell quiet, and the suit again asked what I wanted. When I told him, he turned and walked to Mr. White, who seemed to glare at me as the suit talked. I wasn't feeling warm and fuzzy.

Mr. White left the room, and the suit returned. "You'll find Mr. Corkem on the thirteenth floor," he said smugly.

What an attitude. "Where is that? I just got here. Don't know my way around."

"Where exactly did you come from?" You would've thought I'd insulted his family.

"Provincetown, Cape Cod. The Sandcastle Resort."

"Figures." He smirked and pointed toward the elevators.

People called out their floors on the crowded elevator. "Thirteenth, please," I said.

Seven or eight people turned. Some smiled; others looked pissed off. The place was nuts.

"No such thing," said the guy standing next to me. "Unlucky number. They don't use it."

He was right. The suit and Mr. White were screwing with me.

78

◈

After riding back down to the lobby, I found a concierge who directed me to the administration offices in the building next door. After I introduced myself to the receptionist, she gave me a once-over and motioned toward a seat in the waiting room. A few moments later, I followed her to a door that read "Roy Corkem, Vice President." At his desk sat a fortysomething gray-haired Roy Corkem.

He stood and offered his hand, "Jake Arril," he said. "Welcome to Las Vegas."

Finally, a friendly face.

"Please, sit." He gestured toward a leather chair. "Pretty casual clothes, Jake. Am I looking at Cape Cod?"

I hadn't thought about my wardrobe, but I flashed a wad of cash. "This is what I'll wear tomorrow, Roy. Wanted to get the lay of the land, see what works."

He headed for the door. "Let's get you settled. There's one more show this afternoon. Maybe you can shadow a tour, see what we're all about."

I followed him through the lobby and down the hall to a hotel room. Stunned by the shag carpet and outdated bedspread, I had a feeling Redd Foxx wasn't on this floor.

"You're only here for a week," he said. "This'll do. It's clean, with daily maid service, and it's a quick trip to work."

It was the Las Vegas version of the Barracks.

"No one stays in the room, anyway," he added. "The action is downstairs and on the Strip."

"It'll do. The price is right."

He smiled and turned for the door.

"Roy, I won't make a habit of it, but can I make a call? It's Mom's birthday."

He hesitated but then nodded. "Get cleaned up," he said. "Meet me in the sales center in thirty minutes." He paused at the door. "If you need anything, you can come to me. Anything."

The second "anything" made me uncomfortable.

As I unpacked, I realized Roy was right. I'd have to kick the wardrobe up a notch. I hung my suit coat, a couple of shirts, and a pair of pants in the bathroom. I turned on the hot shower, hoping to steam out a few wrinkles. I sat on the edge of the bed and stared out the window overlooking the crowded pool. Lounge chairs, pool bar, smoking barbecue—it was like the Castle, but bigger.

The phone rang twice. "Coach here."

"How's it going, Dad?"

"Good to hear from you, Jake. Must be cold on the cape."

I paused. "Actually, Dad, I'm in Las Vegas. Just got here today. The cape was slowing down."

The phone went silent, then I heard him talking to Mom. "It's your son. For Christmas's sake, he's in Las Vegas."

She took the phone.

"Wanted to wish you a happy birthday, Mom. You have to see this place. Redd Foxx is staying here, putting on a show in the casino every night."

Again the phone got quiet. "Be careful, honey," she said finally. "And make sure you stay warm."

I laughed. "It's hot here, Mom. I'm looking at hundreds of people in bathing suits. But listen, I love you. Happy birthday."

"No moss growing under your feet, honey. Be careful, Jake, and thank you for calling. Love you."

I held on to the phone for a few seconds after she hung up, suddenly feeling alone. After getting dressed, I paused in front of the mirror. The outfit wasn't perfect, still a little wrinkled, but it would have to do. I laughed again, thinking of the last time I'd worn the sport jacket, and then stashed most of my cash under the mattress.

On my way to meet Roy, I saw the reps filing into the theater, their tours completed. Everything was big here, even the women's hair, and a lot of the guys wore cowboy hats and string ties. It sure was country western.

Since Mr. White and the suit hadn't exactly welcomed me, I didn't barge into the show. I hung around the casino, and when a loud cheer went up at one of the roulette tables, I walked over.

The dealer removed all the chips except the stack on twenty-eight, which he counted. He slid two towers of red chips in front an overweight middle-aged man whose polka-dot shirt was drenched in sweat. He cheerfully tossed one back to the dealer, giving him his tip.

"Not bad," said a guy next to me. "Hundred-dollar tip."

"How much did that guy just win?" I asked. I'd never been in a casino.

"Pays thirty-five to one to hit the number dead on. He had a thousand dollars on the table."

"You mean he won a thousand?"

He shook his head. "Nope, he bet a thousand."

"You mean he won thirty-five thousand?"

"Welcome to Vegas."

No wonder the big guy was sweating. Roy tapped my shoulder. He was shorter than he looked in his office but cut a good figure in a three-piece suit.

"C'mon," he said. "Last show of the day. Our best speaker is on stage."

In the theater, reps and UPs sat at one hundred round tables covered with white cloths. As we took seats in the back, the lights dimmed and the loudspeaker boomed. "Ladies and gentlemen, the Hacienda of world-famous Las Vegas is proud to present Mr. Billy Best, the original Marlboro Man!" The iconic ad of the cowboy on his horse filled a huge screen. The Marlboro theme song filled the theater.

Wearing a cowboy hat, out walked Billy Best. The music died down, and under a spotlight, the show began. He started by warming up the tours, but instead of the one-on-one I was used to, he was pitching to one hundred UPs. I was amazed. The spotlight jumped from one table to the next. Each rep would stand, introduce their UPs by name, and share a quirky comment about the couple. After each introduction, the audience erupted in a thunderous applause.

"Does your family deserve to stay in the Hacienda's luxurious suites?" Billy Best's voice echoed through the room.

After each yes, the room erupted again. The UPs cherished their five minutes of fame under the spotlight. The show finished with a standing ovation. Each rep then went to work on a close, drawing a line down the center of a sheet of paper, another across the top. The left side was filled with the benefits of joining, with the only possible objection—money—on the other. The T close. Brilliant.

There was excitement in the air. The benefits of joining outweighed the rest. The only factor left was cost.

The rep would stand and shout for a worksheet, creating the illusion that a sale was made. In on the game, the other reps would applaud, resulting in a round of cheers from the room. Little did the UPs know that a worksheet didn't guarantee a sale. But that was the game; it was all about the hype.

As rep after rep yelled for worksheets, the place whipped into a frenzy. Everyone was joining. I'd seen it on a small scale at Jiminy Peak, with Niles's antics during the barbecue that got him fired. But this was Vegas.

Soon an army of good-looking girls brought packages to the tables—paperwork for the new owners.

"Does this happen every show?" I asked.

Roy nodded. "Five times a day, seven days a week."

I did some quick calculations. They were doing more than a million dollars a week.

Roy and I walked out to the casino floor, through Reception, and into Mr. White's office. The title on the door was marked "HMFIC." Whatever that means.

Roy introduced me to the man sitting behind the desk, Mr. White. To his left stood Billy Best, sales manager and orator extraordinaire. To his right was the suit, Tommy Winn, second in command.

"That was quite a show, Billy," I said as I extended my hand. "You guys have got it down."

He looked at Winn, then back to me. "You can call me Mr. Best, got it?"

I thought he was joking, but no one else laughed. Slowly, I pulled my hand back.

Best leaned back in his chair. "Where did Roy find you?"

I felt attacked. "I flew across the country to work here. Just finished a season at the Sandcastle, Cape Cod."

Again he looked at Winn and back at me. "You mean Provincetown, don't you?"

"Same thing. Provincetown is Cape Cod."

Best leaned forward. "Sales meeting is at ten. Be here and be ready."

I followed Roy to the door. No handshaking here. As we left, I swore I heard Winn say, "Fags."

Pricks.

"Nice couple of guys," I said to Roy.

He didn't smile. "Jake, Vegas is full of sharks. Eat or get eaten. I get the attitude too. Every day."

I shrugged. "I'm here to make money, not to win a popularity contest."

"I've gotta go," he said. "Two things. First, you need a non-gaming employee license. Second, spruce up the clothes. They'll bust your balls if you don't."

"Where do I get the license? What's it for?"

He looked surprised. "Go downtown to the police department. They'll run a background check, make sure you don't have a record, and take a photo."

This place is tough.

79

It didn't take long for me to realize that casinos weren't designed for spectators. At a roulette table, I handed the dealer three hundred-dollar bills. He gave me two stacks of ten-dollar chips, fifteen in each. Everyone around me scrambled to frantically match their chips with lucky numbers. I leaned over and placed a chip on twenty-eight, Coach's baseball number.

The ball clattered, and the wheel began to slow. The dealer waved his hand across the board. "No more bets."

When the ball came to rest, he called "Black twenty-eight" and put thirty-five more chips in front of me! I'd hit my first bet in Vegas.

The gent next to me nodded toward my chips. "Nice bet." He had a pretty good stack himself.

"Beginner's luck." I told him.

"Hope it's not the most expensive bet you ever make."

Not having a clue what he meant, I put a few more chips on the table.

Twenty minutes later, I pulled out three more hundred-dollar bills. The last seven spins had eaten the original three hundred plus my winnings. The gent just kept playing, minding his own business.

An hour after that, I decided to call it quits. I'd lost track of the money, but I'd spent a lot. When I got up, the gent looked at me sadly. I understood what he'd said earlier.

It was 9:00 p.m., midnight on the East Coast, and I hadn't eaten all day. I checked out the restaurants, passing up a high-end steakhouse for an all-you-can-eat $2.95 buffet. The long line moved slowly. Slot machines lined the path to the buffet, almost as if they were saying, "You wanna eat? Feed me first."

I reached into my pocket and counted what was left. Six hundred dollars. I still didn't know how much I'd lost, because I didn't know how much I had when I started.

A waitress walked up and down the line, providing change for the slots. Almost everyone played, including me, and by the time I reached the buffet, I'd dropped another forty dollars. It was a pretty expensive three-dollar dinner, but I couldn't complain about the food. Monster roast beef, salads, pasta, chicken, seafood, desserts … I devoured the meal and thought about seconds but took a walk instead.

In a nearby men's clothing store, I chose two suits: one blue, one brown. Looking into the full-length mirror, I noticed the salesman staring at my shoes. I looked down too and laughed at the topsiders.

A pair of black dress shoes later, I forked over $552, leaving myself with $7. I'd probably dropped a couple thousand dollars in a few hours. But I wasn't worried. Money was everywhere.

The front desk of the casino was busy. Pretty girls waited at the exit while the crowd left Redd Foxx's show. They were offering gifts as an incentive to attend the next day's sales presentation. Each salesgirl held a clear blue plastic clock that had dice numbers on it. Pretty smart marketing.

The sales center was lit, but considering my earlier welcome, I didn't go in. I passed a roulette table as the ball came to rest on the double green zero, and I knew what the next number would be. I don't know how I knew, but I did.

The ball spun as I swapped my seven dollars for chips and placed my bet. "Black twenty-eight!" the dealer called.

I won a couple hundred, but I wasn't happy. In fact, I was pissed off. Where was the number when I was betting big bucks?

This place is nuts. Even when you win, you lose.

80

Morning came too early, and the line at the buffet made me decide against breakfast. The casino was busy, and so was the front desk. I headed to the sales center.

The reps were a wide range of characters, men and women of all ages wearing formal suits and dresses. I poured a cup of coffee and introduced myself to a few people, getting less-than-friendly responses. Everyone in this town had an attitude.

I was sitting in the pit with the other reps when a round of applause erupted. Billy Best and Tommy Winn came out of the office. "Good morning to those of you who are here to make money," Best began. "Those of you who plan to hang out and drink coffee, get the fuck out of our way!" I could've sworn he was looking at me.

A recap of the previous day brought more applause. The results were impressive—if they were real. Best wrapped up the meeting announcing the SPIF. The top producer over the next two weeks would receive two front-row seats at Caesars Palace on October 3.

The place went crazy. Best turned to Winn, who was preparing for the presentation, and asked, "Who are you going to be today?"

"Ladies and gentlemen," Winn said, "the Hacienda is pleased to welcome Mr. Tommy Winn, the new low-flying, high-speed record holder in a single-engine aircraft!" He bowed.

The reps cheered as a good-looking woman yelled, "How fast were you going?"

"As fast as you want, sweetheart!"

The crowd laughed as a string of receptionists appeared, calling names and handing out UP sheets. The reps scrambled, collecting papers and heading to Reception to pluck tours from the crowd.

"What's with the SPIF?" I asked a young guy. "What's going on at Caesars Palace on the third?"

He looked at me as if I were from another planet. "Ali fights Holmes. Biggest event of the year. Those seats are five hundred a pop—if you can get them."

Muhammad Ali. Going for the heavyweight world championship. For the fourth time. This place isn't fooling around.

A receptionist called my name and handed me paperwork.

"I'm new," I told her. "Got here yesterday."

"Just following Mr. Winn's orders," she said, but then she softened. "Go to Reception, bring the UPs in here for the warm-up. Once you're done, join everyone for the tour of the model suite, then go to the theater. Good luck."

It was the first help I'd been offered in Vegas. I headed to Reception. The young couple waiting for me were wearing blue jeans and matching plaid shirts. I tried not to prejudge, but her missing front tooth paired with his dirty fingernails made optimism tough.

They had driven from Tennessee to spend three days here on their honeymoon in a "great" trailer park complex on the outskirts of town. When I asked about their vacation habits, they stared at me blankly; this was the first time they'd left home. During the next half hour, I learned about the lives of tobacco pickers with three children ages two, four, and seven. That was remarkable, considering she was twenty-one years old.

Finally, the announcement came to begin the tour. Walking the path outside, I felt like a shepherd tending the flock. My new friends were clearly intimidated as we entered the two-bedroom model suite. She marveled at the three televisions. He explained that their trailer back home didn't have electricity.

Christ, the bikers at Jiminy Peak were a better shot.

Back at the theater, after a half-hour improv by Winn, the music started. I did my best, writing out the advantages of joining, doubtful they had gas money to get home.

Thank God it ended. I didn't see any need to call for help, so I read the survey sheet until the room was done selling. In the upper right corner, on a line marked "Source," were the handwritten letters "TPT."

Quite a few sales were announced, and that was encouraging. Not exactly the start I had at the Sandcastle, but hey, nowhere to go but up.

The dealing quieted down, and the reps exited the theater. Standing in the gifting line with my UP, I realized that new members were being gifted Hacienda dice clocks and a free dinner. My couple got a pass for two at the buffet, a six-dollar value, and they were happy.

Another crowd gathered for the next show as I went into the sales area, where the reps who'd scored were high-fiving. I looked around the room and noticed a girl in her midtwenties approach my table; her soft blonde curls danced as she walked toward me. She held out her hand.

"Cassandra," she said. "Cassy."

"Jake Arril. Glad to meet you."

She was pissed off. "That prick is gonna do whatever it takes to make me quit because I won't sleep with him. All I get these days are goddamn TPTs! If I was selling hundred-dollar bills for a buck, they couldn't come up with the buck!"

"What's a TPT?" I asked. "It was on my survey sheet."

Cassy frowned. "Trailer park trash. Some genius figured out that the guests at Jim-Bob's backwoods freakin' trailer park will stay here all day if you throw them a free lunch. Christ, I'm afraid I'll catch a disease from half of them."

I laughed, and after a second, she did too. Over her shoulder, I looked at Mr. White's closed door. "What does HMFIC stand for?" I asked.

She frowned again. "You mean that bastard who's doing this to me? That's his way of telling us he's the Head Motherfucker in Charge. Cute, huh?"

The door opened, and Winn carried a pile of survey sheets to Reception. On the way back, he made a beeline for our table.

"Who do you think you are," he asked me, "not calling a TO before gifting?"

I was onto his game, but I knew a confrontation would end badly for me, so I nodded like a puppy. "Won't happen again, Mr. Winn, sir; I'll call you to every table I have. You're right, I probably let that one slip right through my fingers."

He looked confused, unsure whether I was screwing with him or not.

He headed back to the office but turned to look at me again before going inside.

Cassy giggled. "That was great! Junior prick just had his head stuck up his ass and doesn't know it!"

The same receptionist came over and handed us sheets, whispering, "Sorry."

Written in the right corner of both surveys was "TPT."

Cassy sighed. "Break out the Lysol and the bug spray. This is going to be a long day."

She smiled as we started for Reception. "When this nightmare ends, Jake Arril, why don't you meet me at the pool bar? We'll pick the bugs off each other."

I smiled back. "Are you asking me out, Daisy Mae?"

81

After dragging around four straight TPTs, I knew management was screwing with me. No one had that kind of bad luck—except Cassy. I was hungry, but the nonstop shows didn't allow for lunch. Best and Winn had their catered lunches wheeled into the office, making a point to leave the door open. All I could do was take the next tour and try to revive the dead.

Winn met every NQ I was dealt, and he enjoyed belittling me each time.

"I hope Jean here was courteous today," he'd say. "He's on probation with the sales team, so if you have any complaints, please tell Reception."

Then he'd turn to me and smile. "We'll let you know when the gifting center opens. You guys have fun until then."

I was developing a strong dislike for the guy.

Cassy passed by throughout the day, dousing me with an imaginary spray can. When the final tour was underway, I walked to the suite with TPT number five in tow. Hearing a commotion, I turned to see a guy running across the lawn toward us. Chasing him were two uniformed cops, guns in hand.

One cop took aim, fired, and kept firing.

I hit the ground hard, knocking the breath out of myself. And then I heard the applause. The hit TV show Vegas was filming. Robert Ulrich, playing Detective Dan Tanna, leaned over the fallen guy and cuffed him.

I stood and looked around sheepishly. "Bet you think I thought that was real," I said to the people staring. Grass stains covered half the clothes I'd just bought.

Cassy tried to stifle her laughter. I took a bow.

The day was a wash. No sales and half my wardrobe destroyed. In the sales center, Winn reminded me to get my non-gaming license from the police. *Great.*

Back at my room, I changed into fresh clothes and grabbed some cash. The sun was setting as I walked to the pool bar, the palm trees throwing shadows on the deck. A band played Christopher Cross's *Sailing*. Beautiful.

Speaking of beautiful, Cassy tapped my shoulder as I drank a beer at the bar.

Grinning, I asked, "Did you get all the bugs off in the shower?"

She tossed an imaginary critter over her shoulder. "The pool works better. Chlorine kills 'em dead."

"Makes sense. What are you drinking?"

"Beer's fine."

She'd changed into what looked like a jogging outfit, the top exposing one shoulder, a blue bandanna covering the top of her head. Casual and classy.

"What do you think of Sin City so far?" she asked.

"Well, I lost money gambling, got screwed on the line, made an ass of myself on tour, and right now I'm so hungry I could eat a horse."

"All in one day. Not bad." She got off the barstool. "I swear this place makes me itchy. Come on, I'll show you the town."

A black convertible Mustang pulled up as we stood on the red carpet at the entrance, and a valet wearing the red Hacienda jacket opened the driver's door. "If you ever get tired of this steed, Cassy, let me know. She'd look great in my barn."

Cassy handed him a few bills, laughing. "Thanks, Jimmy, I'll remember that."

The top was down, the windows up. She pulled the stick shift into gear and hit the gas. In the side-view mirror, Jimmy laughed.

"He loves it when I do that," she said.

A greenish tint in the sky blended into a thin orange line on the horizon as we sped toward an oasis of light.

"What do you feel like eating?" Cassy shouted.

"Big steak," I yelled back.

She became a tour guide when the traffic slowed to a crawl, pointing out the Flamingo, the Dunes, the Tropicana, all lit with a staggering number of colored lights. At Caesars Palace, we turned into a driveway encircling a pool filled with magnificent Roman statues. Fountains shot geysers of water forty feet into the air. Cassy pulled up to the front door under a huge pillared overhang, and a valet hustled to open her door.

"Welcome, Miss Cassy."

She knew his name too, and quietly handed him money while I stood gawking at the sights.

"Should have seen the act out here last week," she said. "What a mess."

"What happened?"

She shook her head. "Stunt guy tried to jump the pool on a motorcycle, but he didn't time the fountain."

I looked at her as a geyser blew fifty feet in the air. "Don't tell me the fountain hit him in the ass."

She nodded. "And he nailed one of the statues. The blood in the pool was gross."

I looked back at the scene. "Did he die?"

"No, but he broke a lot of bones." She took my hand. "Come on, this is the best steakhouse in Vegas."

The place was night-and-day compared to the Hacienda. The casino looked like a Hollywood set, with white marble statues, dealers in tuxedos, and decked-out patrons who packed the tables.

Plumes of bluish smoke drifted above the tables as both men and women puffed on cigars. Toga-clad waitresses filled glasses with expensive champagne. A valet opened the restaurant door.

"Good evening, Miss Cassy," he said. "Welcome back."

She smiled. "Thanks, Billy. Would you tell George I'd like to see him?"

In no time, a gray-haired guy in a tuxedo hurried out. "Good to see you, Cassy," he gushed. "What can I do for you?"

"George, this is my friend Jake. It's his first time in Vegas, and I wanted to bring him to the finest restaurant in the world."

George turned to me. "Mr. Jake, it's a pleasure to meet you. Any friend of Cassy's is a friend of ours. Welcome to Caesar's Fire."

He seemed to size me up. "I'll bet a forty-two long will do the trick," he said, and he then disappeared to the rear of the restaurant, which was the most high-end establishment I'd ever been in. The staff wore variously colored tuxedo jackets: black for order-takers, white for servers, yellow for bartenders. The place smelled great.

Shortly, George returned with two sport jackets, one white, one blue. "Your choice, Mr. Jake." I looked at Cassy for help.

"Definitely not white," she said.

I laughed and put the blue one on. No run-of-the-mill jacket, it fit like a glove.

"George, you're a love," Cassy said. "Thank you."

"It's my pleasure," he responded. "Let me show you to your table."

Hope I brought enough cash.

We slid into a back booth, the wall covered with autographed photos of Dean Martin, Ann-Margret, and other celebrities.

"Will anyone else be joining you this evening?" George asked.

Cassy shook her head, George snapped his fingers, and a young guy removed the chairs on the other side of the table.

"Anything you need, Cassy, let me know," George said. "Anything." He looked up at the wall. "Only yesterday, you were that little girl who loved butter mints. Do you remember reaching into my pocket for them?"

Cassy looked embarrassed, but she smiled. "Of course, Georgie. How could I forget?"

He looked pleased as he took his leave. A girl in a white tuxedo filled our water glasses, and a young man in a blue jacket delivered a basket of assorted breads. They kept coming, different coats bringing different treats. The place was off the charts, and Cassy was clearly enjoying herself as we made small talk. Soon a middle-aged guy in a black tux carried two large leather-backed menus to the table. Handing Cassy one, he said, "I already know what the princess will have."

She grinned. "No need to fix what's not broken, Allen."

He asked if I knew what I wanted.

Opening the menu, I shook my head. Allen smiled. "Are we hungry tonight?" I nodded enthusiastically.

"We just got a shipment of fresh lobster in from Maine," he said. "And the Texas aged beef is our specialty, fire-seared with a peppercorn sauce that's to die for. But take your time. In the meantime, Mr. George has sent a bottle of our finest bubbly to the table—compliments of the house, of course." Turning to Cassy, he asked, "May I pour?"

She smiled, and the cork popped.

He turned to me. "Take your time. There's no hurry."

"What are you having?" I asked. "Sounds like it's a given."

She grinned. "A salad—Caesar, of course—and two shrimp cocktails. And for dessert, chocolate cheesecake."

The menu didn't list any prices. I decided on a steak and salad. Allen returned, nodded at my choice, took the menus, and left.

I raised my glass of bubbly. "To UPs who have electricity."

"And indoor plumbing," Cassy added. In the photo behind her, a little girl in pigtails stood with an elder man in front of a twin-engine aircraft. I noticed the bottom was signed "J. P." and, scribbled in crayon, "Cassy."

"George meant it when he said this is your table. Is the good-looking guy your dad?"

She blushed. "We always ate here when I was little, but he's so busy now I don't get to see him much."

Our salads arrived as the piano player segued into *New York, New York*. People at other tables began to applaud as George ushered a group inside. Wearing a tux with a white scarf and dark glasses, a guy in the center looked in our direction, spoke to George, and then headed toward us as his entourage continued to a table.

"Cassy," he said, his arms open. "Good to see you, sweetheart."

She stood and hugged him, kissing his cheek. "Hi, Uncle Frank."

He took a step back, his hands on her shoulders. "You are as beautiful as your mother. Is your father with you?"

She shook her head. "Uncle Frank, meet my friend Jake." Setting my napkin down, I stood and shook his hand.

"You taking good care of my girl, young man?" He seemed serious.

Not knowing what to say, I nodded.

He flashed a million-dollar smile and patted my shoulder. "Let me know if you need anything, Cassy. Say hi to your father, enjoy your dinner, and don't eat too much cheesecake."

He walked across the restaurant to join his party, shaking hands at tables along the way.

"Was that who I think it was?" I asked.

Cassy smiled. "My Uncle Frank. Not my real uncle, but I've called him that since I was a little girl."

Clearly, she wanted to let it go at that, so I did.

Who is this girl?

82

Allen returned with the bill in a small leather folder. I reached for it with one hand, digging into my pocket with the other, but Cassy snatched it.

"My treat," she said. "I asked you out, remember?"

Over my objections, she signed the bill without looking at it, then returned the pen to Allen. He picked up the half-empty bottle. "Want me to send this upstairs?"

She nodded and thanked him. George caught up with us as we walked toward the door, asking if the meal was up to par, and Cassy hugged him. I thanked him and started to take off the jacket. He put his hand on my shoulder. "Keep it," he said. "It's cool outside, and I'm sure you two are going to walk around for a while."

He was right. Cassy and I walked down the driveway arm-in-arm, past a naked Roman statue with no head.

"Don't tell me the guy on the motorcycle decapitated that thing."

She laughed and shook her head, then rested it on my shoulder as we walked in silence to the Strip. She was a mystery, but an easy mystery. When we passed the MGM's glittering Donna Summer sign, she said "I'd suggest we go in, but I don't want to risk ruining a perfect evening. The prick lives here."

"You mean Mr. White?" She nodded.

I pulled her closer, and we walked on in the wonderland, amid the lights and the cooling desert air, me and this beautiful girl. *Magic.*

We walked for hours, listening to musicians, stopping occasionally to take in a street act. When we found ourselves back in front of the fountains at Caesars, we watched the water fall from the sky into the lit pool. She turned to face me. I looked into her eyes.

She tilted her head. Our kiss was long and deep.

She stepped back and took my hand. I let her lead, up the driveway, through the casino, to an elevator marked *Private*. She opened it with a key, pushed the only button, and we went up slowly. At the end of the hall, she used a different key to open the door.

All I could say was "Wow."

We walked across the huge room to a wall of glass overlooking the Las Vegas Strip. She poured the champagne and we sipped, taking in the fantasy below, until she took both glasses and led me down the hallway to her bedroom.

She touched my face and whispered, "Are you all right with this?"

I hugged her and whispered back, "Do you have electricity and indoor plumbing?"

83

As daylight crept across the sky, I looked down at the Strip. A procession of cabs pulled up to the entrance, some dropping off early arrivals, others picking up all-nighters. It was true: Vegas never sleeps.

There was a knock on the door. A white-jacketed Hispanic man wheeled a cart covered with a white linen tablecloth into the room. He removed the cloth, revealing silver-domed plates, polished cutlery, and a solitary long-stemmed rose. He seemed pleased with his tip, and when he left, I wheeled the cart into the bedroom.

Cassy scrunched her nose when I tickled her with the rose, and then opened her eyes. "You cooked breakfast," she said. "How sweet."

"Too bad this place doesn't have room service."

She eyed the rose. "For anyone special?"

"Naw."

She chased me around the place with a pillow until I surrendered on the couch and gave her the flower. She filled the empty champagne bottle with melted ice from the bucket and triumphantly set the arrangement on a glass table. Then she tugged on my hand until I stood. She rested her head against my chest.

"Better eat," I said. "I've got to jump a cab back to the Hacienda for another day of fun at the factory."

She scrunched her nose again. "Today's my day off, thank God." And then she brightened. "Hey, don't you need to get your license at the police station? I'll go with you, and we'll make a day of it. You know how long paperwork can take."

She was excited, and the plan made sense. Roy insisted I get my license. I'd take the day off.

"We'll grab a bathing suit for you downstairs," she said. "I want to show you a cool place."

We wheeled the breakfast cart into the living room and ate, took a long shower, and went to a gift shop. The casino was packed—action everywhere.

Ten minutes later, we pulled up to the Las Vegas Sheriff's Department. "Hope this goes okay," I said.

"It's no sweat, honey. Everybody gets one. Unless you're a criminal or something."

"That's the worry," I mumbled.

The building was packed. Cassy disappeared and came back with a sheriff in tow.

"Jake, this is Sheriff Thomas. He'll get the license for you."

This girl has connections everywhere.

Twenty minutes later, holding my non-gaming photo ID, I shook the sheriff's hand. He sent a big hello to Cassy's dad.

"Thanks, Cassy," I said as we drove away. "I was nervous about that. I could use a beer or two."

She laughed. "Good. We're going to the best bar by a damn sight."

The best bar in this town must be pretty special.

We left Las Vegas and drove through the desert heat. "Good thing we brought our bathing suits," I said.

"Patience," she answered. "We'll be there soon."

We drove southeast for a half hour, then climbed a ridge. When we crested, a body of water stretched in front of us as far as the eye could see.

"My God," I said, "where did this come from?"

She looked over her sunglasses. "Good thing we brought the suits?"

"Okay, okay."

Soon we parked at a small marina. "Hey, darlin'" yelled a big guy wearing cowboy boots, blue jeans, and a Hawaiian shirt. "How's my gal?"

Cassy hugged him and introduced Slim, who had a strong handshake.

"I've had that name for a long time," he said. "Actually was slim, once upon a dream."

I laughed with him as he turned back to Cassy. "Got your message. Everything's on the boat. Have fun."

The view was incredible—a river cut into a canyon. At the fuel dock was an eighteen-foot baby blue Donzi speedboat named *Sassy*. I covered my eyes and moaned. "How classy, Cassy has Sassy."

"Oh, shut up," she said. "By the way, can you swim?"

I laughed. "Just came from old Cape Cod."

84

Cassy pushed the throttle and we jetted into blue-green water nestled in a canyon surrounded by purple and green mountains. It was beautiful. And she was beautiful, her dark hair flowing down her back.

"Wanna drive?" she asked.

I took the wheel but kept her in front of me as I guided the boat. She pointed out a white streak on the mountains about three feet above the waterline. She explained that the lake's water level had dropped in recent years, revealing the bleached rock.

We took our time exploring hidden coves, enjoying the scenery. We spent the afternoon lying in the back of the Donzi, drifting under the hot sun. I was amazed to find such peace and quiet. With my eyes closed, the soft breeze and gentle sway felt good. Moments later, a tap on my shoulder interrupted the serenity.

"Come on, let's go. I want to show you something."

She pulled my arm and headed to the wheel, where we took our seats. She hit the throttle and sped toward a massive concrete structure. Slowing down, she turned off the engine, reached into a red cooler and pulled out two beers.

"Hoover Dam," she said. "Largest in the world. Powers Las Vegas."

She handed me a cold one, and we toasted. "Told you we'd have a beer at the best bar by a dam site."

We ate lunch in a secluded cove and spent what was left of the day swimming and sunbathing. When the sun began to set, we went back to the marina and tied up.

"Want to grab something to eat?" she asked.

"Sure thing, but I need to stop at the Hacienda for a change of clothes."

"Why don't I drop you off and pick you up in an hour?"

After a quick shower and change, I grabbed some cash and went down to the casino. As I stood near a roulette table, I felt a tap on my shoulder.

"Mr. Arril," Winn said, "if you're not too busy playing tourist, I'd like a minute of your time."

I followed him to the sales office. Best was in his office, yelling into the phone. "I don't give a fuck! My job is to bring in the money! Don't mess with me, Roy. You know who runs this place." He slammed the phone down.

Winn stood with his hands on his hips. "Are we paying for your room here?" I nodded.

"Do you have a job here?"

I pulled the license from my pocket. "Roy told me to get it, so I did."

He jabbed his finger in my face. "Do things like that on your own time. During the day, your ass is mine."

I wanted to deck him. "Just trying to do what you guys want. I'm here to make money, that's all, but I don't stand a chance with what you're giving me."

My voice summoned Best out of his office, arms folded across his chest. "What does that mean, exactly?"

"Those TPTs you're feeding me are from the land of the living dead. I've spent the last year pitching at two different resorts, consistently at the top of the line. All I want is a fair shot."

Best sneered. "Then take the tours we give you and find the money. Sometimes you have to eat a shit sandwich. You don't have to like it; just eat it."

He turned to go back into his office, muttering. I swear he said, "faggot."

"Arril," Winn said, "ten guys are lined up to take your spot. Don't do us any favors by staying. Your type never cuts it anyway."

The guy was pushing all my buttons, and frankly, I didn't get it. *Your type?*

"You'll never fit in here," he added. "Your type is too soft."

What the hell was he talking about? I wanted to knock his lights out, but I sucked it up and walked away, pissed off. I understood pricks like Charlie and Herbie; with them it was all about control. But Best and Winn were just a couple of dickheads.

I was lost in thought in front of a roulette table when I felt another tap on my shoulder. I spun around with my fists clenched.

Cassy stepped back quickly. "Easy, tiger, it's just me."

I held my open hands up to her. "Damn, Cassy, I'm sorry. Just had a run-in with those assholes in the sales office. Let's get out of here before I do something stupid."

She took my hand, and we walked toward the door. I looked back at the salesroom, and there they were, standing in the doorway, staring at us.

"Great," I muttered. "Now they'll turn the heat up on you."

Soon we were driving down the Strip. "Look," I said, "if I'm gonna cause you any more problems, I can be on the next flight out."

She gave me a look. "Don't worry about me. I can handle myself."

"They've had it out for me since I got here, but why do they keep picking on you, Cassy? Don't they know who you are? And with your connections, why do you put up with it?"

"I pretty much keep to myself, Jake. I don't use what you call my 'connections.' I stand on my own two feet. They're just punks—little boys with little toys. Let it go at that."

I took a deep breath.

"Did you have fun today?" she asked.

"It was great. It's always great with you."

"That's the nicest thing anyone's said to me in a long time."

I looked out my window, not seeing anything. "I mean it."

She asked what I wanted for dinner, but my appetite was gone.

"Whatever you want," I said. "Your choice."

She was trying to lighten the mood, but I had a lot on my mind. For one, my free accommodations would run out in three days. I put my hand over my face and groaned.

"Snap out of it, Jake. Everything's gonna be fine."

She was right, and I knew it. Look at what happened after Jiminy Peak. And I still had a whack of cash, just in case.

She pulled into a little restaurant with a red neon sign, Luigi's, and happily took my hand. Inside, the smell of oregano, garlic, and everything Italian hung in the air.

An older gentleman called out from behind the bar. "Bella, come give me a kiss!"

Everyone loved her. After the double-cheek kiss, she said, "Luigi, meet my friend Jake."

The guy's handshake felt as if he worked with steel, not pasta. He led us to a table against the wall in the back. "Sit with your friends and family," he said.

Guess who was in the photos.

He winked at Cassy. "Same as always, bella?" She looked at me. "Large pizza, extra pepperoni?" I smiled.

Luigi left to put in the order and returned quickly with a bottle of red wine. "This is from the village where I was born," he said proudly, "in Italy."

"Can't ask for anything better than that." He filled our glasses. After a sip, I said, "That's the best red wine I've ever had."

Looking pleased, he left us to take care of a couple who'd settled in at the bar.

My thoughts went back to the job. "Don't you get hungry during the workday?" I asked. "The buffet takes forever, and there's no time to go out."

"Most reps brown-bag it," she said, "and down something between shows. Did you notice the fridge in the corner of the salesroom?" I hadn't.

A little old Italian lady wearing an apron over her dress ceremoniously placed a huge, steaming pizza on the table. Cassy stood and hugged her. "Momma, you're as beautiful as ever!"

The little lady beamed, and tears welled up in her eyes. "No, Bella, it is you who is beautiful. Let me look at you."

"Don't you start crying, Momma," Cassy said. "She's happy and safe in heaven, not sick anymore."

Momma dabbed her eyes with a napkin. "Extra pepperoni so you can pick off, like when you were a little girl."

Cassy turned to me. "Jake, this is Luigi's wife, Momma." She wiped her hand on her apron and held it out to me.

"Nice to meet you, signora," I said. "The pizza smells great."

She blushed. "You call me Momma."

"Okay, Ma-Ma."

She gave Cassy the double-cheek kiss before returning to the kitchen. In those few moments, I'd learned that Cassy's mom had been sick and passed away. Everything I knew about her I learned from what other people said.

As we ate, Cassy picked up pepperoni slices, held them above her head, and dropped them into her mouth like a little kid. After a slice too many, I leaned back, stuffed, looking at the half that remained.

"That was one big pie. And really good."

"Take the rest," she said. "Have it for lunch tomorrow."

Momma wrapped the slices and put them in a brown paper bag, the Italian flag and "Luigi's" printed on the side. When I asked for the check, it seemed I'd insulted her. Cassy and I hugged her and went to the bar to thank Luigi. He pointed to the bag. "Lunch tomorrow?"

I laughed. "If it makes it home."

Cassy asked whether I felt like doing anything, but my mind was spinning again. Vegas was either a great time or a disaster, nothing in the middle.

"Better head back and get ready for tomorrow," I said. "Those guys have it in for me, and I want to be on my game."

She patted my leg before I got out of the car at the Hacienda. I walked to the driver's side, leaned in, and we kissed.

"It will all be fine, Jake," she said. "Trust me."

She smiled, and I watched her drive away. I wasn't so sure.

85

The second show was exiting the theater, and the sales center was busy. The girls at the front desk worked hard to generate tours. These UPs were buying, and I needed to get my hands on them. I'd die with the TPTs.

A well-dressed couple walked past the desk and sat at a roulette table. I took a chair next to them, exchanged cash for chips, and asked if they'd seen the show. The Jordans were from Wellesley, as it turned out, the town next to Natick. Gene, Pat, and I became fast friends.

As the dealer spun the wheel and the ball bounced around, we placed our bets. I learned that the Jordans came to Vegas every year, staying at the MGM. They were thrilled when I told them I'd come from Cape Cod.

We didn't win. "Don't get excited," I whispered to Gene, "but I know the next number. Wait until the ball is rolling, and then follow my lead." To my surprise, he nodded.

I put four green chips, fifty dollars each, on black twenty-eight. Gene didn't move.

I looked at the ball, at him, and then at the ball again. The wheel slowed.

Gene placed a stack of chips on top of mine just as the dealer waved his hand over the table. The ball kept bouncing, from one number to the next, and then finally settled.

Applause erupted around us.

"Black twenty-eight!" the dealer yelled. He seemed happy until his manager showed up, who didn't seem pleased at all.

Gene slapped me on the back as the dealer confirmed the payout with the manager and handed over a stack of black and purple chips. Gene had won more than $17,000! Without a word, he tossed a black chip on the table for the dealer. I tossed a green chip.

"I'm going to the cashier," Gene said, "then I want to buy you a drink. Okay with you?"

I followed him to the cashier's counter, where he collected a two-inch-thick pack of hundred-dollar bills. Gene hugged Pat as they waited for me to get my cash.

"Let's take a cab back to the MGM," he said. "We'll celebrate."

"Let's grab a drink here," I suggested. "Big day tomorrow. And it starts early."

Once we were seated in a club overlooking the casino, I put the question to Gene. "You meet someone at a roulette table, and the madman tells you to place a bet. Not only do you bet, but you bet big. What made you do it?"

They both smiled, but it was Pat who answered. "Jake, we've been coming here for twelve years and have never won anything. We're not big gamblers. We set aside an amount to lose, and when that's gone, we're finished."

Gene took over. "We're pretty consistent. We reach our limit after four or five days, and that's that. The last two times we were here, someone told me about a hunch, like you did tonight, but I didn't bet. I told Pat that the next time it happened, I would. So there it is. In thirty seconds, we won all our money back from Vegas, thanks to you."

"Right place at the right time," I said. "Do you believe in fate?"

"I do now," Pat replied. "What are the odds of meeting someone from back home who would tell us the winning number?"

"Your luck is just beginning" I told them.

Gene looked confused.

We'd all ordered vodka with cranberry juice, and as we sipped, I started the pitch. An hour and a half and a few cocktails later, with help from a borrowed pen and a lot of napkins, Dr. Gene Jordan and his wife Pat were sold on the program. They were perfect UPs: Vegas, Cape Cod, winter trips down south—it all made sense.

Gene covered a yawn and checked his watch. "What a night," he said. "Better grab a cab and head back."

I thought the shot at a sale had vanished until Pat piped up. "So where do we go from here? How do we join?"

Gene looked at her, then nodded at me. It was time to close the deal.

"If you're comfortable," I said, "I recommend two weeks during high season in a one-bedroom. Use one week here, the other on Cape Cod or down south. The weeks would cost about eighty-five hundred each, the total equaling the amount you won tonight."

Pat laughed. "See what I mean about fate? We came here to see a show and won our vacations for life."

"If I give you a deposit now, can we meet in the morning to do the paperwork?" Gene asked.

I took a clean napkin and wrote up the deal.

"We're going to lake Mead tomorrow," Gene said, "and leaving the next day, so we're going to be busy." He handed me a $3,000 deposit.

I walked them to the door and, after a handshake from Gene and a hug from Pat, headed to my room. Finally, the curse was broken. Yet another way to skin the cat.

As I waited for the elevator, I realized the pen I'd borrowed from a waitress was still in my pocket. When I found her in the bar, she held up a finger and disappeared through double doors, returning with a paper bag. Luigi's pizza—tomorrow's lunch. I'd completely forgotten it at the table.

I reached into my pocket, surprised to find a few green chips I hadn't cashed in, and handed her one.

"Do you know this is fifty dollars?" she asked.

I nodded.

"You must really love pizza."

86

The next morning, with a new ID, lunch, and the Jordans' cash deposit, I was good to go. The casino was busy, as usual. I put the bag inside the refrigerator in the sales center and turned to find Best and Winn watching.

"I've got a deal," I said. "Where can I find a worksheet?"

There were no high-fives. Winn pointed to the receptionist.

Cassy joined me while I was filling out the forms. "What's up?" she asked. "Did you get a deal?"

I was about to tell her about it when the receptionist walked over. "Jake, the Jordans are at Reception for you."

I nodded. "Who do I ask about paperwork?"

"I'll have one of the girls meet you in the theater," she said. "Is the worksheet signed?"

I shook my head and looked down at the napkin.

She laughed. "Just sit at a table. We'll be there in a minute."

I gave Cassy a thumbs-up, went to find the Jordans, and did a quick recap of the numbers. They signed and counted out another $14,000.

As a secretary took over, I shook hands with both of them. I explained that I had to leave for a meeting but would try to see them before they left Vegas. Simple. No problems. Gotta love fate.

After the meeting, I went to Reception to greet my UPs, expecting to see TPT in the corner of the survey. I was surprised to see Gene and Pat inside the theater, talking to Best. Seeing me, he shook their hands and walked away.

After seating my UPs, I approached the Jordans. "Everything okay?"

They looked concerned. "Just got the third degree on how we met, Jake," Gene said. "That guy's a real prick."

"A real prick," Pat repeated.

"Can't say I disagree. But he is the sales manager. Part of his job is marketing, finding out where new members heard about us. Don't worry; I'm your contact. If you ever need anything, call on the toll-free number."

They nodded, and we shook hands a final time.

What the hell? Was Best trying to blow the deal? Management or not, you don't talk to another guy's sale. You don't just barge in like that.

I rejoined my UPs—bona fide, true-to- the-core TPTs—and the look on Cassy's face told me she had the same. When I found myself next to her in the suite, I whispered, "Dinner's on me tonight. You pick the spot."

The next speaker was billed as having led the last successful expedition to the South Pole. He stood about five feet tall and must have weighed in at 250. *Any seals left alive down there?*

The second tour went from bad to bad-er. I gave my couple their dinner vouchers and then, remembering the pizza, went to the fridge. The bag was gone. I soon spotted a Luigi's bag on Best's desk.

Did the prick actually steal my lunch? I couldn't bring myself to believe it so passed it off as coincidence. Maybe Cassy took it.

When the workday finally ended, all deals were on the board except mine, so I began to chalk up the numbers.

"Hey!" Winn yelled. "What do you think you're doing?" I used the chalk to point at the board, then at myself.

"No one touches the board," he said. "Only real deals go up there."

I'd had enough. "A seventeen-thousand-dollar cash sale isn't a real deal?" Other reps were listening.

"Only sales that come from the line are counted," he said. "Not mystery deals that fall from the sky."

Some reps were on his side—the insiders, the ones making money. No one gave a damn what the TPT handlers thought. The opinion of the sheep didn't matter.

I ignored all of them.

I didn't see Cassy for the rest of that day. Or night.

87

Days went by. No Cassy.

I found a small apartment across the road from the Hacienda, in a two-story complex with a grass courtyard. Seven hundred a month up front got me a clean, furnished one-bedroom with a small kitchen. The manager, Agnes, had an uncanny ability to let her cigarette burn to the filter without the ash falling off. Whether walking her mutt in the morning or sitting on the lawn chair outside her first-floor apartment, the old lady constantly had a cigarette burning to the core, ash intact. One of life's great mysteries.

I'd get up early to grab breakfast at the buffet and sneak out a sandwich wrapped in a napkin for lunch. But most of the time, when I went to the fridge, my lunch was gone. I didn't know whether it was Best or Winn, but it was one of them.

After four days, I took a cab to Caesars after work. George said he hadn't seen Cassy since our dinner there, so I took another cab and asked Luigi and Momma if they'd seen her. Momma nodded toward a back booth.

Cassy was sitting alone. I draped a napkin across my arm and walked to her table. In my best Italian accent, I asked, "What would you like for dinner miss?" She looked up and started to cry. I sat, taking her hand in mine.

"What's wrong, Cassy? I've been looking for you."

Her eyes were red. "I thought you left, without so much as a good-bye. I went to the casino and heard you'd checked out. I left messages in the sales center for you."

I was floored. "You disappeared, vanished. I thought we were supposed to go for dinner the other night. I had to move. The pricks didn't give me any messages. I had no idea how to reach you. Christ, I don't even know your last name." I sighed, looking into her sad eyes. "I missed you. Why aren't you going to work? I kept hoping you'd show up. I didn't know what to think."

She frowned. "I'd just had enough. In the middle of the tour with those flea-bitten TPTs, the guy wants to take a crap in the suite. I lead them downstairs to the public restrooms and then notice the woman can't close her purse. She'd stolen too many rolls of toilet paper!"

I couldn't help it. I busted up.

"So I just give them the vouchers, and that fucking Winn starts yelling at me in front of everyone. I told him I was done and walked out. I thought things might get easier for you if I wasn't around. After a few days, I tried to reach you, but couldn't."

She started crying again. I sat next to her in the booth and put my arm around her.

She rested her head on my shoulder and sighed.

"Toilet paper," I said. "That's pretty low. My biggest problem is lunch."

She tilted her head to look at me. "Lunch?"

"Either Best or Winn. One of them keeps eating my lunch."

She giggled. "You're kidding, right?"

I shook my head. "They started with Luigi's pizza. Now it doesn't matter; whatever I bring disappears."

She laughed. "What planet are those guys from?" I had to laugh, too.

She lowered her voice. "Do you know Winn's last name isn't Winn?"

"That's probably true with Best, too, the Marlboro Man. And, for Christ's sake, the fat Antarctic explorer."

"Winn's real last name is Winston," she said, "and there's a warrant out for him in California for selling drugs."

I wondered how she knew all this, but Momma had come to the table. "Ah, Bella, is that my baby laughing again?"

Cassy kissed my cheek. "It was all a mistake, Momma. It's good now."

Momma smiled. "Anyone hungry?"

"I'm starving," I told Momma. "Missed my lunch."

Cassy cracked up. Momma didn't understand, but she laughed because Cassy did. She said something in Italian and left us.

As independent as Cassy was, there was a vulnerable side to her. I moved to the other side of the table. Facing her, I took both her hands again. "I'm sorry these guys put you through this. You don't deserve it."

She smiled. "Thanks. Not many accept me just for me, but you do."

I held on to her hands until Momma delivered a shrimp-and-pasta feast.

As we ate, Cassy cheered up. "I'm going to get that son of a bitch," she said at one point, "just on principle. Don't see how I can get Best, though, that pompous pig."

I laughed. "Guys like that always get what they deserve. Let's enjoy the meal; at least we found each other."

She stabbed the plate with her fork. "Take that, you little shrimp!"

We were both laughing when Momma came back to the table. "You want anything else? Maybe a nice espresso?"

Cassy looked at me. "Want anything, Jake?"

"Would you make me a lunch for work tomorrow?" Momma nodded enthusiastically and asked what I wanted.

"A big roll, with lettuce, tomato, and lots of onions."

Momma frowned. "No meat?"

I shook my head.

"Is this payback?" Cassy asked.

"You could call it that," I told her.

Momma came back a few minutes later with the sandwich in a bag. "I wrap twice so onion doesn't stink. You sure this is sandwich you want?"

I nodded and thanked her. Again she refused my money, and we left.

"What's next?" Cassy asked.

I wanted to put the sandwich in the fridge, so we drove to my apartment. It wasn't exactly the penthouse at Caesars, but Cassy didn't comment. She wrapped her arms around my neck, and we kissed.

"You're welcome to stay with me," she said, lowering her arms to my waist. "Don't get me wrong. There's nothing wrong with …"

I put my finger on her mouth. "Thanks," I whispered, kissing her again.

She took a step back and started to unbutton her blouse.

"Excuse me, miss, do you have a reservation?"

She laughed. "None at all."

Later, lying with her head on my shoulder, she said, "Nice view."

Beaming through the unit's one window was a full moon. At that moment, I couldn't imagine any place I'd rather be.

The next morning, after showering with Cassy, I dressed and grabbed the sandwich from the fridge. She wrinkled her nose. "If you're going to sit next to me tonight, bring lots of breath mints."

I laughed. "Don't worry. I won't need them."

I spotted Agnes as we walked to the car. "Nice nightie, gorgeous," I called. "Sexy."

She touched her hair. "Norma Jean had nothing on me. Not in my prime, anyway."

The mutt was taking his morning crap on the lawn. Cassy gagged. "Ewww. Gross. So much for breakfast."

"That's lunch," I said. I stood by the driver's door and leaned over to kiss her.

"Will you come with me tonight?" she asked.

"Where?"

She looked surprised. "To the fight. Ali and Holmes."

Of course. I leafed through an imaginary calendar. "Let's see what else I have planned."

She laughed as she backed out. "Pick you up at six. Say hi to the TPTs!"

She sped down the Strip, waving through the open roof, as I found a stick on the lawn. I knelt and unwrapped the sandwich—the onion smell was strong—and looked around at the piles of dog shit. Should I serve the freshest stuff, or maybe something aged a bit? Tough decision.

Finally, because I thought I might otherwise throw up, I chose a day-old heap. The stick rolled the whole pile onto the bun, and I fought off a gag as I gently squeezed the sandwich together. After double-wrapping the prize, I went to work.

The receptionist who'd been kind a few days earlier said, "Good morning."

"Morning, Kate," I said. "Think my luck will change today?"

She frowned. "What they're doing to you is wrong. I've seen this before."

I smiled. "Every dog has his day."

I put the mystery sandwich in the fridge and could feel Best and Winn watching. Best smiled and went into his office. Nothing like Luigi's for lunch.

After the meeting, Kate looked sad as she handed me the sheet. It was the same old thing, but I wasn't focused on sales. I was waiting for the bomb to drop. I checked the fridge, and there it was, screaming, "Eat me, you bastard!"

When I returned from my second tour, the sales center door was closed. Hacienda maintenance were busy scrubbing the carpet in front of the casino.

The whole section was taped off like a crime scene.

The rat had taken the bait.

88

"It was nuts!" Kate gushed. "Someone screamed. Mr. Best came running from his office, puking his guts out. He puked more than I thought anyone could puke. Christ, he puked all the way out of the casino!"

I shook my head. "Probably something he ate."

"All shows are canceled," she said. "It'll take days to clean up the mess. It smells like shit!"

"Onions," I said.

She nodded. "Shit and onions."

As I walked out of the casino, I realized Kate wasn't kidding. The crowds were all but gone. Workers were scrubbing the floor all the way to the front doors. I asked a little old lady at a slot machine what had happened.

"A stunt," she said, feeding the machine nickels with a lit cigarette in her mouth. "You know Vegas. Just a show. Overdone, if you ask me. No one could puke that much."

Wondering how much the casino was losing, I asked a valet what had happened.

He looked crazed. "You'd have thought a bomb went off. Dude comes running out, yelling, 'Shit, shit, shit!' Puked the whole casino. Everyone left in a hurry. Fucking place smells like shit."

"And onions," I added.

He agreed.

I walked across the road to my apartment, nervous about whether or not there'd be trouble—as in cops. Nailing Billy Best was one thing; blowing out the casino, another. The stunt had proved more than I'd bargained for.

I wondered whether I'd killed the prick. I'd poisoned him, for sure.

It would be a reach to say I liked my lunch that way, but how would he sound? He stole someone's shit sandwich and then puked all over Las Vegas.

At 6:00 p.m. sharp, Cassy pulled up in front of the apartment. It was the first time I'd seen her dressed up. Wearing a black cocktail dress, her long brown hair slicked in a tight bun, she was stunning.

"Wow. With the way you look, no one's gonna pay attention to the fight."

She giggled. "You clean up nice yourself."

I leaned over for a kiss and headed to Caesars to witness the greatest fighter of all time.

"How was your day?" she asked as we drove down the strip.

I didn't know where to start.

"Why are you smiling?" she prodded. "What happened, Jake?"

I didn't sugarcoat the story, and she laughed so hard I was afraid she'd drive off the road. Every few seconds, she'd turn to look at me and say, "No way! You didn't!" I couldn't remember anyone being so happy. She really hated the guy.

"One down, one to go," she said. "It's the grossest thing I've ever heard, but he deserved it, and not just because of you and me. He's a shithead."

We both broke up as she realized what she'd said. "It's one thing to *hear* the shit coming out of his mouth," I added, "another to see it."

"He really puked all the way to the front doors?"

I nodded. "Who knows how much of the sandwich he ate. Must have been quite a bit."

"I wish I'd seen his face when he figured it out," she said, and then she paused. "On second thought, I guess it's a memory I can live without."

"Onions," I said, and she winced.

89

Cassy slipped her arm through mine as we walked through the lobby and into the packed casino. The high rollers were in town for the fight. Dressed in expensive suits and gowns, they tossed big money around as if it were nothing. We walked around, taking in the sights, hearing an occasional roar from the winning tables.

A group of five played blackjack, two on either side of a bald guy. One whispered to the bald one, who turned and met my eyes. Marvin *Hagler*. The last time I'd seen him was in Provincetown, before Brown ended up unconscious on the floor.

I looked to the first guy, who'd rocked Brown, and then back at Hagler. He looked at me, at Cassy, at me again. And then he nodded.

I was glad the middleweight champion of the world wasn't nursing a grudge.

"Well, well, how do you know Marvin?" Cassy asked.

"We spent some quality time together in a pool hall once." She looked confused. "He trains in Provincetown," I told her, "and I've seen him around."

As we passed a roulette table, the ball stopped on the green double zero. "Watch this," I said.

I put $500 on the table and asked for one chip. The dealer handed it to me and slid the cash into the table's opening. As the wheel slowed, I reached out and placed the chip on my number. The ball landed on black 28.

And then it popped out. Black 26.

Cassy shrugged. "Almost."

"Looks like a black night. Bet the winner of the fight will be black too. Do you think everyone here is going?"

She nodded. "The hotel sold out months ago."

"But there are thousands. How big is the arena?"

She took my hand. "Come on. It's about time to head to our seats anyway."

We didn't go to the entrance everyone else used, but to a private door flanked by two armed guards. One said, "Evening, miss. Enjoy the fight."

"Thanks, Brian," Cassy answered. "Should be quite the show. Hope you can see some of it."

"Working security ringside, thanks to your father."

"Good. You deserve it."

We found ourselves outside in an area that combined a parking lot with a ton of tennis courts. "The resort puts up this temporary stadium for events like this," she said. "Takes fifty guys three weeks to set up. Seats twenty-six thousand Incredible, don't you think?"

It was. It was also hot. "Okay to take off my jacket? Might melt if I don't."

She laughed. "Be comfortable, honey. And by the way, you look nice."

I was wearing my plaid jacket over a dress shirt, with jeans and cowboy boots, nothing special. Our reserved seats were on the floor, five rows back from the ring.

"Is this the best we can do?" I asked. "Look at those stools inside the ring. We could put them next to each other and see what's going on."

Cassy punched my arm.

Hollywood had come to Vegas for the event. The stadium filled quickly, and the crowd was full of familiar faces. It was surreal.

Cassy was unfazed. She turned, hearing a nearby voice call her name. "When are you coming back to the beach?"

She shrugged at Tom Selleck and blew him a kiss. He held a hand to his ear, telling her to call.

"You know Magnum?"

She laughed. "We have a place in Hawaii. He's a family friend."

Of course he is.

90

The lights around the stadium dimmed and fireworks lit up the sky as the announcer boomed, "Ladies and gentlemen …"

First came Ali, trying to regain the championship for the fourth time, his entourage following him to the ring. The crowd went nuts, chanting, "Ali! Ali! Ali!"

His trainer lifted a rope, and Ali climbed into the ring, dancing, throwing punches, and yelling, "I'm the greatest! He's mine in nine!"

Muhammad Ali. I actually got goose bumps.

Next came Larry Holmes, current world heavyweight champ and Ali's ex–sparring partner.

Photographers and reporters filled the front rows around the ring. Howard Cosell spoke into a handheld microphone as the two fighters came to the center of the ring, listened to instructions from the referee, then returned to their corners.

People in front of us stood to make way for an entourage surrounding a massive gray afro that could only belong to one person—Don King.

The bell rang. The fighters met midring and tapped gloves. With a quick snap of his wrist, Holmes tagged Ali right in the face.

The sound of the glove making contact was unbelievable. It was all crazy: thudding body shots, the crowd's roar, trainers yelling from the corners. I'd been in a few fights, but Holmes's first shot would've put me into a coma. The bombs he landed as the fight went on would've killed a horse.

The fight was scheduled for fifteen three- minute rounds. Between the third and fourth, Cassy looked down the row and waved. Uncle Frank blew her a kiss.

The fight was, in a word, sad. Ali was getting his ass kicked. As the blows rained down on him, it seemed his arms were getting heavier and heavier. By the ninth round, he was just about helpless. Blood ran down his face from a cut on one cheek, his left eye was swollen shut, and his right was starting to close.

The chant began when the bell rang to start the tenth. "Ali! Ali! Ali!" It continued through the entire round.

Ali almost went down a few times. Even though I was rooting for him, enough was enough. He could get really hurt. Or worse.

As he went to the corner and sat on the stool, one trainer screamed, "Come on, champ! You're the greatest. You can beat this guy!"

But a trainer I recognized, Angelo Dundee, threw a white towel into the ring.

When the other trainer argued, Dundee raised his voice. "I said, 'It's over.'"

I pointed at Holmes and leaned into Cassy. "Am I seeing this right?"

She looked at him and nodded. The champ, with his corner crew whooping it up, sat with tears streaming down his face, staring at Ali.

Man, what a show of respect.

The two fighters went to the ring center as Holmes was declared the winner by TKO. He hugged Ali, raised his hands above his head, and went back to the corner.

The fighters left the stadium, and the crowd chanted "Ali!" long after he was gone. The sound system played "My Way" as we followed the crowd back to the casino and into the lobby. Cassy was beaming. "Did you enjoy that?"

I shook my head. "Nah. Kind of boring." She took my arm. "Hungry?"

"One condition," I said as we walked toward the restaurant. "My treat."

91

Cassy nodded and waved a few times as George seated us at her table. Hollywood's who's who was already in the restaurant.

"What are you expecting tomorrow?" she asked.

I took a deep breath. "We'll just have to see what happens. Whatever it is, it is."

"There should be more fireworks in the morning," she said coyly.

"What does that mean?"

"It's a surprise. You can't have all the fun."

After dinner, we rode the elevator to the penthouse. Three suites were on the floor. She explained that out of the three, one was hers and the two others were private. Each suite had its own elevator.

We got out as a group went into a suite down the hall. I recognized Don King's thunderous voice: "You'll always be the greatest. We're gonna have a rematch." The one in the middle of the group had a white towel over his head.

"Is that him?" I asked. "Is that Ali?"

She nodded.

"Uncle Muhammad?"

She punched my arm. "Cousin."

We gazed at the Strip for a while and then went to bed. Later, holding her, I said, "Thanks for one of the best nights of my life."

She kissed my shoulder. "My pleasure. I love being with you."

I leaned up to look at her. "I have to tell you something."

She frowned. "This doesn't sound good."

"I have no idea what's going to happen tomorrow, but I know those guys will try to get me. I don't care; it was worth it. I just hope I don't end up in jail. But I want you to know I wouldn't have missed being here for the world. Because of you—"

She put her finger to my lips.

"You are so special, Cassy, and—"

"You could stay with me," she said softly. "We don't have to stay in Vegas. We could go to LA or Hawaii. Wherever you want."

I smiled. "You are so beautiful. I'm lucky you shared time with me. But that's your world, not mine."

She nodded sadly. "Well, I can guarantee you won't be the one who gets arrested."

I was confused.

"Trust me," she said. "It won't be you."

"I love you, Cassy."

She looked as though she might cry. "I love you, too."

The next morning, I woke up early, kissed her gently, and grabbed a cab back to the apartment. After a quick shower, I headed to the Hacienda. *Let's see what you've got, boys.*

I hit the buffet for breakfast, then took a deep breath and went into the sales room. All conversations stopped. A few people looked happy to see me; most didn't. I sat at a round table by myself.

Best's office light was on, but he was nowhere to be seen. After a few minutes, Winn walked out and glared at me.

"Arril," he spat, "you're fired. You will never work in this town again. Get out."

I stood and walked toward him. "Gonna miss touring those TPTs. Pretty great waste of time."

I looked him in the eyes and lowered my voice. "Tell your master, you little bitch, that I hope he enjoyed his lunch. I'll never forget his shit-eating grin."

I stood still for a minute, hoping he'd do something. He didn't move, so I turned and walked out of the room. At the desk, I told Kate to take me off the line.

"I'm sorry, Jake," she said. "You weren't given a fair shot."

I asked her to call Roy Corkem for my paycheck, and she gasped. "I completely forgot. I've got it right here. They sent it down after Mr. Best got sick yesterday."

She gave me the check and pointed to the cashier's window. When I turned, two uniformed officers were walking toward me. *Here I go. Straight to jail.*

I recognized one of them. The sheriff Cassy knew, the one who had helped with my license, nodded as they walked past me and into the sales office.

"Thomas Winston," he announced, "I have a warrant for your arrest ..."

Sassy, classy Cassy.

A cab ride later, I was in the Las Vegas Airport, boarding a flight to Boston.

SECTION V |
| Back to the Castle

P Town

92

"Time to wake up, honey." I received a gentle nudge from the stewardess. "Seat back up. We're landing."

I'd slept through the entire flight.

Marroni was outside the terminal, leaning against his car.

"Welcome home," he said. "What kind of trouble did you cause out there?"

"A few people won't forget me." It was hard to believe I'd only been gone three weeks.

He laughed as we took off for the Castle, and that's what we did most of the way back—laugh. When I told him about Cassy, Uncle Frank, and Ali, he kept saying, "No way," turning to look at me.

"What did you say to Frank when he asked if you were taking good care of the girl?"

"I said, 'It's really none of your business. And by the way, Frank, haven't I asked you not to bother me while I'm eating?'"

Marroni slapped the dashboard. "You are so full of shit. But I don't care. My friend is back. What's Cassy's last name, anyway?"

I shook my head. "Never found out."

"You spent three weeks with her, and you don't know her last name?"

I shrugged.

When the Sagamore Bridge appeared, I called, "Bingo!"

"You played bingo?" he asked.

"No, but I gambled. Won some, lost some."

He laughed like hell when I told him about Best and Winn. "Sounds like Bonnie and Clyde, not Jake and Cassy. Those guys didn't know who they were screwing with. Eat shit and go to jail!"

Soon we were in the Castle's parking lot, in front of Reception. "Why aren't we at the Barracks?" I asked.

"No heat in the rooms, so Barry put the few of us left in the suites. I'm overlooking the pool, and you've got the studio next to me."

I grabbed my pack from the trunk.

"Or you can bunk with me," he added.

"Who gets the sleeper sofa?"

He grinned. "Guess."

"The studio will be fine."

After stashing my stuff and my cash, I knocked on Marroni's door. He opened it holding two beers. "Missed you, my friend." We clinked bottles and drank.

"Let's go to the tiki," he said. "A few people want to see you."

Doug, Donna, Sweets, Becky, and Barry were waiting.

The new bartender, Rita, reached out to shake my hand. "So you're the great Jake Arril," she said. "Heard a lot about you. Welcome back."

It was good to be back, but the place had changed. It was quiet, almost hushed.

Only a few suites were lit, and even the sky seemed darker. It wasn't bad. Just different.

Doug seemed especially happy. "Dinner's on me if you're hungry, buddy," he said.

"Mojo's." I smiled.

I wanted to see the town again, get some chowder and a burger, maybe walk the pier. Marroni, Doug, Donna, and I hopped the bus.

A light blanket of fog settled on the town. The streets were eerie, empty, with most stores closed. I shuddered, feeling the chill in the air.

The hot chowder and burger tasted good, but the pier would have to wait. I was drained. Back in Marroni's room, I asked, "Any drama since I left?"

He thought for a minute. "Barry's more open about being with Janice."

"How's Robby handling it?"

He shook his head. "We're not worried about Robby. We're worried about the guy Janice left Robby for, and I don't mean Barry."

"What do you mean, worried?"

"Every once in a while, he shows up late at night on the pool deck or

318

the beach. Sweets thinks the guy just likes to take walks after work, but I don't know."

I wasn't sure what Marroni was getting at.

"I do know one thing," he added. "That is one big boy. Barry better watch his ass."

93

Marroni was as chipper as ever the next morning, enjoying his coffee with Doug in the restaurant.

"Morning," he said. "Sleep well?"

I nodded and asked what time it was.

"Nine-thirty," Doug told me.

"Great. I missed the meeting. Now I'm on overage."

They both laughed.

"No meetings," Marroni said. "If a tour comes in, Kelli hunts down the next rep on the line."

I went to the sales office. Kelli was excited to see me, wanting details about the glitz and glamour of Vegas. I gave her a fairy-tale account of the city, and she was floored when I started dropping names.

"Tom Selleck? Are you kidding me? I don't know what I love more about Magnum, P.I., his red Ferrari or his ass!"

In the contract office, Janice hugged me. Robby gave me a thumbs-up but kept working. Janice shrugged.

And that was about it for day one back at the Castle. Like a water faucet turned off, the tour flow was nonexistent. We were all waiting for Halloween weekend, our final chance to make money before the Castle shut down for the season.

Only those of us with cash could afford to stick around, and only the cream of the crop had cash. Accumulating it was easy for me, so it wasn't appreciated. Money was nothing more than tickets to the show of life, I told the others. With tickets, we could do anything.

As the weeks dragged on, we slept, ate, and played cards, usually in Marroni's room. Doug was by far the best poker player. He knew when to push, when to pull, and how to bluff. No wonder he took to sales.

To even out the odds, Sweets suggested we switch to a game called acey deucey. After everybody antes up, one player draws two cards and bets—any amount from zero to the total in the pot—on whether the third card will fall numerically between the first two. If it does, the bettor wins the amount he bet. If it doesn't, he adds that amount to the pot. If the third card matches one of the first two, he pays double. And if the first two cards match each other, he matches the pot.

We each threw in twenty dollars. With one hundred dollars on the table, Sweets drew a five and an eight, and passed.

"Why?" Marroni asked. "All you needed was a six or a seven."

I looked at him, not sure whether he was serious.

Doug pulled a ten and a three, bet twenty dollars, and flipped a jack. He added twenty dollars to the pot.

I pulled a king and a three. "Bet the pot."

They couldn't have been happier when the next card was a three. I threw another $120 into the pot. Barry pulled a pair of queens and had to match it, so $480 was on the table.

Marroni groaned. "This is Satan's game."

He wasn't wrong. The cards could kill you. He pulled an ace and a two, calling the ace high, and bet $300.

The next card was a seven. "Knew it, just knew it. I should've bet the whole pot," he grumbled, collecting his winnings.

Sweets pulled a jack and a two, bet the pot, and then pulled a king.

The game went. It didn't take long for the pot to reach $1,000.

Doug looked at a queen and a five, thought it over, and passed. The guys disagreed, but he was right.

The first card I pulled was a king. The next was also a king, so I put ten hundreds and a fifty on the table.

Marroni buried his face in his hands. We'd been playing for ten minutes, and the pot was over $2,000.

Wearing his reading glasses, Barry drew a four and a queen. He tried to appear calm but lit a cigar, forgetting the one burning in the ashtray. Doug smiled.

"All the women better go home," Barry said. "Fifteen hundred." The next card was a three. His hand shook as he counted out the cash.

There was a knock at the door.

"Come in if you have money," Marroni yelled. In walked Becky.

"Right on!" Sweets hollered. "Come to me, Lady Luck." She stood behind him as he said, "Show me the cards."

An ace and a two. Acey deucey.

"Ace high or low?" I was joking, but no one laughed.

Sweets said, "Pot!"

The payoff card turned. A two.

"Honey," he said, "would you go get me some money?"

"Sure," Becky said sadly. "How much?"

He held up four fingers. She left and returned quickly with the cash. The pot was now over $7,000.

Doug looked at a king and a four. Without hesitating, he said, "Pot." I looked at him.

"I came here broke," he said. "Let's see the card." It was a nine.

Doug jumped up, folded all of the cash neatly, and filled his pockets. He'd won six months of a waiter's salary in about twenty minutes. But Doug wasn't a waiter anymore. He was a time-share salesman.

And a damn good one.

94

Owners and their guests started arriving for the big weekend at about 2:00 p.m. on Friday. Mother Nature cooperated, delivering a clear sky and light winds. A band was booked for the tiki bar, and complimentary hors d'oeuvres would be served.

This was it: the season's final shot. Marroni and I were standing by the pool when I heard my name called. Sitting at the tiki bar, Bill and Edna Thomas waved me over.

"Jake, good to see ya!" Bill smiled. "Thought you'd still be in Vegas?"

"I went broke." I said, smirking.

Bill and Edna both chuckled.

"Well, we're glad to have you back. We can't get enough of this place. Those two weeks in September were absolutely beautiful. Just the quiet time we needed."

Bill kissed Edna on the cheek before turning back to me. "Thank you for taking care of our friends. More should be coming in today."

"Thanks for the referrals. The roulette table ate me up. I could use the money."

The weekend was nothing short of controlled chaos. Everyone wanted to buy. Bill and Edna hosted a little party in their suite. I entertained the group with tales of Las Vegas and the incredible Hacienda. The gathering alone netted about $4,000 in commissions.

We were all doing well. The reps who left the Castle at summer's end definitely left money on the table—a lot of it. The unmanned tours were fair game. The band was great, and so was the food, but the sales were incredible. By 9:30 p.m., the dealing was done. Final figures topped $200,000.

Marroni and I hopped on the bus, heading downtown for the parade. "How did you do?" he asked.

I grinned. "Close to seven grand. How about you?"

"Three." He looked happy.

Town was busier than I'd ever seen it, with color everywhere, floats, costumes, and storefront decorations. The air was painted with music, a townwide celebration. I'd heard about Mardi Gras in New Orleans, but I was sure it had nothing on Provincetown.

As a float went by, someone yelled my name. "Jake, come on!" Kelli gestured for me to join her on the float.

I put up my hands. "Nothing to wear."

She threw her head back and laughed, "A dream come true!"

The Main Street bars were packed, but we managed to slip into the Crown & Anchor, where a girl with long, thick black hair sat alone. A butterfly mask covered the top of her face. Her eyes caught mine, and what eyes they were. I felt as if I'd been struck by lightning.

"You are the most beautiful thief I've ever seen," I said.

She giggled. "What did I steal?"

"My heart." I offered my hand.

She didn't take it. "That's why I wear a mask. Don't want the witnesses to recognize me."

"Don't worry. I won't turn you in."

She finally shook my hand, telling me her name was Rachel. The rest of the world, along with the excitement surrounding us, faded away.

Marroni tapped me on the shoulder to let me know he was going back to the Castle.

"You know how to tell if he's lying?" he asked Rachel. She shook her head. "His lips are moving."

She laughed, I thanked him for the endorsement, and he left.

Hours melted away. I didn't realize the time until the bartender rang the bell for last call and she reached into her pocket. I pulled a coin from mine. "Tell you what. Heads, you pay. Tails, I do. Game?"

"Is it heads on both sides?" she asked.

I flipped the coin, caught it, and put it back in my pocket. "Tails," I said, and I paid the tab.

Outside, costumed partiers still walked the streets. When I asked where she was headed, she shrugged. "Home."

"Mind if I walk with you, for security reasons?"

She giggled. "The robbed protecting the robber."

We walked uphill on a side street to her house. She took her mask off, shook out her hair, and, after a few awkward moments, asked, "Would you like to come in?" I nodded. She put a finger to her lips as she opened the door. "My parents are asleep."

In the living room, she asked whether I wanted a drink.

"Just a glass of water."

When she went down a hallway, I looked around the room. The walls were lined with bookcases; an oriental rug sat under a brown leather sofa and chair. To my left, a pair of reading glasses rested on an end table. A photo of President Kennedy hung on the wall, a telephone table beneath it. Pasted on the phone was its number, the last four digits 0525. My birthday.

"Nice room," I said as Rachel came back with the water. "Looks like a law office."

She nodded. "Actually, my father's a lawyer."

I drank the water, then said, "Look, it's late, so I'll go. But remember, you stole my heart. And I always get even."

"Is that a threat?"

"Nope. It's a promise."

When I walked outside, she lingered in the doorway. I waved from the sidewalk. She waved back, then closed the door softly. The bus wasn't running, but I barely noticed the walk back, my feet never touching the ground.

95

The Castle was fun when the weather was good. The next morning, it wasn't. The wind had shifted. It was pouring.

In Reception, Kelli greeted me with a groan, looking as if she'd had a long night.

"Where's the high-spirited filly from the float?" I asked.

"Dead," she said, and she groaned again.

The guys were having coffee in the restaurant, all in good moods in spite of the weather. Doug was especially upbeat—and why not? After his acey deucey win and yesterday's sales, he was swimming in cash.

Eventually the group broke up, leaving Marroni and me at the table.

"That one from last night is a keeper," he said, "a real keeper."

I nodded. "Gonna call her, invite her to dinner."

"That's great," he said. "She gave you her number."

"Not exactly," I told him.

"How'd you get it, then?"

I started to explain, but he interrupted.

"You took it from the phone? God, who knows how she'll take that?"

"It's only fair. I stole her number after she stole my heart."

He groaned like Kelli. "You didn't say that to her, did you?" I admitted I did. He shook his head.

As for sales, the day was a flop, and rain was forecast for the next three days. Some guests left early.

When Rachel answered, I said I was calling about a theft. She laughed and asked how I'd gotten her number.

"Swapped my heart for it. Told you I'd get even."

She was quiet, and I thought maybe I'd blown it, until she giggled. "I can't believe you stole my number," she said, but she agreed to have dinner with me.

Marroni opened his door. As I walked by, he caught me smiling.

"She said yes!" he shouted. "You dog. Where are you going to take her?"

I went into his room and sat down. "Don't know. Maybe Rose's."

"Where are you meeting her? What time?"

Christ, I hadn't even thought about that. It was pouring, and she didn't know where or when.

"Take my car," Marroni said. "That'll help."

"Thanks."

"Man, do I have to do everything for you? Get back on the phone."

I called her again. Laughing, she admitted, "After I hung up, I didn't have a clue what the plan was. Rose's sounds great. See you at seven."

She opened the door wearing a dress under a light jacket, her wavy black hair cascading over her shoulders. She was beautiful.

"Sorry," I said, turning to walk away. "Must have the wrong address."

She followed. "Would you give me a lift to Rose's? I have to meet a thief."

"Hop in. Heading that way anyhow."

When we arrived, Aaron looked surprised to see us. "Jake, Rachel, welcome."

He shook her hand, then mine. "Heard you went to Vegas, Jake. Everything go okay?"

I nodded, and he turned to Rachel. "How's your family?"

"Everyone's good, Aaron. Thanks."

At our table with menus in hand, I asked what she'd like to drink. She asked what I was having. In no time, two Cape Codders appeared.

"So," she said after a sip, "Vegas. Business or pleasure?"

"Went for business, but it turned into pleasure."

She studied the menu, asked what I wanted. I couldn't decide and asked what she was going to have.

"I was planning to order what you ordered," she said.

"Do any of the appetizers look good?"

She laughed. "They all look good."

I glanced over at Aaron, who hurried to the table.

"Ready to order, Jake?"

"Appetizers," I said.

He nodded. "What is your choice tonight?"

"All of them," I said. "Two at a time. You decide what's first."

"Wine or champagne?" he asked. Rachel's smile said champagne.

Our glasses stayed filled, and the appetizers kept coming. She told me she worked at a cosmetics booth in Hyannis, rationalizing the two days she worked as time well-spent, as she was usually shopping anyway. I told her I was a time-share salesman.

Sipping the hundred-dollar bubbly, she said, "You must be good at it."

"It's actually kind of fun."

As we plowed through the appetizers, she asked, "What was your favorite meal in Vegas?"

I tipped an oyster Rockefeller into my mouth. "I'll never forget a lunch I had with the sales manager. It was the best."

She waited.

"Long story," I said.

When Aaron brought the bill, she grinned. "Want to flip a coin?"

"Only if we use my coin."

We left Rose's and drove toward the Castle in the rain. "Do you play cards?" I asked.

She looked at me. "Poker?"

In Marroni's room, the game was on. "You a card shark?" he asked Rachel. "Did he bring you here to steal our money?"

"You bet." She held her cards close, refused a second draw, put two dimes and three pennies in the pot.

Sweets groaned. "Oh, man, betting big right from the start."

"You go, girl," Donna said. "Show them how it's done."

I matched her bet, and so did Becky. Donna and Marroni folded.

I laughed, "Stakes a little high?"

Marroni nodded.

With the dealing done, Rachel threw in two more dimes, and everyone folded.

She'd won the pot.

When I leaned over, she tilted her cards so I could see. Pure bluff. She didn't even have a pair.

"Good thing we all folded," I said, looking around the table. "The lady knows how to play the game."

We left at about ten thirty, heading back toward town.

"Good bunch," she said. "Marroni has a great laugh."

"Feel like hitting a club?" I asked.

"Let's just go back to my house."

As we walked up her steps, the front door opened. "Rachel, I've been worried," said a stout, silver-haired woman. "You didn't leave a note."

"Sorry, Mom, forgot. Say hi to Jake."

Mom gave me the once-over. "Nice to meet you."

Inside, they walked into the parlor, and the smell of a burning cigar drifted out.

"Daddy, meet Jake," Rachel said.

I hurried in from the hallway. Her father was sitting in the leather chair, reading a newspaper, the photo of JFK on the wall behind him. He looked at me for what seemed like forever, then cleared his throat, folded the paper, and rested his glasses on the nearby table.

"Good evening, young man," he said. And that was it. I shook his hand, feeling less than welcome.

"I'd better get going," I said to Rachel. "Have to work tomorrow."

Turning to Mom, I added, "Nice to meet you. Hope to see you again."

Rachel took my hand, looking as if she were about to laugh. "Come on, I'll walk you out."

At the door, she whispered, "Sorry. They're usually in bed by now."

"They seem nice," I managed.

"Call me," she said. "I think you have my number."

Marroni was alone when I returned his keys. "Moving up in the world," he said. "That one reeks of class."

"The parents weren't impressed."

He laughed. "They'll warm up. How did the night go?"

I shrugged. "At least she wants me to call her."

"There you go, then," he said. "It went well."

I said good night and went to my room.

The next morning, Jimmy came out of a suite carrying tools. "Jake, heard you were back. Good to see you."

"Shutting the place down for the winter?"

He nodded. "I know they want everyone out by next week. If you need a place, I've got a spare bedroom."

I thanked him, realizing I didn't have a plan. The rain wasn't letting up. And it felt as though it would soon turn to snow.

Barry invited all of us to dinner at the restaurant that night, to say good-bye.

Later, sitting in my room, I called her. "I had a really good time last night," she said. Her end of the line went quiet, then she added, "I didn't think you'd call."

"Well," I said, "things are wrapping up here. I've got some decisions to make."

96

The sky was black the following morning, still raining cats and dogs. I went to the sales center to say good-bye to Kelli. Doug was collecting his stuff in the pit when a car pulled up and stopped. The driver hurried to the door, leaving his wipers and lights on.

"Want to flip for the shot?" I asked. "If it is a shot?"

Doug agreed, and I lost. When he went into Reception, the guy said, "I just invested two-hundred grand on a real estate deal downtown. Got anything I can sink another eighty grand into?"

That was one coin toss I wished I'd won. Twenty minutes later, Doug rushed back into the pit. "Eighty-two grand, cash, all blue weeks!"

He'd just made close to $20,000. What a way to end the season.

Marroni was packing when I got back. He told me he was heading to his apartment in Framingham, maybe to sell cars. I gave him my parents' phone number and went to my room to call Rachel. We met for lunch, and that was all it took. This was no time to leave.

She gave me a lift to Jimmy's house, and I put my things in the guest room. She told me she had things to do, promising to come back later.

"I need to know one thing if I'm staying," I called after her.

She turned.

"I need to know your last name."

She looked puzzled. "Frost. My last name is Frost."

Jimmy didn't seem surprised to see me when he got home. I offered to pay for the room, but he refused. "Keep us supplied with Budweiser," he said. "That'll be good enough."

The next month flew by. Rachel and I spent all of our time together; in bed, at fine restaurants, shopping in Hyannis, and walking the snow-covered dunes. I couldn't remember being happier. But on a late November day, Rachel's face told me that something bad had happened.

One evening while Rachel, Jimmy, and I were sitting in the living room, Farnsworth called.

"Watcha doing?" he asked. Just the sound of his voice made me laugh.

He went on and on about Florida, the great weather, and, more importantly, the business opportunities. I asked whether the Matecumbe was hiring. It was, and the housing was free. I took his number and told him I'd be in touch.

The next day, I made two phone calls. First I called home and told my family I'd be home for Christmas. It was coming fast, and I missed them. Next I called Marroni, to run the Florida idea by him. He was glad to hear from me, said there was no work to be had in Framingham and he was bored. Florida made sense.

We agreed to leave the day after Christmas. I didn't know how to tell Rachel. So I didn't.

97

Rachel was disappointed that we wouldn't attend midnight Mass together, but she understood that I hadn't seen my family in a long time. On December 23, I packed a few things, walked to the highway, and stuck out my thumb. Three rides later, I was home.

I opened the door at 1:00 p.m., yelling "Merry Christmas!" Squeals and running feet answered. The kids bounded down the stairs and jumped all over me.

Mom came from the kitchen, drying her hands on a dishtowel. She held my face, then gave me a hug and a kiss. Coach was at school, she said, but he'd be home soon.

When the kids disappeared and Mom went back into the kitchen, I went upstairs to my room. It was just as I'd left it a hundred years ago. I heard the front door open and went back to the top of the stairs.

"I'm home," Dad shouted.

"Welcome back, Coach," I said.

He looked up. "Jake! You're here!" When I went down the steps, he held out his hand, but I hugged him.

We went into the kitchen together, and after the small talk, I said, "Listen, I want to take everyone shopping for Christmas presents."

Mom, being Mom, said, "No need for that, Jake. It's enough that you're here."

I shook my head. "It would mean a lot to me. I've planned it for a while. Got enough gas in the tank to get to the Chestnut Hill Mall, Coach?"

He took a moment to think about it.

"Give me the keys," I said. "I want to see the town anyway. Get everyone ready. I'll be right back."

Mom winked. "Maybe grab a couple of hot dogs at Casey's?"

It's funny how quickly old feelings come back. I filled the gas tank and then walked into Casey's, breathing in the familiar aromas of grilled burgers and steamed hot dogs. Townies huddled on the stools. Everything was just as I remembered.

I took two dogs with catsup and mustard to go, got back in the car, and drove through town, past the high school and athletic fields. Town pride was everywhere. Then I pulled back into the driveway at home, the hot dogs long gone.

Everyone was scrambling to get ready, yelling at each other to hurry up in the bathroom. Soon we all piled into the station wagon and headed down the highway.

The Chestnut Hill Mall was full of high-end shops. Our first stop was Holt's, for Mom. I told the salesgirl I'd treat my mom to whatever she wanted.

"And if you can keep her from seeing the prices, I'd appreciate it. We don't do this every day."

An hour later, Mom had narrowed the choice down to two dresses, each with matching shoes. After taking advice from Joanne and Sessy, she settled on one. I suggested that she and Coach take the kids to the toy store, where I'd meet them after I paid the bill.

"Let's get both," I told the salesgirl when they left, "and both pairs of shoes."

She smiled. "This is awfully nice of you."

"Trust me, she deserves it," I said. "She raised me."

The sales rep handed me the bill. Good thing Mom didn't see it.

In the toy store, Sessy had found a whole wall of Barbies and accessories. Thirty minutes later, we were considering two dolls, each with a car and an airplane, all pink.

I told Joanne about a New Wave-style clothes shop and Blaine about the sports store.

"Mom, why don't you take Joanne? And Dad, do you know anything about sports?"

He laughed. "Not much." And off they went.

By the time I caught up with them, Blaine was trying to choose between a baseball glove and a soccer ball, kneepads, and sneakers. He picked one. I bought it all.

And then I did it again with Joanne.

The trick would be to give each of them the chosen gift and hide the others until Christmas morning. As we walked through the mall, Sessy tugged on my arm. "You forgot Daddy, Jake!"

I pretended to be surprised. "Should he get a present too?" She nodded.

Inside the men's store, I pulled the same drill I'd pulled at Holt's. Coach looked great in every suit he tried. In great shape, he did a suit justice. He narrowed it down to two and tried on a pair of shoes. "These are the most comfortable shoes I've ever worn," he said. He took one off, revealing a hole in his sock, and turned it over to inspect the sole. There was the price tag.

Shaking his head, he looked up. "Can you tell me what in the world makes a pair of shoes worth three hundred dollars?"

The salesman laughed and in a nice way said, "Sir, you said it yourself. Those are the most comfortable shoes you've ever worn."

Deals done, we headed home. With everyone talking a mile a minute in the station wagon, I felt lucky—really lucky. *What a family.*

At the house, I asked everyone to sit in the living room so I could hand out presents in front of the decorated tree. I sifted through the packages, unloading only the gifts they'd chosen, and looked up to find Joanne watching. She knew.

I put my finger to my lips. She smiled and joined the others.

The kids applauded when I suggested pizzas for dinner, and Dad offered to come with me to pick up the pies. On the way home, we stopped by the snow-covered baseball fields and got out of the car.

"Some of my favorite memories are of watching you play here," he said.

I was shivering. "You're a great coach, Dad. I was proud to play for you. Let's get the pizzas home while they're hot."

The engine groaned when I turned the key, but the car started. Soon we were all in the kitchen, eating pepperoni and green pepper pizzas.

We settled in the living room after dinner, the tree lit, the scent of pine in the air.

Each of us told a story of a Christmas past. Blaine's story stole the show, but Mom told it. "One Christmas morning, after unwrapping a

335

mountain of presents, little Blaine looked up and said, 'You know, with all these presents I got, not one was from Mom or Dad.'"

As the rest of us broke up, Sessy looked confused. "Why didn't you get Blaine any presents?" she asked.

We stifled our laughter. We still had a believer among us.

Joanne told the story of the Christmas party my parents threw for their friends during which Mom prepared an appetizer tray with a walnut-crusted red wine cheese ball as its centerpiece. It was the size of a softball. "Merry Christmas!" she called as she left the kitchen.

Mom butted into the story and took over. "I was walking toward the living room, and all my guests, when I tripped. The damn cheese ball flew off the plate and rolled across the living room rug!" We all howled.

Coach changed the subject. "Did you just come from the airport, Jake? Last time we talked, you were in Las Vegas."

"No," I said. "Vegas was great, but I had an opportunity to finish the season big at the Sand Castle, so I took it."

"Was Vegas fun?" Mom asked.

I nodded.

"Did you meet anyone famous?" Joanne asked.

"Frank Sinatra," I told her. "And I saw Tom Selleck."

To my surprise, Coach was impressed. "You actually met Sinatra?"

"Yeah. But the coolest thing was sitting ringside at the Ali–Holmes fight. That was wild."

"I thought I saw you on TV!" Blaine yelled. "I told Dad. Remember, Dad?"

Coach confirmed Blaine's account, then said, "You were at that fight?"

"Sure was."

"What's next for you, Jake?" Mom asked. "Where are you off to?"

I looked at each of them and said, "Florida. Leaving the day after Christmas."

Everyone got quiet for a minute. Coach said, "Whatever you're doing seems to be paying off."

"Anyone special in your life?" Mom asked.

I paused, then nodded. "I think so. That's why I have to go back to the Cape tomorrow. I need to tell her I'm leaving."

"Well, then," Mom said, "we'll have Christmas Eve lunch instead of dinner."

The room fell silent until Sessy announced, "When I grow up, I wanna be just like Jake!"

We all laughed. The kids left the living room with their loot. I sat with Mom and Coach a little longer, then stood to go to bed, receiving hugs from Mom, a handshake from Coach.

I felt like a guest. And it was my doing.

I went to the garage, took the rest of the presents from the car, and hid them in a corner—all but Joanne's. Hers I brought upstairs, putting them in Mom and Dad's room before going to mine. After a knock on my door, it opened.

"If you want," Joanne said, "I'll wrap the rest of the presents."

"What about yours?"

She hugged me. "I already know what they are. Thank you. Love you."

I told her about the stash in the garage and closed the door. Then I looked around the room, feeling as if I might cry. It wasn't my world anymore.

98

The next morning, I took the keys to the car and went downtown. At Maybardi's, Michael welcomed me back. I asked what Coach's car needed.

"Battery, tires, and a tune-up," he said. I handed him the cash and asked him to take care of it the next time Coach came in.

I drove to the center of town and went into Main Street Jewelry, a store I'd never been in. After a quick survey of the choices, I bought a gold cross and chain. I headed home for Mom's famous Christmas Eve dinner—now lunch—lasagna.

After we ate, I hugged everyone, and then Coach gave me a lift to the highway.

"Thanks for coming home," he said as I got out of the car. "We're always here for you, Jake, but go for it!"

I was choked up, couldn't say anything, so I gave him a thumbs-up.

At the bridge, I had a decision to make. It would be dark soon. If the next ride didn't get me all the way to Provincetown, I'd be stuck in the dark on a highway with no lights. A truck pulled over: "P-Town Fish!"

Jimmy was watching TV when the truck dropped me off. I asked if he'd drive me to the package store, and soon we were loading ten cases of beer into the car.

"Merry Christmas," I said. "Thanks for everything."

I asked him for another favor—a lift to the church for midnight Mass.

She was easy to spot. She had the blackest, thickest hair on the planet. And her mother sat beside her.

After excusing myself ten times in their pew, I was next to her.

"Oh my God!" she said, loud enough to interrupt the sermon. The people sitting in front of us raised their hands in the air, saying "Praise God!"

Sliding into the space next to her, I put my arm around her shoulder and gave her a quick kiss on the cheek. Mom glanced in my direction, winked and smiled.

After mass, we drove to Jimmy's house. He was nowhere to be found, probably asleep. The house was cold, so we quietly made our way to the bedroom, slipped under a pile of blankets, and slipped off to sleep. I'd tell her I was headed south in the morning.

The sky was turning a light grey and I could see that a light snow had fallen. I shifted onto my back, careful not to wake Rachael, who slept in the curl of my arm. She slowly opened her eyes and gave me a sad smile. She knew I'd come to say goodbye.

Walking arm-in-arm on the dunes later that morning, we paused and looked out at the frozen Cape Cod bay. A receding tide left car-sized ice chunks on the barren sand. The sky had turned a steel grey. It was cold. Silently I pulled her present from my pocket, and gently put it in her hand. Shifting her gaze from the gift to my eyes, she whispered "I just want to tell you, I had a great time with you. My only regret is there just wasn't enough." I mustered a smile. "Open your present." Holding a delicate strand of gold, she turned her back and I fastened the clasp behind her neck. Turning to me, the cross hung nicely. Not too big, not too small. It was nice. I really didn't have any pre-planned goodbyes. We hadn't really spent that much time together, but it worked. It felt good to be with her. Looking into her eyes, I mustered "look, this isn't goodbye. When I get to wherever I'm going, I'll give you a shout." She put her finger to my lips and shushed me "Jake, chase what you're looking for." With that, she smiled, reached slowly to touch the cross hanging around her neck, and whispered "thanks for everything."

The next morning, I got into the passenger seat and we drove off. Marroni didn't say a word and neither did I until we were crossing the Sagamore bridge. At the crest, he said "don't look back. We'll come back when we've both made it big." The car headed South.

The End

Printed in the United States
by Baker & Taylor Publisher Services